LOST PROPHETS

Also by Alfred L. Malabre, Jr.

Within Our Means
Understanding the New Economy
Beyond Our Means
Investing for Profit in the Eighties
America's Dilemma: Jobs vs. Prices
Understanding the Economy: For People Who Can't Stand
    Economics

LOST PROPHETS

An Insider's History of
the Modern Economists

ALFRED L. MALABRE, JR.

Harvard Business School Press

Boston, Massachusetts

Photographs were kindly furnished by the following sources: John Maynard Keynes and Harry Dexter White, International Monetary Fund. Arthur Burns, Alan Greenspan, and Paul Volcker, the Federal Reserve System; John Kenneth Galbraith, Harvard University News Office; Gardner Ackley and Walter Heller, John F. Kennedy Library; Gardner Ackley and Arthur Okun, Lyndon B. Johnson Library; Otto Eckstein, Harriet Eckstein; Milton Friedman, Stanford University's Hoover Institution; Arthur Laffer, USC News Service; Martin Feldstein, National Bureau of Economic Research; Paul Samuelson, MIT News Office; Geoffrey Moore, Columbia University.

Library of Congress Cataloging-in-Publication Data
Malabre, Alfred L.
   Lost prophets : an insider's history of the modern economists /
Alfred L. Malabre, Jr.
      p.   cm.
   Includes bibliographical references and index.
   ISBN 0-87584-441-3 (hard : alk. paper)
      1. Economics—United States—History—20th century. 2. United
States—Economic policy. 3. Economists—United States. I. Title.
HB119.A2M34   1994
330'.0973—dc20   93-4616
                                                                      CIP

The paper used in this publication meets the requirements of the American National Standard for Permanence of Paper for Printed Library Materials Z39.49-1984

This book is dedicated to Lindley H. Clark, Jr., the best business journalist of his generation—despite his monetarist proclivities—and proof that reporters and editors can be kind, gentle people.

Contents

Acknowledgments

My heartfelt thanks go out to the many people who helped me along the way toward this book. Thanks to you Dick Luecke for helping me conceive the project and for your unflagging encouragement. And to you Nick Philipson, my cheerful, understanding editor and friend. And to you Paula Duffy for your good counsel and understanding. And to you Bob Heilbroner, my most admired friend, for your oh-so-useful commentary, which has made this a much better book. And ditto to you Lacy Hunt and to you Henry Kaufman, old friends and solid sources both; I have benefited greatly from your sage advice which you so generously supplied. My thanks as well to you Paul Steiger, my sterling boss and admired colleague, who sets a high journalistic standard. And to you the multitalented staff of the Hoover Institution who facilitated this project. And finally, my loving thanks to you Mary Patricia, for the never-failing support that makes all things possible.

LOST PROPHETS

Introduction

In the years since World War II, economics has acquired a huge, though not altogether enviable, reputation. Increasingly, economists have become the butt of unkind jokes, such as: you can tell that economists have a good sense of humor by their use of decimal points in their forecasts. Or: economics is obviously the world's oldest profession since only economists could have created the chaos from which God created the world.

Even so, economics and its practitioners have come to dominate political and business decision making to an extent unimaginable decades ago. This influence is in marked contrast to the situation in the century's early decades. Calvin Coolidge had no team of economists to advise him. For all the troubles that the sinking economy caused him, Herbert Hoover's memoirs show no sign that he sought or received counsel from the leading economists of that time. The most notable of economists in Hoover's day was surely Irving Fisher of Yale, but his name appears only three times, and never in a consultative connection, in *The Great Depression*, Hoover's exhaustive personal account of the years from 1929 to 1941. Until the time of Franklin D. Roosevelt, in fact, there were no national income accounts—gross national product and its various components—to help presidents monitor the economy's health. Instead, the pulse of economic affairs was taken primarily from the stock market's gyrations and changes in so-called car loadings, a tabulation of railroad freight activity. The unemployment rate, now a keenly followed monthly barometer of the economy's condition, appeared only yearly.

By comparison, the economy, now closely monitored in scores of ways, was the overriding issue that propelled Bill Clinton into the White House in 1993—and sent George Bush packing to Houston. As the sign over the desk of James Carville, Clinton's savvy campaign strategist, shouted: "It's the economy, Stupid!" Unthinkable even in the early years after World War II, there is now an annual Nobel Prize for contributions to economic science. Economic forecasters, for all their perennial inaccuracies, now possess such clout that stock markets often hang on their prognostications and business planners frequently alter course because of what they say. Their counsel can even shift the fate of presidencies—as Bush's disastrous reelection campaign demonstrated.

This book will probe just how solid or mushy are the various theories, the economic thinking, behind the advice—the forecasts and the policy guidance—that economists have been serving up in recent decades to corporate chieftains as well as to political leaders. What does the record tell us about the reliability, even the usefulness, of what economists preach? How, for better or worse, have their insights, as well as their miscalculations, shaped our lives and our world?

Some findings are disturbing, showing how misguided, even wrongheaded, economists have often been in their assessments of the economy and, as a consequence, in their counsel to policy makers. Occasionally, the resulting damage to the economy— and ultimately to our living standards—has been considerable. One such instance, recounted in Chapter Five, occurred in the late 1970s and early 1980s, when rigid monetarist doctrine briefly ruled the roost at the Federal Reserve Board. Another, discussed in Chapter Six, took place in the early Reagan years, when unbridled supply-side theory held sway at the White House.

Often, the practical effect of an economic theory conceived in an ivory tower and then eagerly applied by planners has proved embarrassingly different from the anticipated result. An egregious case in point, examined in Chapter One, is the notion that a stable, prosperous international monetary system, constructed around fixed currency exchange rates, could somehow endure indefinitely, benefiting all participants. Another casualty of real-world experience, described in Chapter Three, is the mistaken belief of many economists loyal to John Maynard Keynes that governmental fine-tuning, through deftly executed adjustments in taxing and spending, would largely eliminate a business cycle that has endured for as long as the economy's performance has been observed.

A disconcerting footnote is that the economy seems, at least by one important measure, to have fared best in those brief periods of the post–World War II era when the President's Council of Economic Advisers (CEA) in Washington was, for one reason or another, without a chairman. This, at least, is the finding of a prominent member of the Harvard economics faculty, Robert J. Barro. Barro has constructed a so-called misery index, reflecting economic growth, joblessness, and unemployment and interest-rate levels, and he has concluded that misery seems to diminish most pronouncedly when the chairmanship of the CEA has been held by an economist named "vacancy." In these special periods, ranging from some months in early 1953 to some months in the early and mid-1980s, misery declined at an average annual rate of 2.3%, according to Barro. This was a far sharper rate of decline than occurred during the tenure of any flesh-and-blood chairman. In fact, misery *rose* nearly 2% a year during the CEA chairmanships of such eminent economists as Herbert Stein (1972–1974) and Charles Schultze (1977–1981).

For all of this, economists do have something to offer as the Clinton presidency, with its attention to economic planning, unfolds. Their performance through the postwar decades is by no means without notable achievements, as this book will document. The challenge is to ferret out the sensible and useful precepts from those that have been, or should be, discarded— and to do so in a manner palatable to readers who may not care to distinguish between a Laffer curve and an IS-LM curve. We can benefit by eschewing ideas that have proved to be cockeyed, or worse, and by embracing those parts of this or that theory that seem to have worked reasonably well. There may be little to salvage in the shambles of supply-side economics, for example, but the failure of Keynesian efforts to fine tune the economy should not obscure such helpful insights as the crucial link that runs between labor income and consumer spending—a connection much on the minds of policy makers in the early months of Clinton's presidency, when a two-year-old business recovery did not produce any significant growth in jobs.

The troubles of monetarism, by the same token, should not allow us to neglect the monetarist lesson that prolonged, accelerating monetary growth can lead to worsening inflation. In a similar fashion, though there may be much to question in the idea of rational expectations, surely such an idea can help us appreciate more fully how private attitudes shape the economy's course.

The approach to be taken here is somewhat unusual for an economic accounting. This is by no means a traditional, dry history of the economy and its expert observers. Rather, it is an adventure designed to introduce readers firsthand to the thinkers behind the ideas, to bring to life the individuals whose theories have helped, for better and for worse, shape our world: a bouncy Arthur Laffer, prescribing deep-knee bends, performed in the lavatory, as a way to stay in shape on long flights between high-paying speaking engagements; a diminutive, feisty Milton Friedman, arriving in high style at a fancy Phoenix resort to lecture a gathering of his disciples, as well as some gullible but influential reporters, on the virtues of monetary policy; a pipe-puffing Arthur Burns, walking in the Vermont woods behind his summer home, showing a visitor the small cabin where he planned, but sadly never found the time, to write the memoirs of a busy, important life; a naively optimistic Otto Eckstein, proclaiming to admiring corporate executives the arrival of a new, recession-free era for the economy.

When one surveys the circumstances that surround the economics profession and its modern practitioners, the dramatists of ancient Greece spring to mind. In the plays of Aeschylus, in the early Greek period, the tragic hero inevitably suffered but learned from this suffering and emerged a better person, blessed with a heightened awareness. In the plays of Sophocles, in the middle Greek phase, the hero once again suffered but learned little from his suffering. There was still some benefit, however, since the audience, and perhaps the chorus, did gain insights. In the plays of Euripides, in the final phase, however, suffering persisted but was pointless, with no discernible good coming out of it. All was senseless, and cynicism prevailed.

Something like this disheartening progression has occurred over the last few decades on the economic front. In the early postwar years, there was a feeling among government and business leaders, as well as people generally, that America's economy, while hardly immune to difficulty, could at least be made to expand smoothly and continuously if only the proper mix of economic policies were assiduously applied.

But in the mid-1960s, something akin to what the Greeks called *hubris* set in within policy-making circles. Eminent economists who should have known better grew convinced that a sort of perpetual prosperity was possible. What the future held, in fact, was what the Greek playwrights called *ate*, the inevitable aftermath to hubris: devastation, defeat, despair. Or, in terms of the U.S. economy, spiraling inflation, wrenching downswings in business activity, surges in joblessness, swelling, huge deficits in both the federal budget and foreign trade.

Late in Jimmy Carter's White House tenure, there was a shift to the so-called monetarist approach to economic management. The hope, once again false, was that monetarism would usher in uninterrupted economic gains, turning slumps, high inflation, and severe unemployment into memories from a benighted time. This was not to be, and after monetarism's failure came the so-called supply-side theorists who convinced Ronald Reagan that the path to sustained prosperity was through something called the Laffer curve, a parabola promising that steep tax-rate reductions would unleash such a burst of economic activity that the economy's various woes would disappear. Nothing of the sort occurred.

Against such a background, it is tempting now to be cynical, to conclude that efforts to attain a higher level of prosperity through the thoughtful application of economic analysis—of what economists have to say—are pointless. As in the plays of Euripides, there appears little to be learned.

I submit, however, that this temptation should be resisted, especially as a young, optimistic president seeks ways to achieve a better time for Americans, particularly within the economic arena. So, cynicism is not what emerges here. The effort, rather, is to provide some valuable perspective in a worrisome, confusing time. By recalling events surrounding the collapse of the Bretton Woods system in the early 1970s, we become more critical observers of the European Community's current, troubled effort to tie together the exchange rates of its wildly dissimilar member nations. By witnessing the Federal Reserve's dismal failure to manage the monetary aggregates during Paul Volcker's chairmanship, we are better able to appreciate the Fed's present reluctance to attach its operating procedures too closely to any monetary aggregate—despite the urging of some monetarists. By remembering the inability of economists in the Johnson White House to achieve recession-free growth through Keynesian fine-tuning, we know to be suspicious of similar calls emanating from some within the Clinton administration.

Reflecting on the repercussions of the French Revolution, Edmund Burke observed that the age of chivalry was gone, replaced by one of economists and calculators (the human sort). Now, the age of economists—if not of calculators (the electronic sort)—may soon be gone as well. But let us hope not, for what economists have to say, as they continue to come along and lecture us, remains important. Their counsel may not be all golden, but neither is it dross. They remain our special guides to the good life—uncertain ones to be sure, but that may be a blessing, for uncertain guides will be less likely to hurry us off in wrong directions.

1

An Impossible Dream

It is widely—but mistakenly—supposed that Thomas Carlyle labeled economics the "dismal science" because it seems, at least to some of us, such an uninteresting, unclear, even foggy business, full of ifs and maybes. But this is not at all what the Scot had in mind. He viewed economics in the other sense of the word dismal: showing or causing gloom or depression. To Carlyle, economics was a science, the study of which led inevitably to the conclusion that prosperity would diminish and financial misery just as surely would spread and deepen.

A minor quibble that I have with Carlyle's judgment is his notion that economics can be described as a science. A more accurate description, I submit, would be that it constitutes, at best, a pseudoscience and, at worst, a guessing game, often wildly inaccurate, frequently carried on by clever bamboozlers whose academic credentials may far exceed any possible contributions they may make to the betterment of mankind.

My far larger objection to what Carlyle has to say about economics, however, involves the implication that economists themselves, like the "science" they practice, are a dismal, pessimistic lot. Surely, what follows here must show that economists in fact possess a degree of optimism that strains belief. Who but a cockeyed optimist could possibly imagine that relationships between the currencies of widely diverse national economies could remain rigidly fixed over prolonged periods, if not indefinitely? Only economists, residing in their special, heavenly world, can muster such optimism.

A SOMBER INTERVIEW

Without a doubt, I should have known and offered my condolences right at the start of the interview. But I didn't know what had just happened and so was taken very much aback when Otmar Emminger—balding and moon-faced as always, slightly resembling President Eisenhower—told me in his clear, Germanic-accented English: "You have come at a terribly sad time for us." I knew that the international monetary situation was worsening, but I hadn't imagined that things had grown quite as bad as Emminger's frowning physiognomy seemed to indicate. I soon discovered, however, that he had a far more personal matter on his mind. "This afternoon I have to bury my friend Dr. Blessing," he explained, not quite in tears. "We have suffered a terrible loss. He was a great man, a great central banker."

Since I had been traveling for several days, in and out of planes and airports that all looked much alike, I was embarrassingly unaware that Karl Blessing, the brilliant, energetic, seemingly healthy president of West Germany's Bundesbank, had been ill, much less that he had died. My visit was poorly timed, to say the least. Accordingly, I much appreciated that Emminger, ever the gentleman, had managed to make time for me even though his late friend's funeral was only hours away.

In other ways, however, the timing of my visit to the headquarters of the Bundesbank in Frankfurt on that Monday morning of May 3, 1971, could hardly have been more appropriate. For as I look back now, after more than two decades, it's clear that the day marked not only the funeral of a great central banker but also the beginning of the end, as Emminger himself would concede, of the monetary arrangement that had bound the economies of the major nations of the non-Communist world since World War II: the Bretton Woods system.

Permit me to backtrack a little. I had scheduled my trip to

Frankfurt several weeks earlier while I still was in New York. From my *Wall Street Journal* perch in downtown Manhattan, I had particularly sought—and finally managed to land—an interview with Emminger, the notably straight-talking and affable vice president of the increasingly powerful Bundesbank, West Germany's (and now Germany's) central bank.

At the time, Emminger was functioning as the Bundesbank's main liaison with policy makers at the Federal Reserve Board in Washington. I had interviewed him several times over the past decade, usually catching him during his periodic swings through New York and Washington, and I admired him for his no-nonsense assessments of what was happening and was likely to happen in the international economic arena. His candid commentary was always a refreshing change from the couched palaver that all too often emanated from many of the U.S. officials who determined economic policy in President Richard M. Nixon's White House.

My interview with Emminger would be, I was sure, the most important, most informative of the interviews I had scheduled with influential West Europeans during the two-week reporting trip that would take me to London, Paris, and Brussels, as well as to the West German financial center. (A measure of the low regard in which most West Germans held their then-capital of Bonn in 1971, more than two decades after the end of World War II, was that their nation's central bank was still situated up the Rhine in Frankfurt.) My European reporting trip, I was sure, would provide at the least some good grist for perhaps one or two fairly routine contributions for *The Wall Street Journal*'s "Outlook" columns, the page-length essays on some aspect of the economic scene at home or abroad that occupy column five of the paper's front page each Monday. I would appraise Western Europe's economic prospects in a leisurely fashion, I supposed, recording my impressions in my own sweet time after returning to my comfortable New York base.

This, as things turned out, was not to be. Instead, as Emminger spoke, I began to perceive that our talk was turning into a most extraordinary interview, as important as any I had ever conducted, one that demanded prompt submission to my editors back in New York. With remarkable candor for a top government official, especially for a central banker, he told me in unequivocal terms that the rules by which international financial dealings had been conducted since World War II were about to be changed: a new monetary era was at hand.

"This is a very tragic story," Emminger said, no longer referring to Blessing's death. He explained: "The U.S. dollar inflow has made all our measures to control our own economy futile. We have had dollar crises before, but nothing like this. It is creating very big tensions that the international monetary system simply can no longer stand." He added, "The inflation coming to us now is what Dr. Blessing spent many years trying to prevent." His message was clear: only two days later—on Wednesday, May 5, 1971—West Germany made it official, announcing to the world that it was suspending its support for the U.S. dollar in flagrant violation of the International Monetary Fund's (IMF) long-standing Bretton Woods rules.

The significance of this West German action, which Emminger had previewed for me, can hardly be overstated. The IMF's rules had been set years earlier, in the latter part of World War II, at an international conference at Bretton Woods in New Hampshire. The so-called Bretton Woods plan aimed ultimately at encouraging and facilitating the free movement of capital and goods across national borders, a flow deemed conducive to global prosperity in the war's difficult aftermath. To accomplish this, the major currencies, it was believed, would have to be readily interchangeable.

In practice this meant that a West German auto maker selling cars to a U.S. auto dealer, for instance, would deposit the dollars received in a German commercial bank. The bank in turn would deliver these dollars to the Bundesbank in exchange for marks. Under the Bretton Woods system—at least until May 5, 1971—the Bundesbank would pay a narrowly set price in marks for the auto maker's dollars; in Germany at that particular time, the price was approximately 3.6 marks per dollar.

The dollar was in effect a fixed link connecting all major currencies, and the immutable anchor for the dollar, in turn, was gold. Under the Bretton Woods system, the United States was pledged to pay out gold from its once-substantial, post–World War II stock at a rate of one ounce for every $35, if a foreign government were to request it.

By May 1971, the United States for years had been spending far more abroad than it had managed to take in from other nations. As a consequence, a large fraction of the U.S. gold supply had moved abroad, largely, but not entirely, as a result of gold purchases by the chrysophilitic French. In early 1961, the U.S. gold stock totaled $17.6 billion; by late 1967, it had shrunk to $12 billion and by the spring of 1968, to $10.7 billion. In addition, more than $50 billion—dollars not cashed in for U.S. gold—were estimated to be in foreign hands. This total was up from about $23 billion a decade before and up from only about $8 billion in the early 1950s.

After so many years of imbalance in its international accounts, the United States in early 1971 had only enough foreign currencies and gold—measured at the $35 per ounce Bretton Woods price—to cover a quarter of these foreign-owned dollars. If foreign holders had sought gold for their dollars, it would have been impossible to pay at the $35 price and would have brought down the Bretton Woods system. Therefore, the claims were not made, and the dollars were swallowed, to use Emminger's word, fueling inflation abroad. The emperor had no clothes, but so far most foreign leaders had not dared to say so.

The result abroad was worrisome, unwanted inflation, as Emminger had indicated to me in the May interview. In the last 12 months, he reported, West Germany's money supply had risen 22.5%. This, he said, was "entirely due to the dollar inflow." He added, "We feel anything over a 10% rise in our money supply is much too much. We're in a pretty desperate situation, with our monetary policy in effect being dictated to us by Washington." On Tuesday, May 4, it was later reported, the Bundesbank had swallowed the then-unprecedented sum of $1.2 billion. The only prompt remedy, of course, was for the Bundesbank to stop swallowing dollars at the fixed rate of 3.6 marks, which was precisely what had happened on Wednesday, May 5, within 48 hours of my interview with Emminger.

The repercussions of Germany's suspension of the Bretton Woods system were immediate and dramatic. My early glimpse of a world without agreed-upon currency exchange rates between the major nations was vivid. I was still in Europe on May 5, when the Bundesbank took its action. I had just traveled from Paris to the Hilton Hotel in Brussels. Upon arriving at the Hilton, I found that the hotel had stopped exchanging dollars for Belgian francs or, in fact, for any other currency. I had looked forward to a pleasant dinner at a small neighborhood restaurant, La Chourenne, just off the city's magnificent Grand Place, which I remembered fondly from an earlier visit. But with no Belgian francs, and not being able to obtain any using my dollar-denominated traveler's checks, I found myself dining in the Hilton's rather Spartan coffee shop and charging the modest meal to my room.

I thought ahead to what I would do if the Hilton was still not exchanging dollars when I checked out later in the week. I would have to try to use my credit card to pay the bill, of course, and have American Express bill me at whatever rate of exchange was eventually set between the dollar and the Belgian franc. This is what I did, in fact, and when the bill came to me in New York weeks later, the dollar was again being accepted in European centers, but reluctantly and at far less favorable rates for itinerant Americans than before May 5.

Paradoxically, however much these countries may have detested the influx of dollars, they couldn't get along without them in those years. Imagine the repercussions if the sort of situation that I encountered at the Brussels Hilton had continued indefinitely. There would have been a recession in Western Europe to curl even a central banker's hair. More than half of the guests at my Brussels hotel were Americans, traveling as either tourists or on business. The hotel doubtlessly would have had to close its doors if these guests couldn't come because their dollars, and eventually their credit cards, were no longer acceptable. And not just the Hilton's doors would have closed. Americans were ubiquitous in that spring of 1971 in Europe, whether quaffing down a pint of bitter in London's Grenadier pub or sipping a glass of wine at the Crazy Horse saloon in Paris or simply strolling along the Rhine in Frankfurt.

So the reality was that Europe had to accept dollars because it couldn't get along very well without the people who carried them. In fact, there was even a little-recognized danger if, in suspending the Bretton Woods exchange rates, countries such as West Germany paid very much less for dollars. To the extent that these moves would make trips to Europe more costly for Americans, they would also tend to reduce the volume of this all-important business. And this would constitute a mouse-sized problem compared with the potential drag on Europe's exports to the United States, which, of course, would cost much more.

The analogy is imperfect to be sure, but there was some resemblance between Europe's need for dollars and a drug addict's need for heroin. The addict can't really live with the drug, and yet he can't really live without it. The addict comes to hate the drug precisely because he has found he cannot get along without it. The American dollar wasn't hated in Europe in the spring of 1971, but it most certainly was no longer adored. It was viewed with an increasing amount of distrust and even ill will. Inevitably, this ill will spilled from the economic sphere into political and social relationships. A young woman who served as a cashier at the Intercontinental Hotel in Frankfurt was visibly annoyed when I insisted on May 3, before the Bundesbank's announcement, that she give me change in marks rather than dollars. A Paris bellhop grunted disapprovingly when I tipped him in U.S. currency.

The final blow to the Bretton Woods system, with its narrowly fixed linkages between the major currencies, came in mid-August 1971. On the evening of August 15, a Sunday, President Nixon went on national television to announce the closing of the gold window: no longer would the United States exchange gold for dollars at the Bretton Woods price of $35 per ounce. The system's anchor was being hauled up. The decision was reached during a secret meeting between the president and a few of his top advisers at Camp David. The president of the Federal Reserve Bank of New York, Alfred Hayes, wasn't even consulted. Hayes, as we will see, was a staunch supporter of the Bretton Woods fixed-rate arrangement.

In the week before Nixon's move, nearly $4 billion of "hot money" had fled the United States for foreign currencies. In a last-ditch effort to protect the nation's dwindling gold stock, which would have been gone but for the forbearance of foreign governments, the Federal Reserve with the Treasury Department's approval borrowed some $2.2 billion in other currencies through prearranged credit lines with other central banks. Charles A. Coombs, a senior vice president at the New York Federal Reserve Bank and the special manager of the Fed's powerful policy-setting unit, the Federal Open Market Committee (FOMC), relates a disquieting encounter during a trip to Washington on August 6. Coombs recalls "one distinguished Federal Reserve figure"—presumably Chairman Arthur F. Burns—who said "as I entered his office that Friday, 'I don't know about you, but I'm getting scared!'" Coombs came away worried that the "situation could turn into panic within a matter of days" and concluded that "drastic policy action" could no longer be averted.[1] That drastic action came with Nixon's August 15 closing of the gold window. The Bretton Woods system was finished.

HARDLY A "GOLDEN" PERIOD

Monetary chaos, of course, wasn't what the architects of the Bretton Woods system, primarily economists, envisioned when they laid the framework for it in 1944. With the system's collapse in 1971, currency values in much of the world were free to float daily in relationship to one another, responding only to the forces of supply and demand. As a result, no government is now obliged to swallow American dollars at a fixed rate of exchange if dollars start to pile up excessively within its borders. Today when the Federal Reserve's monetary policy grows overly expansionary, much of the resulting inflationary pressure stays at home; inflation no longer can be so readily exported to such places as Germany. Now, excessive dollars quickly generate domestic inflation, and the dollar's value in international currency markets is likely to drop if the Fed pumps out too much money. Any such drop, of course, tends to intensify inflationary pressure at home, inasmuch as it makes imported goods costlier for Americans and spurs demand for U.S. goods abroad. As Milton Friedman, the Nobel laureate at Stanford University's Hoover Institution, once told me during an interview at his mountain summer home in Ely, Vermont, "Fixed rates allow inflationary policies to be disguised."

To this day, I should note, considerable disagreement continues to exist among economists over whether a fixed-rate system, à la Bretton Woods, or a floating-rate arrangement is preferable. Proponents of a fixed-rate system point to the fact that inflation in most countries worsened after the Bretton Woods system collapsed. Analysts who favor floating rates, however, contend—correctly in my view—that much of the world's post–1971 inflation is derived from practices in effect during the Bretton Woods years. These economists blame much of the post–1971 inflation on the enormous hoard of American dollars that was allowed to accumulate abroad while the fixed-rate arrangement was in effect. This never would have occurred, they argue, without fixed rates of currency exchange. The Bretton Woods system, they further claim, could never have survived the economic shocks that have occurred since 1971, particularly the repeated shortages and price surges that have marked the oil business. The old system was simply too brittle to accommodate such disruptions.

There remains a widespread misconception, harbored to this day on the editorial page of my own newspaper, that the Bretton Woods system somehow engendered the relatively inflation-free growth and rising international prosperity that marked the early postwar decades. This simplistic notion holds that fixed rates brought a high degree of certainty into international transactions, which in turn fostered the early postwar expansion of commercial and capital flows across national borders.

Ideally, to be sure, the Bretton Woods system was conducive to such benign developments. In the abstract, it promised to eliminate uncertainty from international financial dealings. For instance, a widget maker would know, when an order arrived from abroad, that the money to be received for the widgets would be worth as much as in the past.

In practice, however, fixed rates brought intense uncertainty. Between 1944, when the Bretton Woods system was conceived, and August 15, 1971, when the system collapsed, 45 countries changed the international rates for their currencies. In some instances, the changes were repeated many times, so that a total of 74 currency-rate changes occurred under the Bretton Woods system. Fritz Machlup, a noted Princeton University economist, once joked to me that the postwar fixed-rate system was actually a jumping-rate system.

Even so, attempts to maintain fixed-rate relationships between various key currencies persisted until 1973. In December 1971, under the so-called Smithsonian Agreement, the currencies of the 10 major trading countries in the non-Communist world, the G-10 group, were realigned in what amounted to a fixed-rate arrangement. Under the agreement, the United States consented to devalue the dollar to $38 per ounce of gold, which in turn brought an average 10% devaluation of the dollar against the other currencies.

Most important, however, the dollar's convertibility into gold was not restored, and the United States no longer committed itself to supporting the dollar. Then, in February 1973, the dollar was further devalued to $42.22 per ounce of gold, which again raised the worth of the other major currencies 10% against the dollar. A month later, after massive interventions by various monetary authorities, the shattered system of fixed exchange rates disintegrated into generalized floating.[2]

For currency rates to remain fixed for long periods, the countries involved must retain their relative competitive positions in the global marketplace indefinitely—an impossibility that many eminent economists nonetheless had come to believe. In the two decades after the collapse of the Bretton Woods system, the value of the dollar, finally reflecting marketplace forces, fell against the mark, for example, from the aforementioned 3.6 rate to below 1.6. The market price for gold, meanwhile, soared more than tenfold.

Some nations, like the United States, saw their standings

erode in the continual global economic race, while others gained ground. To be sure, a government can attempt to cling to an outdated exchange rate, but this only means that when an eventual rate change comes it will be greater, and therefore more disruptive of international transactions, than a change made promptly. Under the Bretton Woods system, as we have seen with Germany, countries often clung to existing rates of exchange too long, prompting speculation on a large future exchange-rate change. A case in point from the Bretton Woods years is Britain, an architect of the system. Britain struggled along for years attempting to preserve the fixed value of the pound, which was overvalued. Finally, expedients ranging from tax increases to protectionist trade measures were exhausted, and devaluation was resorted to; in November 1968, the pound's value was cut by 14.3%, to $2.40 from $2.80. This happened despite a move by U.S. authorities to prop up the pound with massive dollar infusions. Under freely floating rates, such a big, sudden change in the pound's value wouldn't have been possible. Instead, there would have been constant, but relatively minor, changes, and therefore, none of the disruption and speculation that accompanies a major devaluation.

Among other things, overdue changes in a currency's rate of exchange allow speculators to make a tidy profit. Clearly, in the Bretton Woods years, exchange rates were getting out of line a lot faster and by far larger degrees than the system's planners had anticipated back in 1944. Strictly speaking, the Bretton Woods system did permit a slight fluctuation of rates, up to 1% on either side of the designated parity between particular currencies. But the many forced devaluations and revaluations usually were of far larger magnitude than 1%.

Nostalgia for the Bretton Woods system notwithstanding, a more reasonable explanation for the rising international prosperity of the early postwar decades rests in the ready availability of U.S. capital, especially in the early years. This capital was sorely needed to rebuild the war-ravaged economies in Western Europe and elsewhere. As the reconstruction proceeded, world economic activity expanded quickly. It was the U.S. decision to make its capital available, rather than the existence of a fixed-rate monetary system tied to gold, that was responsible for the impressive early postwar record.

At the start of the post–World War II era, Uncle Sam held roughly two-thirds of the world's gold supply. This accumulation dated back to the 1930s, when a capital flight from Europe intensified as fears of a new war mounted. During World War II, understandably, gold continued to flow into the United States not only in the form of capital flight but also to pay for weaponry and various military endeavors undertaken by America on behalf of its allies.

Now, of course, there is no longer a superprosperous, supergenerous Uncle Sam waiting in the wings to fatten up other economies with bulging amounts of capital. Ideally, the smoothest-running international monetary system would be one managed by a world central bank. Such an institution would be able to regulate monetary policies in all countries and, in effect, decide what currencies should be worth in terms of one another. It's a fact of political life, however, that no government—even those in Western Europe—thus far appears willing to yield so much authority to an international body. It has been difficult just to establish a central monetary authority for only a part of the European Community (EC).

The best practical alternative to a world central bank, most economists now agree, is to continue to let currency values move freely in response to the supply-and-demand forces of global markets. Perhaps the most cogent case for such a loosely knit arrangement was made soon after the collapse of the Bretton Woods system by Darryl R. Francis, at the time the president of the St. Louis Federal Reserve Bank. He argued that a floating-rate system "would best solve our current difficulties and would assure a permanent exchange-rate mechanism which should be free of the type of trade slowdowns we are experiencing now." He conceded that "continuous small changes in exchange rates would induce marginally greater daily risks" for people engaged in international business. However, precisely because constant adjustments to marketplace forces would occur with floating rates, the danger of occasional, but large and highly disruptive, rate changes, such as took place under the Bretton Woods system, would virtually be eliminated.[3] Other attributes of a floating-rate system include the likelihood that no unwanted accumulations of currencies are necessary, since rates are free to respond immediately to the forces of supply and demand. Moreover, floating rates make it possible for governments to pursue independent domestic economic policies without the burden of a trading partner whose currency is held at an unrealistically low rate of exchange.

In retrospect, then, it is apparent that the Bretton Woods system was hardly the success it is sometimes still considered. Rather, it was an unrealistic plan, doomed to fail once the limits of U.S. largesse were reached.

Still, the dream of fixed rates dies hard. Even as the Bretton Woods system was beginning to crack in the late 1960s, influential voices continued to be raised in its support. In Frankfurt, in mid-July 1968, Bundesbank President Karl Blessing confessed to me his deepening "concern" that "one day" the Bretton Woods system might break down, to be followed, in all probability, by a period of floating rates. "Floating rates," Blessing warned, "could bring on a lot of trouble, but the possibility [of their being implemented] cannot be ruled out." At about the same time in Paris, Jacques Rueff, the eminent French economist, continued to advocate a return to a fixed-rate system even more rigid than the Bretton Woods system: a gold standard unblemished by any special treatment for the American dollar. This, he told me in his comfortable Paris apartment in mid-1968, was the only "logical solution" to a "precarious" international monetary situation.

For still more evidence that the Bretton Woods dream dies hard, one need only turn to the EC's persistent effort to establish a common currency. In 1973, two years after the collapse of the Bretton Woods system, key members of the European Community agreed to set up a system among themselves that would be similar to the Bretton Woods system: their currencies would be fixed in relation to one another but would increase or decline in value in relation to the rest of the world. Six years later, the arrangement was formalized and made more binding with the creation of the so-called European Monetary System, with the goal of a common European currency.

However, some EC members, notably Britain, remain reluctant to surrender control of their money supply to an international body. Meanwhile, the German mark has served as the standard for the group. But because the mark has been relatively strong, reflecting Germany's very competitive economy, some EC members have had to struggle to keep the value of their own currencies from dropping sharply against the mark. These efforts have led to high interest rates, high unemployment, and sluggish or nonexistent economic growth. So painful were such efforts for Britain and Italy, for example, that in September 1992 both left the system—wise decisions that show once again the impossibility of fixing currency rates between economies whose capabilities may differ greatly.

In the United States, as recently as December 31, 1991, Lawrence Kudlow, the chief economist of the powerful New York investment firm of Bear, Stearns, claimed at the top of *The Wall Street Journal*'s editorial page that the Bretton Woods era had been a "golden" period. Kudlow urged U.S. policy makers to strive to reinstitute such a system.

THE INTERWAR EXPERIENCE

The Bretton Woods system, as unworkable as it ultimately turned out to be, was the brainchild of a select handful of top economists on both sides of the Atlantic Ocean. On July 1, 1944—with World War II still raging but with the prospect of an Allied victory clearly increasing—no fewer than 730 representatives, mostly economists, from as many as 45 nations convened at a large old hotel—the Mount Washington—in the tiny, rural New England community of Bretton Woods, New Hampshire. From this historic conference, three organizations were born: the IMF, which was by far the most important of the three, the World Bank, and the International Trade Organization. The crucial task of ensuring exchange-rate stability was assigned to the IMF. It and the World Bank were to draw financial support from the participating nations at Bretton Woods according to each nation's particular economic resources.

IMF members not physically occupied by the enemy during the war were required to establish par values for their currencies in terms of either gold or the dollar; by the end of 1946, 32 nations had done so. Current-account transactions, such as trade in goods and services, were required to be made within bands of 1% of the designated values, and changes were not permitted for any reason but to correct any "fundamental" disequilibrium in a country's balance of payments—and even then, this could be done only after extensive consultation with IMF officials. The "stick" in this arrangement was the loss of IMF financial aid if a country altered the value of its currency without the agency's approval. In practice, the stick was rarely employed. Often, the IMF granted countries access to financial aid even if their currencies were trading at values well below levels prescribed by the rules.

The original quotas for the IMF totaled $8.8 billion, with the U.S. contribution of $2.75 billion amounting to the lion's share. It was further arranged that a country's contribution would determine its voting power within the IMF, based on a formula of one vote for every $100,000 contributed. The rules called for members to pay one-quarter of their quotas in gold and the remaining amount in their particular currencies.[4]

As things worked out after the war, the transitional period to a fully operating international monetary system proved far longer than the Bretton Woods architects anticipated. Indeed, full convertibility of all the major currencies did not occur until 1958, a full 14 years after the meeting in New Hampshire. In the meantime, many countries had employed exchange controls, and bilateral monetary agreements between trading partners were widespread.

"Until the Western European industrial countries made their currencies convertible on December 27, 1958, the [Bretton Woods] system did not operate as intended," notes Michael Bordo, a Rutgers professor who has extensively studied the evolution of the Bretton Woods system. In reality, Bordo contends, the system functioned fully as intended for only 12 years—or only 9 years "if we date its termination at the end of Gold Pool and the start of the two-tier system on March 15, 1968."[5]

For many years, the so-called Gold Pool helped the United States hold the yellow metal's price in all transactions near $35 per ounce. The United States, Britain, and several other major industrial countries ran this pool through the Bank of England in London and controlled the release of the non-Communist world's yearly output of freshly mined gold. But by the fall of 1967, private speculation against the long-term value of the dollar was such that the pool's members could no longer feed enough gold into the pool to meet demand at the $35 price. In March 1968, the pool was disbanded, and the metal's price was allowed to float in the marketplace. Within a few days, gold was selling privately in Switzerland for as much as $45 an ounce, even though Washington continued to hold its official dollar-gold rate at $35 per ounce as prescribed by Bretton Woods rules.

Although the monetary plan for fixed rates was hatched at Bretton Woods in July 1944, its true genesis extends back to the troubled interwar years of prosperity that were abruptly halted and then reversed in the 1930s by a deepening global depression. The economists responsible for what emerged at Bretton Woods—notably John Maynard Keynes of Britain and Harry Dexter White of the United States—were profoundly influenced by events in the interwar years and had come to share a conviction that only a closely managed international system could foster prosperity in the postwar era.

This conviction, unfortunately, was rooted in a widely held—but deeply mistaken—interpretation of the interwar experience. The prevailing, conventional view of the time held that a major factor in the depressionary interwar period was insufficient monetary cooperation among the major nations. But this view glossed over important facts. In country after country in the 1930s, economic recovery—not depression—began soon after a particular country's currency collapsed. Indeed, economic contraction usually occurred during the precollapse period when ill-fated efforts to save the value of the British pound or the French franc or some other currency were still under way.

The British experience is a case in point. The pound sterling collapsed in September 1931, when Britain, after heavy gold losses, stopped selling gold for pounds at a prescribed price. In the quarter before the devaluation of the pound, the British index of industrial production, for example, stood at only 80% of its 1924 average. This was after a long decline from a high in 1929 of 113%. No sooner did the pound fall, however, than the index (which was based on physical volume and thus not distorted by inflation or deflation) began to climb. By the end of 1931, it stood at 88%; it reached the 90% mark in the first quarter of 1932, 103% by early 1934, and 127% three years later.

The French example shows striking similarities to the British experience. France's currency was among the last to fall in the 1930s, finally succumbing to devaluation near the end of 1936. By no coincidence, France's economy was also among the last to turn up in the 1930s. In fact, records show that French industrial production did not begin to turn clearly upward until as late as 1938. In 1936, when the franc collapsed, French output stood at 93% of its 1913 average.

Other key economic yardsticks display a similar pattern. On the employment front, for instance, the percentage of the British labor force with jobs fell persistently through 1930 and during most of 1931, then briefly leveled off, and then, by late 1932, began to increase. In the United States, where the currency collapse came early in 1933, similar patterns of production and employment can be traced.

A detailed study of the global monetary situation in these depression years was conducted 50 years ago by Ragnar Nurkse, an economist working for the old, long-defunct League of Nations. In a volume titled *International Currency Experience—Lessons of the Inter-War Period*, Nurkse drew some intriguing conclusions. In country after country, he noted, "Devaluation was followed by a domestic expansion of investment and national income." Moreover, he found that this domestic improvement tended "to stimulate foreign trade all around." In addition, Nurkse found that after the dust of all the devaluations had settled, the relationships between the major currencies were not very different from before.[6]

Currency data from those years bear this out. The table below shows the exchange values of particular currencies in relation to the dollar. The 1930 relationships are used as the base of 100. For example, the value of the British pound in relationship to the dollar fell sharply between 1930 and 1932, as the pound was devalued, and then rebounded, so that in 1936, the pound's value in dollar terms was only slightly higher than in 1930.

Country	1930	1932	1934	1936
Britain	100	67	102	101
France	100	100	168	119
Italy	100	100	162	100
Canada	100	87	101	100

What did the currency chaos of the 1930s prove if, in the end, the major currencies returned to roughly the same relationships? Nurkse had an answer. "In the default of simultaneous antidepression measures," he concluded, "successive devaluations leading to monetary expansion were the only practical alternative, if exchange control was to be avoided." Moreover, the currency collapses that marked the period were hardly a cause of the deepening hard times. Rather, the collapses tended to coincide with the advent of economic improvement in one country after another. In brief, the breakdown of unsustainable fixed-rate arrangements led to better times.

A NEGLECTED LESSON

Seldom has such an important historical lesson been so badly neglected and misunderstood as in the planning that preceded the multinational conference at Bretton Woods. To appreciate how this could possibly happen, one must first take a closer look at the system's architects: John Maynard Keynes and Harry Dexter White and their colleagues on each side of the Atlantic. The planners in the time leading up to the conference were dreaming a dream that was truly impossible. As Michael Bordo puts it, "The architects of the Bretton Woods system wanted a set of monetary arrangements that would combine the advantage of the classical gold standard—exchange-rate stability—with the advantages of floating rates—independence to pursue national full-employment policies." As Bordo notes, they sought to eschew the supposed defects of floating exchange rates—for example, competitive "beggar-thy-neighbor" devaluations—as well as the undeniable defects of a fixed-rate, gold-standard system with its tendency to subject domestic economic activity to stern international constraints.[7] The ambition may have been worthy, but it was also blind to some very recent history.

An early draft of Keynes' proposals for a postwar system reveals his misreading of the interwar experience, as he claimed that during the depression "the world explored in rapid succession almost, as it were, in an intensive laboratory experiment, all the alternative false approaches to the solution."[8] Floating rates, as we have seen, hardly constituted a "false" approach to a dire situation.

A similar misreading, as well as a naive devotion to managed currencies, can be detected in an early paper of Harry White. In it, he labeled as a "hangover from a 19th century creed" the belief "still so widely held" that "interference with trade and with capital and gold movements, etc., are harmful." He scoffed at the idea that without governmental intervention "international economic adjustments . . . would work themselves out toward an 'equilibrium' with a minimum of harm to world trade and prosperity." He concluded, "It is doubtful whether that belief was ever sound."[9] Again, we see a woeful misreading of the interwar experience.

Seldom have economists been accorded the power and importance that Keynes and White, with their shared faith in government intervention, enjoyed during World War II. The war served, as wars often do, to draw economists into governmental posts in both Britain and America. This predictable pattern, moreover, came on the heels of the prolonged international depression that, for better or worse, had severely shaken old beliefs, particularly the belief in the ability of free-market forces to set things right. On top of the wartime need, from a purely military standpoint, for economic brainpower in Washington and London, there was the need for a fresh approach to economic matters generally. As G. John Ikenberry of Princeton University observes, "All increments of historical time are not equal: There are junctures or 'breakpoints' when possibilities for major change are particularly great and the scope of possible outcomes are unusually wide. In this century, the several years surrounding 1945 would surely be one such moment." At such moments, Ikenberry goes on, "the removal of obstacles to change occurs simultaneously with the presence of impulses to change," and when this happens, "fundamental change is possible."[10]

For Keynes and White and their respective colleagues, the upshot was, as Ikenberry puts it, a "privileged position" to advance proposals—a position made all the more privileged, I should add, by the complexity of the issues. John Kenneth Galbraith of Harvard has said of Bretton Woods, "There can have been few international meetings in the history of such convocations where public comprehension of what was occurring or even of what was being attempted was so slight [but] this was far from a handicap [since] what people do not understand, they generally think important."[11]

It is difficult to imagine two more different men than Keynes and White working so successfully together in a profession that is well known for intramural squabbling. The former was a renowned economist and British aristocrat whose name remains synonymous with pathbreaking economic ideas. The latter was an obscure U.S. Treasury official who, unlike Keynes, was devoid of the social graces and who, Galbraith recalls, was "impolite and irascible" as well as, like Keynes, arrogant. While the name of Keynes continues to occupy prominent space in encyclopedias and on biographic bookshelves, White's is all but forgotten. The end to his important life was sorry indeed; he was drummed out of his Treasury job after the war, accused of being a Communist sympathizer. Galbraith recalls the final days: "On August 13, 1948, he answered the charges to the Un-American Activities of the House of Representatives with poorly restrainted contempt, omitting to mention only that had he been a Communist, he would have been not their servant but their master—a fact to which all who knew him would attest. Then, a day or so later, he too died of heart disease from which he also had previously suffered."[12] Keynes, it should be explained, had died in 1946 of similar causes.

The philosophy shared by these economists of such disparate backgrounds was clear enough: economic order in the postwar world should be a closely managed, multinational affair with monetary and trade practices subject to strict international agreement and supervision to promote the fullest possible employment and the social and economic goals embodied in what had come to be known as Keynesian economics.

The arrangement hammered out at Bretton Woods, it should be added, grew out of quite distinctive plans, constructed a good deal earlier by the respective sides. Keynes' approach to Bretton Woods was rooted in his view that social progress and economic prosperity should be the overriding mission of international planning for the postwar era. As early as 1943, he had put forward plans for a so-called International Clearing Union—nearly tantamount to a world central bank—to be empowered not only to manage but to create a new global currency, dubbed the "bancor," for settling payments imbalances between nations. The International Clearing Union, through financial penalties if necessary, would be authorized to pressure both deficit and surplus countries to even out their imbalances. The bancor's value was to be set in terms of gold, with each national currency then set in terms of the bancor. Nations with international accounts in surplus would be required to maintain interest-bearing credit balances, and those in deficit would have to balance their accounts through interest-bearing overdrafts transferred to the surplus nations' credit. Gold could also be used in these settlements.

At about the same time as Keynes developed his plan, White and his colleagues in the United States produced a plan wherein each nation would contribute gold and a set amount of its own currency to a so-called United Nations Stabilization Fund. In its disciplinary details, the White proposal was even stricter than Keynes' plan. Each country was required to maintain a predetermined par value for its currency in terms of a "unitas," or international unit of account, worth 10 gold U.S. dollars. This par value could only be changed if a "fundamental dise-quilibrium" developed in a country's balance of payments. Even then, changes could be made only with the fund's permission, and if the change was more than 10%, three-quarters of the fund's membership would have to approve it. Substantial penalties would be inflicted for rules violations.

A compromise between the two plans emerged in April 1944, bearing the ungainly title of "Joint Statement by Experts on the Establishment of the International Monetary Fund." This was to serve as the working draft at Bretton Woods and ulti-mately provided the basis for the IMF's articles of agreement. As Ikenberry recalls, the "crucial breakthrough" that brought the compromise was achieved in September 1943, when the British side agreed to abandon the idea of unlimited liability for creditor countries that was embodied in Keynes' International Clearing Union. Under the compromise, the responsibility for restoring international equilibrium would fall in practice on the overburdened shoulders of nations in deficit and would not be carried as well by creditor nations, as Keynes quite sensibly had urged.

As this suggests, the final plan on balance was somewhat closer to White's position then to Keynes'. Still, Keynes' influ-ence throughout the planning process and in the final draft was considerable. By the time of the conference, Keynes himself commanded a wartime office within the U.S. Treasury in Wash-ington, and his disciples could be found throughout key sectors of the Washington bureaucracy, particularly at the important National Resources Planning Board, where they pressed for an expanded federal role in managing the economy. The aim was full employment and greater social welfare, an ambition strongly and loudly supported by such liberal elements of Amer-ican journalism as *The Nation* and *The New Republic*. In fact, Ikenberry observes, many of the Keynesians in Washington "believed that the maintenance of high levels of employment and the development of national planning throughout the world should take precedence over the opening of economies to the free flow of investment and trade." The remarkable—and lamentable—fact is that few economic planners "saw any real alternative to Bretton Woods," Ikenberry reports. "Moreover, the coalition against Bretton Woods—New York bankers, high-tariff advocates, silverites and isolationists—were soon seen as an odd bunch, outside the political mainstream."[13]

WHAT MIGHT HAVE BEEN

What if? What if Keynes and White and their fellow interventionists had not gained sway in Washington and in London during World War II? What if there had been no conference at Bretton Woods or elsewhere to establish—or more properly to reestablish—an international monetary system based on fixed relationships between major currencies? What if, after the war, currencies had been allowed to float freely in terms of one another, promptly responding to marketplace forces of currency supply and demand—much as would happen after the collapse of the tottering Bretton Woods system in the early 1970s? What if these unrealistic planners of the postwar world—Keynes, White, and their disciples—had been believers in the efficacy of free-market forces?

After the end of World War II, as we have seen, the United States had possession of an enormous amount of capital, much of it in gold that had flowed into the nation during the troubled years preceding the outbreak of hostilities in Europe. In those years, even more than today, America was the ultimate safe haven for capital. As Guido Carli, the Italian central banker, told me many years ago, a rich Italian's favorite nest egg, along with gold, was a large cooperative apartment on New York's Fifth Avenue. He said this, I should add, while ensconced in precisely such a location.

It was primarily American capital, plus the remarkable altruism and generosity of its possessors, that fueled the sharp, sustained economic expansion that marked much of the non-Communist world in the early postwar decades. In those years, of course, many of the major IMF participants—the Communist nations had chosen not to join—had enormous import requirements but could offer little to the United States or other nations in the way of necessary exports. This difficulty was resolved through the willingness of the United States to make available its great store of wealth. First, there was a "special loan" of $3.75 billion to Britain, made under the Anglo-American Financial Agreement of 1945. Then, of course, came the Marshall Plan with its appropriation of some $12.5 billion, still a large sum today and a truly gigantic amount in those years.

If there were indeed "golden years" under the Bretton Woods system, this generous outpouring of U.S. capital, not the fixed-rate system itself, was largely the reason. And, given America's unswerving (as well as, it can be argued, self-serving) generosity, this outpouring would surely have occurred even if the monetary arrangements devised by Keynes and White had not come into being. Indeed, the remarkable postwar expansion would have occurred no matter what was decided at Bretton Woods. Surely there is no reason to suspect that the generosity level in early postwar America would have been lower had currencies been allowed to float.

Had floating rates ensued, however, many of the troubles that developed as America's circumstances grew more strained in the 1960s and early 1970s might not have taken place. Germany, for instance, probably would not have been placed in the position of having to "swallow," as Emminger described it, dollars and, as a result, import unhealthy doses of inflation from the United States. For its part, the United States without fixed rates might not have been so easily lulled into living beyond its means, in effect printing supposedly fixed-rate dollars—35 of them to an ounce of gold—for use in the global marketplace. Had the dollar's value been floating in those years, its value probably would have diminished, and the money-printing gambit would have soon grown less attractive.

In late 1973, soon after the collapse of Bretton Woods and the subsequent, predictable drop in the dollar's international worth, the global economy was subjected to the shocks of steeply higher oil prices and a squeeze on oil's availability, the result of a highly successful cartel established by the Organization of Petroleum Exporting Countries (OPEC). Some analysts, I should note, claim in retrospect that these two events were related. "The long-smouldering resentment of the Middle East oil-producing countries over earlier heavy losses sustained in selling off a precious natural resource in exchange for depreciating paper money, first sterling and then the dollar, now found an excuse for retaliation in the form of price demands that went far beyond the bounds of reason," argued Charles A. Coombs in 1976. The OPEC price surge, Coombs concludes, was a "by-product of the breakdown of world financial order."[14]

Of course, as a manager of this "broken-down" financial order, Coombs, who served at the New York Fed for 33 years, has a very large ax to grind. A more reasonable assessment of the OPEC move is that it would have come whatever monetary system—fixed or floating rate—was in force. Moreover, it is highly likely that oil price increases would have had a far more egregious impact on the global economy had the Bretton Woods system still been in operation. The OPEC action led to—indeed, necessitated—an enormous increase in international capital flows. As Henry Kaufman notes, "The Bretton Woods era was basically one of limited international capital mobility and therefore subject to particular strain in times of unexpected shocks in the global economy." The period of "floating rates," he continues, "by contrast has been marked by growing internationalization of capital markets."[15]

For all of the international economic strains that OPEC's actions precipitated, the global flows of capital and commerce expanded markedly in the post–Bretton Woods years. It is highly doubtful that such expansion would have materialized under the previous, more rigid monetary system. In 1972, near the end of the fixed-rate arrangement, international bank lending, for example, totaled less than $5 billion; by the mid-1980s, after more than a decade of floating rates, the total exceeded $50 billion. Similarly, the amount of international bond issues in 1972 approximated $10 billion; in 1985, the total reached $175 billion. Such enormous increases, Kaufman notes, were "particularly striking, since many observers had expected high currency volatility [stemming from floating rates] to inhibit international capital mobility."[16]

There is no doubt that such volatility did accompany the early shakedown phases of floating rates. In a 24-month period after the move to floating rates, the dollar's rate against the mark plunged 31%, as Charles Coombs recalls. Then, however, it rebounded 30%, slumped 17%, rose 12%, and finally fell 10%. But for all of this volatility, world trade and international capital flows continued to rise. Not only was there volatility soon after the breakdown of the Bretton Woods system, as currencies readjusted their values, but there was also, it should be noted, some continuing governmental interference with the emerging supply-and-demand forces affecting particular currencies. Central bank officials were accustomed to holding the monetary reins, and not surprisingly, many persisted in intervening when possible in the global currency marketplace. The result was a prolonged period of what economists call "dirty" floating.

As Coombs relates, the Federal Reserve chairman at the time, Arthur Burns, along with key officials at the Fed's regional bank in New York, such as Coombs himself, "shared an acute distaste and distrust of free-floating exchange rates."[17] With somewhat reluctant White House approval and the ready cooperation of Swiss and West German monetary authorities, there was soon an increase in central-bank intervention in foreign-exchange markets. The intervention hoped to reestablish more stable currency relationships at levels deemed most appropriate by the particular monetary authorities. This was attempted through massive, jointly conducted central-bank buying or selling of one or another currency. In only six months of 1975, for instance, the Federal Reserve alone intervened to the tune of about $1 billion, attempting to push up the dollar's international value. Ultimately, such administrative moves proved insufficient to overcome more fundamental forces; in the end, currencies tended, despite efforts to prop them up or push them down, to seek levels appropriate to the circumstances of the economies they represented.

Perhaps the most reasonable explanation for this futile attempt to rig currency values can be found in human nature. In 1970, while the Bretton Woods system was still in operation, I tried to illustrate this point through a brief fable that appeared on the editorial page of *The Wall Street Journal*. As the scene opens, the seven governors of the Federal Reserve Board and other top Reserve officials are gathered behind closed doors in Washington. At the head of the table is Chairman Arthur Burns. After discussing domestic matters, the conversation turns to the international arena. Very much on the officials' minds is a recent call for the implementation of floating exchange rates, issued by Milton Friedman. Friedman, who at the time was teaching at the University of Chicago, had been loudly urging in *The Wall Street Journal*, *Newsweek*, and elsewhere that fixed exchange rates be scrapped and a currency's value be allowed to float freely in foreign transactions in response to supply and demand. Part of the imaginary discussion among the officials follows:

CHAIRMAN BURNS: We mustn't forget we also have responsibility on the international front. We're expected to work closely with other central bankers to preserve our system of fixed exchange rates. As you know, Mr. Alfred Hayes, president of the New York Federal Reserve Bank, and other members of his staff make periodic trips to Switzerland to confer secretly with foreign central bankers.

MR. HAYES: Indeed, Mr. Chairman, I'm off to Basel, by way of London, this very afternoon. As you know, there's been increasing speculation about another realignment in certain exchange rates.

GOVERNOR GEORGE MITCHELL: If I understand Professor Friedman correctly, there would no longer be any fixed exchange rates for us to worry about. Is that correct?

CHAIRMAN BURNS: Professor Friedman would have us let the dollar float freely, like a commodity, subject only to the demands of the marketplace. Let me quote from an old *Newsweek* column of his. "We should say to the people of the world: a dollar is a dollar. You may borrow dollars in the United States or abroad from anyone who is willing to lend. You may lend dollars in the United States or abroad to anyone who is willing to borrow. You may buy dollars from or sell dollars to anyone you wish at any price that is mutually agreeable. The U.S.government will not interfere in any way."

GOVERNOR SHERMAN MAISEL: No more trips to Basel. No more worrying about what country is buying gold on the sly. No more buying this currency and selling that currency to preserve this or that exchange rate. No more battling to avoid a devaluation of this currency or to promote a revaluation of that currency. Is that what we have here?

GOVERNOR DEWEY DAANE: I'm beginning to think Professor Friedman wants to do us out of our jobs.

GOVERNOR ANDREW BRIMMER: No more rescue operations for the pound sterling?

MR. HAYES: No more secret meetings in Basel?

GOVERNOR J. L. ROBERTSON: No more secret changes in monetary policy?

CHAIRMAN BURNS: Gentlemen, gentlemen. One at a time please. It's obvious we've got to do a lot of hard thinking about implementing Mr. Friedman's ideas. Let me suggest we postpone consideration of his ideas until some later meeting. In the meantime, let's turn our attention to the matter of monetary policy. Let's see now, I believe when we met three weeks ago, we voted to tighten up considerably. In light of recent economic statistics, I suggest it would now be prudent to change course and adopt a monetary policy of substantial ease. Perhaps each of you would comment on this suggestion.

As the curtain falls, Governor Robertson, vice chairman of the board, is about to speak. Mr. Hayes excuses himself because he has to catch a plane for London.[18]

There is a real-life, highly coincidental epilogue to this little fable. Shortly after my fanciful tale ran in the paper, I went to London to gather grist for a couple of columns. To pass the time one lonely evening, I visited a somewhat raunchy nightclub called Raymond's Revue Bar, situated in the heart of London's

Soho district, where strippers were peeling before an audience of mostly middle-aged and slightly inebriated males, many of whom I judged to be traveling American businessmen. Among the attentive group, I observed through the smoky haze, was none other than Alfred Hayes, as trim and WASPy-looking as ever with his closely-cropped gray hair and prim, silver-rimmed spectacles. Having interviewed him many times at his home base at the New York Fed, I decided to sidle over and inquire whether I might—on the paper's generous expense account, of course—buy him a late dinner after the show. Clearly embarrassed at being spotted by a member of the New York financial press in such a far-off, voyeuristic den, he rather brusquely declined my invitation, explaining that he had pressing business later in the evening and also had to catch an early-morning flight—guess where—to Basel. Almost immediately, in fact, Hayes exited Raymond's, departing in the same limousine that I had noticed parked outside the club when I arrived.

Even without the dinner, however, my chance encounter with Hayes was of journalistic use. I had been searching for some catchy way to lead off a column I was preparing on the considerable troubles of the British pound and the futile U.S. efforts to shore it up. Now, I realized, I had my lead: "Alfred Hayes, president of the New York Federal Reserve Bank, was here in London the other evening, studying the gyrations of the pound—the pound of flesh, that is. His examination was conducted, accordingly, not within the confines of the Bank of England or the British Treasury, but at a joint in Soho called Raymond's. . . ."

On a more serious note, there can be no doubt that a considerable degree of comfort was drawn on both sides of the Atlantic at this time from the fact that central bankers such as Hayes maintained close, regular contact with their international counterparts. It was somehow reassuring that at least once a month these monetary authorities would convene behind closed doors in Basel to ponder the health of the international monetary system and to consider ways in which monetary crises might be avoided. I submit, however, that a far more significant meeting of international monetary experts—none of them in governmental positions—took place in early 1969 in Oyster Bay, New York, at a luxurious conference facility called Planting Fields.

The meeting, which ran for three days in late January and was financed by the Ford Foundation, brought together two groups that had previously had relatively little contact—academic economists who specialized in international monetary affairs and commercial bankers whose daily business involved buying and selling different currencies. Its purpose, according to a brief press release, was to explore issues that were "raised by the various proposals for adoption of greater exchange-rate flexibility." Among the academicians present were professors from such institutions as Princeton University and the Fletcher School of Law and Diplomacy. Among the practitioners—as the professors called their counterparts—were representatives from such key banks as Morgan Guaranty Trust and First National City Bank of New York, now Citibank. About 30 people, half from the United States and half from major foreign nations, attended. None was a central banker.

The participants agreed not to divulge precisely what was said during the three days. It was felt, particularly by the banking representatives, that the discussion would progress with greater candor if Basel-like secrecy could be maintained. Nevertheless, it was possible to piece together from interviews soon after an approximate outline of what transpired. At the start, the two sides appeared hopelessly far apart. The economists, unlike many of their more influential colleagues in Washington and other capitals, generally held that the prevailing monetary system of fixed exchange rates was a bad arrangement and should be replaced as quickly as possible by a flexible system in which currencies would be allowed to float freely or within a wide band. The bankers, on the other hand, generally held that a flexible system would be utterly unworkable and that the fixed-rate system should be continued.

The viewpoints were not new or surprising. The academics maintained that the fixed-rate idea was unrealistic. A vote-seeking national leader, they said, simply could not be expected to take the sort of restrictive economic measures that often were necessary to uphold a currency's international value. Such a leader would also be reluctant to devalue the currency as long as there was even a slim chance that devaluation could be avoided. In the end, because of the delay, highly disruptive and long overdue devaluations would become necessary. If exchange rates were allowed to be flexible, the academicians concluded, such disruption would be much less likely. Exchange-rate changes would be more frequent and therefore smaller and less traumatic.

The practitioners argued that flexible rates would introduce unacceptable uncertainty into their daily currency-trading operations. Moreover, they attributed the great post–World War II growth of international business largely to the fixed-rate system. Their essential argument against flexibility was as follows: uncertain of what a particular currency might be worth a day or a week or a month in the future, a businessman would hesitate to go ahead with an international transaction. Eventually, international business would begin to contract. This, in turn, would lead to recessions in nations where international business played an important role. Eventually, a worldwide depression could develop.

As the Oyster Bay meeting progressed, however, it became clear that the positions of the two sides were not as rigid as they had appeared at the outset. "I learned some things about the technical problems that foreign-exchange dealers occasionally encounter in their daily operations," recalled an academic participant. And a banker who also attended told me: "I feel I really gained something from thrashing things out with the professors."[19]

An indication of the meeting's success was evident in two informal polls that one of the participants conducted. The first poll, taken near the start of the conference, found that nearly all the practitioners were flatly opposed to any shift toward flexible exchange rates. The second poll, taken at the end of the conference, found that a decisive majority of the practitioners now felt that they could live with at least a modest degree of rate flexibility.

There remained, to be sure, a considerable gap between the

degree of flexibility that most academicians favored and the
degree that most practitioners thought they could tolerate.
Some of the professors present, such as Princeton's Fritz Machlup, had long advocated freely floating rates, and most had
already campaigned for a monetary system that would allow a
currency to move at least 5% above or below its fixed relationship with other currencies. Even the most receptive practitioners at Oyster Bay balked at the idea of a band that would exceed
2.5%. Nevertheless, the meeting signified an important first
step in establishing a dialogue between the ivory tower of economists—ones unwilling to endorse the view of their policy-making colleagues—and the real world of business people.

Unlike the meetings held monthly by central bankers at
Basel, the one at Oyster Bay had no immediate impact on the
monetary arrangements binding the economies of the major
industrial countries. But if these private citizens from the campus and the marketplace could somehow establish a common
ground, as began to happen at Oyster Bay, it would ultimately
prove far more important that anything taking place at Basel.

Even now, long after the Oyster Bay meeting and the eventual end of the Bretton Woods system, central bankers still
travel abroad occasionally, and in the process, I suspect, they
enjoy a bit of fun from time to time whether at Raymond's or
at the Louvre in Paris or perhaps at the opera in Milan. They
may do these enjoyable things now, I should add, without the
nagging worry that some fixed rate may come unstuck just
when, for example, the stripper is getting ready to discard her
last bit of lingerie. This newfound peace of mind, it would seem,
is yet another benefit of floating rates: they do manage to make
life less worrisome even for some of their most diehard oppo-
nents.

What *is* worrisome, at least for those of us whose daily lives
continue to be affected by policies that economists initiate, is
that an arrangement as unworkable as the Bretton Woods system could so readily come into being, conceived and promoted
by the leading economic thinkers of the time. Clearly, the lesson

is to be cautious about embracing theories, however brilliant the economists promoting them may appear to be. And the Bretton Woods plan, as I will show in the pages that follow, was only the first of many unrealistic, often damaging concepts that well-intentioned, but overly optimistic, economists have concocted in recent decades for policy makers to implement—always in the name of constructing a new and wonderful economic era.

2

Back to the Home Front

"Full employment." The very words convey an optimism that belies the idea of a dismal science engaging misanthropic practitioners: work for all willing to work in an economy readily able to expand to accommodate a growing, able labor force. If exchange rates could be fixed among the major currencies to facilitate international flows of trade and capital, then surely employment could be arranged to hold joblessness at irreducible minimums. If not entirely eliminated, at least unemployment would never again approach the double-digit rates of the latter interwar years. Like that period's chaotic currency relationships, such joblessness would henceforth be impossible.

The Employment Act of 1946 was a logical sequel to the Bretton Woods system. Herbert Stein, an economics professor at the University of Virginia who served as President Nixon's chief economic adviser, has called the legislation "the Magna Carta of the American economy." President Truman, who signed the act into law, declared that the legislation would commit the federal government to "take any and all measures necessary for a healthy economy."

According to the act, the economy ought to provide "useful opportunities, including self-employment, for those able, willing and seeking to work." The act directed the federal government to use "all its plans, functions, and resources . . . to promote maximum employment, production, and purchasing power." It called on the president to set appropriately high levels of activity for the U.S. economy, created a three-member Council of Economic Advisers (CEA) in the Executive Office of the president and established a Joint Economic Committee of Congress (JEC). With the passage of the act, economists were to occupy an appreciably larger role in determining domestic policy, just as their role had expanded on the international stage with the creation of the Bretton Woods system.

The passage of the 1946 act was a victory for the Keynesian view that an entire economy, like the exchange rates of individual currencies, could be neatly managed over a prolonged period. The act was designed "to put the economics of John Maynard Keynes firmly and fully into law," recalls John Kenneth Galbraith, an ardent admirer of the Englishman. Even so, Galbraith laments that an earlier version of the proposal, which was a good deal stronger and more specific than what finally emerged, failed to make its way through Congress. The earlier version, pushed by Keynesian economists in the executive branch and four senators, led by New York's Robert Wagner, declared that "to the extent that continuing full employment cannot otherwise be achieved, it is the further responsibility of the federal government to provide such volume of federal investment and expenditure as may be needed to assure continuing full employment." Galbraith calls this proposal "the highwater mark, not alone in the United States but in all the industrial lands, of the Keynesian system."[1]

Opposition to the earlier version was led by the National Association of Manufacturers, which warned that enactment would dangerously increase the power of the executive branch and foster socialism. The compromise that became law affirmed only that the legislation was designed to aid individuals "able, willing and seeking to work" and that it would be carried out gingerly, only "to foster and promote free competitive enterprise and the general welfare." Galbraith wryly recalls the final legislation as "a model" for "admirers of the art of legislative emasculation." Nonetheless, he concedes that the act did finally establish economists in what he deems their proper place in the

American scheme of things. Indeed, he regards the legislation as "a step of marked importance in the history of economics: It established economists and economic counsel firmly in the center of modern American public administration [and] there would be similar if less formal steps in the other industrial countries."[2]

A less charitable assessment of the 1946 act comes from Michael Harrington, an avowed Socialist whose 1962 book, *The Other America*, documented in arresting detail the plight of the "invisible" poor across the nation; the book, which I reviewed favorably in *The Wall Street Journal*, inspired much of President Johnson's poverty fighting in the 1960s. Lamenting the 1946 legislation, Harrington notes that as early as 1944 President Roosevelt had advocated a legally guaranteed right to work but that with Roosevelt's death and peace in the world, "a conservative Congress [took] that excellent idea and reduced it to the generalities and pious wishes of the Employment Act of 1946." In fact, Harrington derides the act as "a statute so broad that Eisenhower [when president] was to use it to rationalize deflationary policies that led to chronic unemployment and recession." Even Harrington, however, concedes that over the long run the legislation affected policy, encouraging, for example, President Kennedy in the early 1960s to employ "Keynesian state intervention in a carefully planned way."[3]

A SPLENDID RECORD

As World War II ended, many Americans feared that the postwar period would witness a resumption of the economic stagnation that had marked the immediate prewar years. This widespread worry was based on assumptions that seemed entirely reasonable. With peace, the enormous governmental spending that the war had necessitated was clearly at an end. In a peaceful world, it was argued, such outlays would drop precipitously. For the millions of adult Americans who had endured the wretched 1930s, then, the future threatened to be a painful replay of hard economic times. After all, the reasoning ran, the Great Depression most certainly would have dragged on had not the war intervened, prompting a surge in federal expenditures that made Roosevelt's New Deal seem almost niggardly by comparison. For all the New Deal's good intentions, it seemed that only the massive fiscal stimulus of World War II had managed to pull the economy up from the depressionary abyss.

When the war ended in 1945, only 1.9% of the labor force was unemployed. As low as this may seem by recent standards, it was actually a whisker above the previous year's reading of 1.2%, which remains the lowest jobless rate ever registered in records that trace back more than a century. Such superlow wartime readings were, of course, in sharp contrast to those prevailing through most of the preceding decade. The sorry record: 8.7% of the labor force was unemployed in 1930, 15.9% in 1931, 23.6% in 1932, a still-standing record of 24.9% in 1933, 21.7% in 1934, 20.1% in 1935, 16.9% in 1936, 14.3% in 1937, 19.0% in 1938, and 17.2% in 1939. Even in 1940, with military spending already sharply on the rise, fighting under way in Europe, and war clouds gathering elsewhere, unemployment remained as high as 14.6%. As late as 1941, when the United States finally was drawn into the war, the jobless rate was a painful 9.9%. Not until 1942 did unemployment—at 4.7% of the labor force—reach a rate that seemed consistent with a moderately healthy, if not vigorous, economy.

The upswing in joblessness in 1938, after the rate had fallen more than 10 percentage points between 1933 and 1937, had convinced many previously hopeful analysts that economic stagnation had somehow grown intractable. Something, it appeared to many economists, was woefully amiss with the entire economic system, and the daring innovations contained in President Roosevelt's New Deal were plainly insufficient for setting things right. Accordingly, with the war ending, the economy's outlook seemed all too likely to repeat the prewar experience.

For a brief while, this grim assessment appeared to be right. At 1.9% in 1945, the jobless rate then more than doubled in a single year, reaching 3.9% in 1946. The swift rise continued, and before the end of the decade unemployment had reached 5.9%. In November 1948, a full-fledged recession set in, according to the National Bureau of Economic Research, a nonprofit

think tank in Cambridge, Massachusetts, that serves as the
official arbiter and record keeper in such matters. The 1930s
were beginning to return, it seemed. As the postwar era continued to unfold, the prospect appeared to be for further increases in joblessness, eroding incomes, a gradually diminishing
level of overall business activity, and, ultimately, eroding living
standards.

Seldom have so many forecasters been so very wrong about
the economic outlook. Instead of continuing its climb, the unemployment rate edged down—to 5.3% in 1950, 3.3% in 1951
and 3.0% in 1952. By 1953, with the Korean War in progress,
the jobless level was only 2.9%, which remains the lowest rate
attained since the abnormally low levels recorded during World
War II. The 1949 high of 5.9% was not reached again until 1958,
after the economy once again had entered a recession.

Why had there been such widespread miscalculation about
the postwar economy's prospects? Why were the prospects so
vastly underestimated, especially by economists whose miscalculations normally have been on the side of overoptimism? Why
did the overall level of business activity hold up so much better
than was generally expected?

It is tempting, but entirely incorrect, to attribute the economy's surprising vigor, after such an uncertain start, to the
influence of the Keynesians and impact of the Employment Act
of 1946. However, the measure that finally became law was so
vague that it failed to pinpoint its own goals and did not place
policy makers under any real pressure to stimulate economic
growth. The act merely urged them to pursue full employment.
It did not define either the means to be used or the precise goal
to be achieved.

As for Keynesian influence, in truth it proved to be a relatively minor factor in the economy's surprising performance. In
his *The General Theory of Employment, Interest and Money*,
originally published in 1936, Keynes had warned that "insufficient aggregate demand" would tend to render unemployment
intractable, necessitating highly stimulative governmental measures to revive the flagging "animal spirits" of consumers and

producers.[4] The idea, of course, was that the federal government, through fiscal pump-priming, could achieve vigorous economic growth and hold joblessness to a minimum level, repre-
senting only the "frictional" unemployment of individuals who
were inept or were in the process of moving from one job to
another. If enormous federal outlays seemed appropriate to pep
up business, so be it. If deficits in the federal budget were
deemed a necessary stimulation, so be it.

In fact, if an economist from Mars were to descend tomorrow
and peruse the economic data of the early post–World War II
era, he or she (or it) would surely conclude that Keynesian
economists, for all their influence at Bretton Woods, had little
sway in Washington in those early postwar years.

Consider, for example, the pattern of governmental debt. The
amount of such debt outstanding rose swiftly during World War
II as military outlays—and budgetary red ink—soared. Between 1933, at the nadir of the Great Depression, and 1939, on
the eve of World War II, governmental debt rose from $40.6
billion to $59 billion. Though a modest increase by modern
yardsticks, it amounted to a rise of more than 45% in barely
more than half a decade. Clearly the spending programs of the
New Deal were not without an impact on the nation's finances.
And the increase accelerated as the war years unfolded. With
the United States not yet directly involved in the fighting but
lending increased support to the European allies, the level of
debt rose to $61.2 billion in 1940. Then came the wartime debt
explosion: to $72.4 billion in 1941, $117.1 billion in 1942, $168.9
billion in 1943, $225.8 billion in 1944, and a record-shattering
$265.9 billion in 1945, or 1.25 times that year's gross national
product (GNP). Even in the late-twentieth century, this stands
as an awesome rate of debt to GNP, high enough to rattle even
the bones of Keynes himself.

But now, with our Martian economist, let us consider the
early postwar record of debt. Instead of continuing to climb,
even at a reduced rate, it fell substantially. The total dropped
to $243.2 billion in 1946, to $237.4 billion in 1947, and to $232.9
billion in 1948—a shrinkage of nearly 13% in three years. In

the same span, it should be added, the economy as measured by the GNP, expanded by nearly $46 billion, reducing the debt-to-GNP ratio to .9, sharply below the record-high 1945 reading.

Helping to pare the postwar debt burden, of course, was a steep reduction in federal purchases of goods and services. Spurred by wartime necessity, these outlays had reached a peak in 1944. The total edged down 15%, after adjusting for inflation, in 1945 as the war came to an end and then plunged more than 85% in the next two years. It was a most un-Keynesian decline, sufficient to delight even the most hidebound conservative.

To understand why these trends did not precipitate a resumption of the economic distress that had marked the prewar years, our Martian visitor would need to glance at data quite apart from the federal government's financial doings. With wartime rationing and the outright unavailability of many goods and services, personal savings were sky-high as the war ended. At only $719 million in 1938, the savings total reached $37.3 billion in 1944 before easing to $29.6 billion in 1945 and then falling sharply to a postwar low of $7.3 billion in 1947. Corporate savings traced a similar, if somewhat less abrupt, decline. Meanwhile, private-sector spending, suppressed during the war, rose apace. Personal consumption climbed by one-third in five years, after adjusting for inflation, and business investment jumped nearly fourfold. Outlays by state and local governments also rose sharply.

Despite these spending increases, nonfederal debt remained at minimal levels. In early 1947, consumer installment loans amounted to barely over 2% of personal income. For perspective, the rate in recent years has been close to 20%. Business debt was also low. For example, the so-called quick ratio of manufacturing firms—their cash and cashlike assets, such as Treasury bills, divided by their debt obligations due within a year or less—was at 1.07, several times as high as in recent years. All the while, inflation remained at enviably low levels. Between 1940 and 1946, the consumer price index rose about 40%, even with wartime price controls through much of the period. In pleasant contrast, the consumer price level barely budged from 1947 to 1950. It was no higher in the 1950 than in 1948, and actually fell slightly in 1949.

In all, the early postwar years proved far more prosperous than had been feared by most economists, whatever their theoretical allegiance may have been. Unemployment held at remarkably low levels and private-sector spending climbed sharply. Yet, inflation remained at negligible rates, and the debt burden for consumers and corporations was, by today's measures, feather light.

A leader among the Keynesians, Robert Heilbroner of the New School in New York, calls those years, and on into the mid-1970s, "a golden age of capitalism." They constituted "the longest, strongest, and least-interrupted period of growth in capitalism's history," says Heilbroner, himself a noted economic historian. And, he alleges, "Keynesian economics gave us" this golden age, even though Keynesianism was "always regarded with uneasiness by the business community."[5] Keynesians such as Heilbroner may credit Keynesianism for the heartening course of economic events after the war. A more accurate explanation, however, is simply that the economy was bound to move ahead with peace and victory and enormous pent-up demand after the years of wartime austerity.

A RARE BREED

At 1,153 pages, *The Oxford History of the American People* by Samuel Eliot Morison is among the most comprehensive U.S. histories ever produced. Written by a recipient of the gold medal of the American Academy of Arts and Letters and winner of two Pulitzer Prizes, the thick, fact-packed volume, published in 1965, remains in wide use in colleges and universities in the United States and abroad. Yet, nowhere in it will you find mention of a certain economist named Edwin G. Nourse or the CEA. In fact, the book's 30-page, name-filled, category-filled index contains not a single entry for economists of any sort.

For all the influence of Harry White and John Maynard Keynes in wartime, for all their lasting impact on international monetary arrangements, and for all the contribution of Keynesian ideology to such postwar measures as the full employment act, with the resumption of peace the clout of economists seemed minimal in Washington in 1946. Still, there were developments afoot that even Morison's exhaustive history neglected.

Ed Nourse is hardly a household name, but he does occupy a special niche in U.S. history—Nourse was the first chairman of the CEA. Those who followed in that role include some of the most illustrious names in American economic history. Among them: Arthur F. Burns, CEA chairman in 1953–1956; Walter W. Heller, chairman in 1961–1964; Arthur M. Okun, chairman in 1968–1969; Paul W. McCracken, chairman in 1969–1971; Alan Greenspan, chairman in 1974–1977; and Martin Feldstein, chairman in 1982–1984. Burns and Greenspan went on to become chairmen of the Federal Reserve Board, arguably the most powerful post in the nation after the presidency itself. Other economists who were members of the CEA at one time or another over the postwar years include a Nobel laureate in economics, James Tobin of Yale University; a pioneer in the use of computers in business forecasting, Otto Eckstein, the Harvard professor who founded Data Resources, now DRI/McGraw-Hill, a large economic consulting and forecasting firm; and the highest-ranking woman executive at General Motors, Marina Whitman.

Nourse took the oath of office on August 9, 1946, and served as chairman of the infant institution for more than three years, until November 1, 1949. He was, by all accounts, a pleasant man with no pronounced convictions other than to serve Harry Truman faithfully in whatever ways the president wished. As Galbraith recalls sardonically, Nourse possessed "orthodox credentials and mature years [and] was free from any evident Keynesian taint; it is unlikely that he had ever read *The General Theory* or thought it was a worthwhile use of his time."[6]

Nourse, who was sixty-three years old when he assumed the CEA chairmanship, had labored obscurely for many years at the Brookings Institution, a Washington think tank usually sympathetic to the Democratic party. The Brookings Institution was not averse to the tenets of Keynesianism, but neither was it tightly bound to them. With a Ph.D. from the University of Chicago, Nourse was also a past president of the American Economic Association, which was then and still is dominated by academicians. The association provides a sort of communications network for economists seeking to change jobs. Described by one economic historian as only a "mild" Keynesian, Nourse regarded his council as nonpolitical and therefore "above advocacy and politics [but] on hand to provide answers to questions of a technical nature."[7]

The importance that President Truman initially attached to the CEA is best suggested, perhaps, by his allowing several months to elapse between the passage of the employment act and the appointment of Nourse and the two other CEA members—Leon H. Keyserling, the CEA vice chairman, and John D. Clark. Keyserling, a former aide to Democratic Senator Robert Wagner, was not a trained economist but a lawyer. Even so, when Nourse stepped down in 1949, Keyserling was tapped to succeed him, first as acting chairman and then, in the spring of 1950, as chairman. His CEA service ended with the arrival of Dwight D. Eisenhower at the White House in January 1953.

CEA members were not required to have an advanced degree in economics but should be, according the 1946 law, "exceptionally qualified to analyze and interpret economic developments, to appraise programs and activities of the government [and] formulate and recommend national economic policy to promote employment, production and purchasing power under free competitive enterprise."

Still, the CEA's influence at the outset of the postwar era was minimal. Walter Heller, who joined the CEA as its chairman in 1961 when John F. Kennedy became president, was a strong believer in his profession's importance in determining and setting the nation's course. But even Heller conceded that it was only with the onset of the New Frontier and Great Society in the early 1960s that economists really "arrived." "We at last accept in fact," he declares, "what was accepted in law 20 years ago in the Employment Act of 1946: namely that the federal government has an overarching responsibility for the nation's economic stability and growth." Some 30 years after "Maynard Keynes fired the opening salvo," he goes on, "the political economist [is] at the president's elbow."[8] Heller further notes that professional economists had recently come to occupy "high places" in such Washington policy centers as the budget bureau, the White House, the Pentagon, the departments of State, Treasury, and Agriculture, and the Federal Reserve Board, as well as the CEA.

Neither Ed Nourse nor his noneconomist successor, Leon Keyserling, could make such claims. In their time, those economists so fortunate as to possess any influence at all in Washington were rarely near the presidential elbow. Still, with the 1946 act, the CEA existed. It was a start.

The JEC, which also came into existence with the 1946 act, is comprised of 10 members from the Senate and 10 from the House of Representatives. The chairmanship rotates between the House and the Senate with each new Congress. When the chair is from the Senate, the ranking minority member is from the House, and vice versa. The committee attempts to oversee the federal government's role in improving the economy's performance. It holds hearings and launches studies on a wide range of economic issues and then submits its recommendations to Congress. It also issues its own annual reports on the state of the economy, much as the president, through the CEA, issues annual economic reports to Congress.

The JEC's first annual report, issued on January 31, 1947, was mainly concerned with finding ways to prevent a new depression and achieving and maintaining "full" employment. But the committee could offer no concrete legislation toward these noble goals because, under the 1946 act, it lacked legislative authority and therefore could not write or report out bills to the House or Senate. Still, as with the CEA, a start had been made.

With its staff of professional economists, the JEC did have some impact on the economy's performance in the early postwar years. And, as the years passed, its influence expanded as its staff slowly broadened to include experts on tax and budget policy, health care, social welfare, labor matters, international trade, and technology issues. In 1955, it began issuing regular studies of the Soviet and Chinese economies and periodic assessments of the economies of Eastern Europe.

Debra Silimeo, a JEC staffer who has reviewed its history, lists what she regards as some of the committee's more important achievements over the years: laying the groundwork for President Kennedy's economic program to "get the country moving again"; spearheading a campaign that resulted in a $5.6 billion cut in the 1969 defense budget; providing a platform for the "new economics" of Walter Heller, who taught with a Keynesian slant for many years at the University of Minnesota, and for the "Chicago school" of Milton Friedman, the leading monetarist who taught for many years at the University of Chicago; giving impetus to the poverty programs of the 1960s after producing studies of low-income American families; providing grist for President Eisenhower's attack on the "military-industrial complex" in his 1961 farewell speech; turning the attention of policy makers to the nation's crumbling infrastructure through an exhaustive 1984 study of the problem; spurring a greater federal effort to improve the quality of economic statistics; and, in the committee's 1989 annual report, citing the federal budget deficit as the nation's number one economic problem and, to deal with it, calling for a package of tax increases and spending cuts, which was eventually enacted.

One may argue indefinitely over the merits and demerits of these JEC endeavors, but they do illustrate the committee's rising influence as the postwar era went along. Even though the JEC was born without legislative teeth, and continues to lack them, it has clearly served, like its CEA sibling, to expand economists' domestic policy-making role.

Meanwhile, away from Washington's power centers in corporate offices around the country, economists played virtually no role at all in those early postwar years. Few private businesses employed economists other than in jobs that had little or no connection with their expertise. In fact, economists were a rarity even at financial firms, where one would imagine there existed even then a special need for forecasting and number crunching.

For instance, no economist was employed, at least as a practicing economist, at such large Wall Street institutions as Merrill Lynch or Salomon Brothers. More than two decades passed
before Merrill finally hired as its economist a bright young man,
still in his twenties, named Gary Shilling. His tenure at Merrill
was short-lived, however, in part because he attempted to take
his role as in-house economist seriously, seeking to be candid in
his forecasts and resenting the repeated muzzling that came
from higher-ups at the securities firm. His departure was
largely a consequence of a particularly frank and somewhat
pessimistic appraisal of the economic outlook during an interview with me that I subsequently published on the Dow Jones
news wire, which *The Wall Street Journal* operated and often
quoted.

It wasn't until 1961 that Salomon Brothers finally hired Sid-
ney Homer to establish an economic and financial research department for the firm. Later that year, Homer, with only an
undergraduate degree from Harvard, hired as his assistant
Henry Kaufman, who brought with him a master's degree from
Columbia and a doctorate from New York University. Kaufman
also had served briefly in the credit department of People's
Industrial Bank, later acquired by Manufacturers Trust, and as
an economic researcher at the Federal Reserve Bank of New
York.

When I first encountered these two men in 1962, they worked
in small, cluttered offices, seemingly forgotten outposts of the
securities firm, which could only be reached in labyrinthian
fashion after circumnavigating the obstacle course presented by
Salomon's sprawling trading floor. Homer retired from Salomon
in 1972, but Kaufman remained to build and lead a large contingent of young, highly trained economists. Their yearly research output was of admirable quality and voluminous enough
to strain even a speed reader's capacity. Such was the department's prestige that Salomon eventually took to renting the
grand ballroom of the Waldorf Astoria as an appropriate setting
for Kaufman's much-awaited and widely reported appraisals of
the economic and financial outlook.

The paucity of economists in private businesses in the early postwar years is evident in the fact that the professional organization that now represents them—the National Association of Business Economists (NABE)—did not exist. NABE wasn't founded until 1959. Though NABE was open to any economist employed in private business, in its early years, it claimed only about 250 members. Its annual get-togethers in those years were low-budget affairs, usually in second-rank hotels in such places as downtown Detroit and downtown Cleveland—as I can testify, having been among the pioneer attendees. It was only years later, after NABE's membership swelled to 4,000 in the mid-1980s, that far more lavish locales became the rule for meetings.

When I joined *The Wall Street Journal,* shortly before the founding of the NABE, the paper employed not a single economist on its staff and ran almost no freelance articles from economists on its editorial page. Now, such articles appear almost daily. Indeed, the editorial page sports a prestigious array of regularly contributing economists, including several former chairmen of the CEA. Moreover, in recent years, the paper has employed an economic news editor and an international economic news editor, as well as a staff of reporters in bureaus across the country who contribute to its increasingly broad economics coverage.

The sophistication of the *Journal's* economic reportage has also risen considerably since the early postwar years. In the 1950s, it was assumed—probably correctly—that many, if not most, of the paper's readers were near-ignoramuses in matters economic. It was a standard rule, accordingly, that such fundamental economic terms as *balance of trade* and *gross national product* had to be defined in an elementary fashion in any story. Unfortunately, this meant that perhaps half of a routine article about the economy's behavior in a particular week or month might well consist of definitions. This, of course, tended to make an often dull report even duller. In the process, it also restricted the space available for reporting new economic developments or subtleties.

In the early postwar years, economists were a rarity even at the largest corporations. Robert J. Eggert, who went on to considerable fame and fortune as the editor of "Blue Chip Economic Indicators," a widely circulated and highly regarded economic newsletter, recalls his hiring by Ford Motor in 1951. A trained economist with 11 years of research experience at the American Meat Institute, Eggert arrived at Ford in Detroit to find only two economists on the entire staff. "There was virtually no market research effort," he says, "nor any serious attempt to appraise the general economic outlook, or how it might affect the automobile business or Ford Motor." Though he encountered considerable resistance initially, Eggert managed slowly to build a research staff that numbered 23 by the time he left Ford in 1968 to teach at Michigan State University. His staunchest supporter in this effort, he remembers, was a fast-rising young Ford executive named Robert McNamara, who of course went on to become the nation's secretary of defense during the Vietnam War and later headed the World Bank. "We just couldn't satisfy Bob with enough data and facts about the economy and our position in it," Eggert says. "It was quite a change from when I first arrived at Ford, before Bob was in the driver's seat, and economists were about as numerous and popular as dodo birds."

RISING CLOUT

Leon Keyserling lacked the professional training in economics that Ed Nourse had possessed. Keyserling's advanced degree was an LL.B. from Harvard Law School, where his professors included Felix Frankfurter, who was later on the Supreme Court. Yet it was Keyserling, the noneconomist, who perhaps did more than anyone to expand the role of economists in early postwar Washington. Though he lacked an advanced degree in economics, he had received considerable training in the subject and was deeply concerned about the U.S. economy's postwar prospects. Like many analysts, he greatly feared a resumption of the depressed prewar conditions. In 1947, he wrote an article entitled "Must We Have Another Depression?" His formula for avoiding one followed the standard Keynesian prescription of a strongly stimulative fiscal policy to offset what he viewed as the tendency of productive capacity to outrun the public's buying power.

Toward this end, Keyserling had helped to draft the 1946 employment legislation when he was an aide to Senator Robert Wagner and worked hard to establish the CEA as a sort of organizational center, tied tightly to the presidency, for a national effort to avert a return to 1930s-like conditions. While the cautious Nourse worried about the possibility that inflation would worsen, Keyserling pressed President Truman for tax cuts and spending initiatives and was perfectly willing to clamp on new wage and price controls should inflation prove worrisome. Unlike Nourse, who abhorred appearing before congressional committees, Keyserling delighted in such appearances. At Keyserling's urging, Truman subscribed to a range of supposedly pro-growth measures, including public works, an increased minimum wage, higher Social Security payments, and greater financial support for farmers. "The ideas of Keyserling and the political requirements of the President coincided," recalls Robert Sobel, the noted economic historian at Hofstra University.

With the outbreak of the Korean War in June 1950, military needs made the sort of expansionary tactics that Keyserling espoused impossible to pursue. Inflation, for example, began to worsen severely. Along the way, Senator Joseph McCarthy charged Keyserling with being soft on communism, an accusation that Keyserling vehemently denied. With Eisenhower's arrival at the White House in January 1953, Keyserling, of course, was out as CEA chairman. He was replaced by Arthur F. Burns, a staunch Republican as well as a bona fide economist with eminent academic credentials. Still, as a result of Keyserling's leadership, the CEA had finally gained a degree of recognition as an influential policy-making voice in Washington. Robert Sobel calls Keyserling "the first major economic soothsayer of the modern era" and notes that Keyserling "helped establish the ground rules under which future economists would operate in the White House." This would not have happened so readily, if at all, had Nourse, despite his training as an economist, stayed on. Indeed, it is questionable whether the CEA itself would have continued.

For a brief while, in fact, it seemed that the CEA might not even survive. The Democrats who controlled Congress as Eisenhower came to office were in an economizing frame of mind and voted to reduce funding in fiscal year 1953 by some 25% for several government agencies, including the CEA. For a while, it seemed possible that Eisenhower might seize on this emasculation of the CEA as an opportunity to do away with it altogether. After all, under Keyserling the agency had grown closely identified with interventionist Keynesian policies that did not sit well with the new president.

Largely on the advice Gabriel Hauge, an experienced economist on the incoming White House staff, Eisenhower decided instead to seek new funding for the CEA and to strengthen it. In fact, under Eisenhower, the CEA eventually occupied "a highly influential position" in the administration, recalls Raymond J. Saulnier, a New York economics professor who joined the CEA as a member in April 1955 and then succeeded Burns as the chairman in December 1956. The council, according to Saulnier's memoir of those years, "figured prominently in all policy making activities of the White House having significant economic content and, with the regrettable and unnecessary exception of some debt-management operations conducted by the Treasury, was involved in the planning and carrying out of all Executive Branch actions likely to have significant economic effect." Saulnier adds that "all legislative proposals of an economic nature, whether originating within or outside government, were submitted to the council for comment directly to the president [and] the council's chairman or another of its members attended all cabinet meetings and all meetings of the president with legislative leaders, making presentations at many of them."[9]

Arthur Burns is usually remembered as a pipe-puffing, scholarly conservative with close political ties to the Republican party. To an extent, this is true. However, his conservative rhetoric, as we will observe, tended to exceed his performance, not only during his tenure as chairman of the CEA from 1953 to 1956 but especially later when he assumed a far more important Washington role as chairman of the Federal Reserve Board. Burns did espouse free markets and cautious fiscal and monetary policies that would protect against inflation. But his main concern, and in retrospect his most important contribution, was his keen appreciation of how overall economic activity had progressed over the years: in a highly cyclical manner. Burns realized that the economy expanded for several years and then contracted for a while, with long-term growth resulting from the fortunate fact that the cycle's expansion phases usually have proved a good deal longer and stronger than the contraction phases.

This understanding of the business cycle was, in large measure, a result of Burns' long association with the National Bureau of Economic Research, headquartered for many years in New York City before it was moved to Cambridge, Massachusetts. Burns' mentor at the National Bureau was its founder, Wesley Mitchell, whose many books and articles included *Business Cycles*, a definitive study of the economy's cyclical tendencies. In a memorial to Mitchell, which he wrote in 1949 while serving as the National Bureau's research director, Burns called the book "a landmark in the development of economics." He asserted that "no other work between [Alfred] Marshall's *Principles* and Keynes' *General Theory* has had as big an influence on the economic thought of the Western World." Business cycles, as Mitchell had taught and Burns agreed, were "not minor or accidental disruptions of equilibrium, but fluctuations systematically generated by economic organization itself." As Burns wrote in his 1949 memorial, with prosperity, "costs in many lines of activity encroach upon selling prices, money markets become strained, and numerous investment projects are set aside until costs of financing seem more favorable; these accumulating stresses . . . lead to a recession [until] the realignment of costs and prices, reduction of inventories, improvement of bank reserves and other developments . . . pave the way for a renewed expansion."[10]

At the time of his appointment to the CEA, Burns was, in

the words of his future CEA colleague, Raymond Saulnier, "the country's leading student of the business cycle," and his presence within the Eisenhower administration "was assurance that cyclical changes would be monitored closely, as they were." For example, as Saulnier recounts, "the CEA had been at work well in advance of the 1953 downturn developing contingency plans to combat recession, should one occur"—as one did. Perhaps Burns' lasting contribution from his time at the CEA was to initiate and to establish, as Saulnier puts it, "the systematic use in government of economic indicators that are now widely employed in economic forecasting."[11]

Before Burns' arrival in Washington, the economy's cyclical behavior—its tendency to become overstrained and then, through contractions, to renew itself—had received rather short shrift. Implicit in the views of such planners as Keyserling was the Keynesian idea that the economy's progress could be closely managed and amplified. With Burns' arrival, however, a new emphasis was put on the idea that the economy, left to its own devices, would prosper at least moderately over the long haul, notwithstanding the difficult recessionary interludes that its cyclical nature necessitated. Indeed, it was Burns' conviction that governmental efforts to spur economic activity, if injudiciously applied, could prove dangerously counterproductive.

The prevailing view had been that the government should strive to minimize, perhaps even to eliminate, the cycle's contraction periods and to perpetuate its expansionary phases. One potential source of stimulation, of course, was the Federal Reserve Board, which through its FOMC could move to spur monetary growth faster than the economy's ability to advance, which in turn fueled inflation. This could be done through the buying of Treasury securities by the Federal Reserve to pump money into the economy. A second stimulative source was the federal government's penchant to spend far more each year than was taken in through taxes. If nothing else, such outlays seemed, at least in the short term, to help generate jobs and spur demand for all sorts of goods and services. It was a broadly held conviction when Burns took command of the CEA that monetary and fiscal stimulation would invariably prolong, with impunity, expansions and limit contractions.

But Burns worried that in this forced-draft effort to alter the economy's natural cyclical patterns—its tendency to slump, cleanse itself of excesses, and then recover with renewed vigor—a rigidity might develop that would transcend the business cycle. He feared that each stimulative measure drained a degree of natural resiliency from the economy so that larger and larger doses of such stimulatives would achieve smaller and smaller results. Fiscal and monetary stimulation implemented to prolong expansions and shorten recessions, Burns believed, worked like a drug, masking symptoms that should be attended to directly. The upshot, in his view, was that in recessions the economic system would never get properly cleansed of the excesses—for instance, excessive borrowing—that typically accumulate during preceding periods of economic growth. With larger doses of stimulation, Burns cautioned, there would develop an increasing brittleness in the economy, and the business cycle would take on a dangerous new aspect: with each new contraction phase, the possibility of a real collapse would increase.

It is a measure of Burns' influence during his tenure at the CEA that the economy was marked by relatively modest ups and downs—moderate growth until July 1953, a 10-month recession of moderate severity, and then a resumption of moderate growth. There was no worrisome buildup of debt in the period, and the consumer price index was virtually unchanged, rising only from 80.1 to 81.4 (on a base of 1967 = 100). Allowing for inflation and for expenditures reflecting the Korean War effort, the government's purchases of goods and services actually declined over the four years. The federal budget, which was $7.1 billion in the red when Burns arrived in Washington—a considerable amount by the standards of those years—showed a $6.1 billion surplus during his last year as Eisenhower's economic chief. One can only speculate on what the record might have shown for this period had Truman remained president with Keyserling as his economist. Most likely, there would have been more federal spending, more debt, more budgetary red ink, more inflation, and perhaps swifter growth and a briefer, shallower recession—but with a price surely to be paid later on.

Burns served, in fact, as a restraining influence on Eisenhower during the 1953–1954 recession. Before the recession set in, Burns had established, with Eisenhower's blessing, an Advisory Board on Economic Growth and Stability (ABEGS). The ABEGS included high-level representatives of the Federal Reserve Board, the Budget Bureau, and various parts of the president's cabinet. Eisenhower put Burns at the helm, which enabled the economist to channel the deliberations and pass them along to the White House. Sooner than most, Burns saw the recession coming and urged modest countercyclical measures to limit it, such as a more relaxed monetary policy. He also formulated a mix of somewhat stronger stimulants for use only if the recession proved long and deep. These included an assortment of public works proposals, accelerated depreciation allowances for various production facilities, and more liberal requirements for home mortgage loans.

By April 1954, the recession had dragged on for nine months, and Eisenhower, concerned and impatient, was increasingly anxious to implement the standby measures and pile on additional ones as well. But Burns, with his long study of the business cycle, urged the president to hold off. Scrutinizing the various indicators of future economic activity that he had helped to develop during his time at the National Bureau of Research, Burns concluded—correctly, as things turned out—that a recovery was near. It should be noted that Burns, unlike many economists of that time, was not much concerned about the threat of a return of the Great Depression. His studies of the business cycle had convinced him that the economy's performance in the 1930s was aberrational. Accordingly, he urged Eisenhower to be patient. The economy, Burns asserted, would be far healthier in the long run if the approaching upturn were to develop naturally. It was a risk that Eisenhower reluctantly and nervously accepted. The recession, in fact, ended the very next month, in May, and a sustained expansion ensued, marked, as we have noted, by low inflation and surpluses in the federal budget. More than three years passed before the economy again turned down. Meanwhile, Burns understandably gained a remarkable degree of influence within the White House. He had "reached a summit," Robert Sobel says, adding, "No previous economist had ever exerted so great an influence in the inner circle during peacetime."[12]

This rising clout was ironic inasmuch as Burns, unlike Keyserling, eschewed a bluntly political approach in his dealings with Congress and other power centers. "Watching Keyserling testify before a congressional committee put one in mind of a partisan scrapper eager to score points," Sobel recalls. He continues, "A Burns appearance on the other hand resembled nothing more than a graduate seminar in a very good university, which somewhere along the line is transformed into a lecture."[13]

Although Burns was no longer a member of the Eisenhower administration after 1956, he continued to advise the president on an informal basis from his perch at the National Bureau in New York. In 1960, for example, he warned the president that a recession appeared imminent and urged him, with a presidential election coming up, to do more to prolong the expansion. The appeal was unsuccessful, and a recession struck in April and persisted until February 1961. It is possible that the recession could not have been averted even if Eisenhower had sought to spur the economy. Economic activity had been distorted earlier by a national steel strike, and some analysts fault the Federal Reserve for being too slow to ease the monetary reins. In any event, more as a result of the new economic slump than any TV debate between the candidates, the Democrats under the leadership of John F. Kennedy regained the White House. However, the defeated Republican candidate, Richard M. Nixon, was deeply grateful to Burns for at least anticipating the recession, which turned out to be a relatively mild affair, and for urging countermeasures. When Nixon finally did assume the presidency in 1969, he rewarded Burns by offering him the powerful chairmanship of the Federal Reserve Board, a position previously monopolized by bankers.

Burns' rhetoric during his eight-year tenure at the Fed remained scholarly and nonpolitical, but it should be noted that his performance seemed increasingly partisan. While he repeatedly warned of the dangers of inflation, he allowed the nation's money supply to surge in a manner bound to induce worsening inflation. The rate of growth of the so-called M1 money supply, which includes demand deposits (private checking accounts) and currency, approximately tripled between mid-1969 and mid-1971. The speedup was even sharper for the broader M2 version of money, which includes most savings deposits; M2 growth rose fivefold in the two-year stretch.

All the while, Burns professed to be a staunch foe of inflation. In testimony before a hearing of the JEC, for example, in February 1971, Burns warned that rates of monetary growth "above the 5% to 6% range, if continued for a long period of time, have typically intensified inflationary pressures." He went on to lecture the legislators that "an excessive rate of monetary expansion now could destroy our nation's chances of bringing about a gradual but lasting control over inflationary forces." The Federal Reserve, Burns promised, "will not become the architects of a new wave of inflation."

But Burns did not practice his preaching. The money supply continued to rise far faster than he had warned would be dangerous, and in due course corrosive inflation developed. In mid-August 1971, President Nixon felt compelled to institute a 90-day wage-price freeze and to let the dollar's value sink in terms of gold, as I described earlier. Surprisingly, Burns supported the wage-price freeze. How could he do this, given his long-standing faith in the virtues of leaving the economy pretty much to its own devices and allowing the business cycle to work its course? He offered a clue to his thinking at a congressional hearing held about that time. "The rules of economics are not working in quite the way they used to," he stated. Wage-rate increases did not seem to moderate, he remarked, despite "extensive unemployment," and commodity prices continued to climb steeply despite "much idle plant capacity." From the same economist who years earlier had persuaded Eisenhower to be patient while waiting for the economy to recover, such commentary seemed out of place and suggested a loss of long-held convictions.

Burns, as we shall observe, is by no means the only prominent economist to have had his convictions shaken by the economy's behavior since World War II ended. But his loss of faith was particularly striking since he seemed in public—before the Congress and elsewhere—so scholarly, even omniscient. At the Fed itself, Burns was widely regarded by underlings and even other governors as something of a tyrant and was not at all popular despite the professorial demeanor and pipe puffing. In his seminal book about the Fed, *The Secrets of the Temple*, William Greider remarks that Burns' manner was "bullying." He could be cruel, Greider reports, "humiliating staff economists with nasty remarks on their competence [and] was also capable of shamelessly juggling the monetary numbers" to score points. His colleagues also displayed "considerable cynicism about the chairman's pious rhetoric" on the dangers of inflation, which worsened a great deal during his chairmanship.[14]

My own impressions of Burns, I should note, are somewhat more complimentary. My first interviews with him were in New York in the early 1960s, when he was running the National Bureau of Economic Research, and I found him somewhat stiff and reticent; he would usually turn me over to his close friend and research director at the bureau, Geoffrey H. Moore, who was invariably cordial and most helpful. Burns became more open with me, somewhat incongruously, *after* he assumed the powerful Fed chairmanship. In November 1971, for instance, I encountered Burns, by then the chairman, at a Manhattan cocktail party given in his honor by Elizabeth Manning, the publisher of a financial journal. While sipping a straight-up martini, he asked me, to my amazement and delight, whether I wouldn't like to hop the shuttle down to Washington to visit with him at the Fed and perhaps conduct an interview for the *Journal*. This was far friendlier treatment than he ever accorded me during his less auspicious tenure at the National Bureau. "Simply ring up Mrs. Mallardi [Catherine Mallardi, his long-time secretary] and tell her I said to set up an appointment for you," he instructed me.

Of course, I did so the very next day and was promptly scheduled for an hour with the chairman in his office on the

afternoon of November 24, Thanksgiving Eve. Burns was a
gracious, welcoming host and, remarkably, spoke on the record,
granting me the only exclusive, for-attribution interview that,
to my understanding, any sitting Fed chairman has given a
reporter in recent decades. The interview appeared prominently in the November 26 edition of the *Journal* under the
headline: "Burns Sees Progress on Inflation, Economy Fronts:
Reserve Chief Undisturbed by the Sharp Slowdown in Money-
Supply Growth." Burns actually gave me nearly two hours, and
when the interview was finished, he generously arranged for
me to be chauffeured back to the airport in his Federal Reserve
limousine. Meanwhile, Joseph Coyne, the Fed's tight-lipped,
protective chief of public relations and a former Associated
Press reporter, didn't know that I had even spoken to his boss
until he picked up the November 26 newspaper. To this day, I
don't know who upset Coyne more—Burns for granting an exclusive, on-the-record interview or me for conducting it.

My last meeting with Burns—who died after a successful tour
of ambassadorial service in Bonn—took place more than a decade later under very different and most pleasant circumstances. I was taking my daughter Ann, a high-school senior at
the time, for an interview at Dartmouth College in Hanover,
New Hampshire, and decided to phone Burns at his vacation
home in nearby Ely, Vermont, where I had visited several
times. I intended merely to chat on the phone, but Burns insisted that I bring along my daughter and have a meal with him
and his son Joseph, a federal agency lawyer as I recall, at a
country inn about halfway between Ely and Hanover. The meal
was delightful, and Burns a most gracious host. While scoring
repeated points in sporadic arguments about various weighty
matters with his contentious son, he also managed to indulge
in amiable small-talk with my daughter about topics far removed from the dreary world of economics. Among other topics,
the two of them spent a good deal of time exchanging views
about the merits of coeducation. The only sign of aging that I
could detect in Burns that evening was that he no longer was
drinking straight-up martinis; instead—for the evening was
warm—he downed two gin and tonics.

Sadly, Burns never produced his memoirs. On one of my visits to his home in Ely, he told me that he intended to write them. In fact, he walked me into the woods on a hillside behind his house, which was in the middle of a lovely valley, and showed me a small cabin where, he said, he intended soon to begin the writing. But the work did not get done, which is unfortunate because I suspect he had considerably more to say about exactly why "the rules of economics are not working in quite the way they used to." He might also have offered some useful advice for the many economists who, following in his footsteps, have ascended to positions of considerable policy-making power. He might even have provided some indication of the extent to which he really believed his own inflation-fighting rhetoric as he went about pumping up the money supply at a pace that ultimately fueled inflation.

His memoirs, had Burns found the time to write them, would have been interesting quite apart from his thoughts on the economy. His last public service was during the Reagan presidency as U.S. ambassador to West Germany, an important political assignment that he handled with tact and skill. In fact, he was far more popular among the Germans in Bonn and elsewhere than he had ever managed to be among his own staff at the Federal Reserve. He didn't live to see the two Germanys reunified, but he strongly favored it, and I can recall on more than one occasion his predicting that reunification would eventually occur.

Had Burns written his memoirs, readers would have discovered that he was hardly the Scottish-named WASP that he appeared to be in public. They would have learned that he was born in 1904 in what was once the Austro-Hungarian empire and his real name—Burnseig—was Jewish, not Scottish. They would have learned that his father Nathan, who brought the family to America just before the outbreak of World War I, earned his living as a house painter in Bayonne, New Jersey, and received occasional help from young Arthur, who was working his way on a scholarship through Columbia University, across the Hudson River. Horatio Alger had nothing on Arthur Burns.

FRESH IDEAS

Between his many other activities, Burns served as an economics professor at Columbia, and today the university has an economics chair in his name. Much earlier in his career, however, he labored briefly as an instructor in economics at Rutgers University, and among his students was a brilliant young man named Milton Friedman, who went on to win the Nobel Prize in economics. I once asked Friedman why he had chosen to take Burns' course, and with a perfectly straight face, he replied that "only a couple of people had signed up for the course and I figured with so few in attendance there would be a good opportunity for close individual instruction."

Milton Friedman never gained the policy-making clout that Burns eventually wielded in Washington. But his ideas on how the economy should be managed exerted a growing influence that ultimately transcended any achievement of his Rutgers instructor. Friedman himself went on to teach economics at the University of Chicago. Lindley H. Clark, Jr., a longtime editor and columnist at *The Wall Street Journal*, was among Friedman's students in the late 1940s. Clark remembers him as an "exciting, even exhilarating" teacher who, unlike some of his colleagues in the economics department, "wasn't always canceling classes because his advice was wanted in Washington."

In these early postwar years, of course, the economic ideas of men like Keynes and Keyserling still were a force in Washington's policy making. But other voices were beginning to be heard, and of these none was more striking than that of Arthur Burns' former student, now an exciting young professor at the University of Chicago.

When I first met Friedman in the mid-1960s, he was beginning to attract national attention for his ideas, but he had not yet found a receptive audience among the nation's policy makers. In business and financial circles, however, he was already gaining considerable attention. Sam I. Nakagama, an investment adviser on Wall Street and also a former Friedman student at Chicago, told me, "If this can be called the age of any economist, it's not the age of John Maynard Keynes, of John Kenneth Galbraith or some other big name—it's the age of Milton Friedman." If Nakagama was perhaps premature in his judgment, he also was prophetic.

Considerably more modest in the early years than after the many honors he received later, Friedman himself found such praise embarrassing. "I don't claim originality for any ideas," he told me during an interview at his home in Ely, near Burns' house. "But I like to keep good ideas alive," he added, "in the hope they will eventually be put into practice."

The most important policy-making idea that Friedman managed to "keep alive" in the early postwar years when Keynesianism still predominated, involved the conduct of monetary policy. To anyone who was willing to hear him out, he advocated that the Federal Reserve pursue a policy that would permit the country's money supply—defined as demand deposits plus currency in circulation—to grow at a reasonably steady rate. He put this rate at roughly 3% to 5% per year, a rise that he estimated would be consistent with stable prices, given what appeared to be the U.S. economy's long-term growth potential; that potential has since narrowed appreciably.

Friedman's view of money's central role in the economy had all sorts of implications for the way in which government policy in general should be carried out. For instance, an easy money policy traditionally had been regarded as conducive to lower interest rates. But as Friedman saw things, easy money would only serve to reduce rates early on and then tend to raise them. This concept stemmed from his observation that a rapidly rising money supply ultimately increases the amounts that people earn and spend, which in turn tend to produce rising prices in general, including the price of credit—interest rates. By the same logic, Friedman claimed that a tight money policy, while tending initially to drive up rates, eventually serves to reduce them.

Friedman blames monetary policy in large measure for the magnitude of the economic collapse in the 1930s. "We learned something from the Great Depression," he remarks. "We learned that you do not cut the quantity of money by a third over three or four years," as the Fed in fact did in the early part of the Great Depression. Because the importance of money in policy making is much more widely appreciated today, thanks largely to Friedman, a rerun of that dismal episode seems far less likely to occur than had Friedman not come along with his monetary message.

The Fed's mistakes in the Great Depression and at other times are painstakingly documented in *A Monetary History of the United States, 1867–1960*, Friedman's most important book, which he wrote with Anna Schwartz, an economist at the National Bureau. The history, which first appeared in November 1963, is considered by most to be the definitive work in its field. Some 8,300 copies were either sold or given away, mostly to other economists, when the 860-page volume first was published. Although this wasn't many copies by the standards of such economist-writers as Harvard's John Kenneth Galbraith, it still stands as a remarkably good showing for a serious, highly technical economic work.

To this day, Friedman is thought of as a conservative, just as Keynes is remembered as a liberal. But the ideas that Friedman developed in the early postwar years really defy such simple categorizing. His recommendation that the Fed induce a fairly tightly controlled expansion of the money supply, for instance, was anathema to conservatives on Friedman's right, such as Friedrich A. von Hayek, the Austrian Nobel laureate, who would minimize any governmental interference in the economy, including interference in the availability of money. On the international front, Friedman was an unrelenting foe of fixed currency-exchange rates or the gold standard. Instead, along with such economic liberals as James Tobin of Yale and Emil Depres of Stanford, he espoused freely floating exchange rates. In 1950, for example, he wrote an essay titled "The Case for Flexible Exchange Rates" that Harry G. Johnson, a professor at the London School of Economics, hardly a conservative institution, once called a "modern classic" that should be studied by "all serious writers on this subject." The breakdown of the Bretton Woods system would have come as no surprise to anyone who had read Friedman's 1950 essay.

On the domestic front, Friedman urged a so-called negative income tax to help the poor. A paper written by him in 1948 argued persuasively that the welfare system was woefully in-effective and that a procedure putting cash in the pockets of the poor to spend as they wished would be vastly preferable. This was hardly a standard conservative notion, nor did it ma-terialize. It did, however, constitute a prominent part of George McGovern's highly liberal Democratic platform when he ran unsuccessfully for president against Richard Nixon in 1972.

"It's absurd to categorize Milton as a conservative or a liberal or whatever," recalls a long-time colleague of his at the Uni-versity of Chicago. "He's simply a man with a marvelously logical mind who follows where the logic leads him." Because his nature was essentially logical and not inclined to action, Friedman spent relatively little time in Washington as the years passed and his influence mounted. For many years he served as an outside consultant to the Federal Reserve Board, a duty that necessitated trips to Washington about twice a year. He also served as an adviser to Barry Goldwater in the Arizona senator's disastrous effort to unseat Lyndon Johnson in the 1964 presidential race, and he provided informal advice to Presidents Nixon and Reagan.

All the while, the Chicago professor gradually gained a broader lay audience for his ideas. In the mid-1960s, he launched an opinion column for *Newsweek* that introduced the magazine's huge readership to his thoughts on monetary policy, a negative income-tax, and other important matters. At the same time, he began to write occasional essays for *The Wall Street Journal*'s editorial page, which provided a friendly forum for much that he had to say. His real breakthrough to a mass audience, how-ever, occurred years later, in 1980, when he was chosen by public television to host a series titled "Free to Choose." In the various segments, the diminuitive economist, all five-feet-one-inch of him, unabashedly extolled free-market economics—lots of entrepreneurial competition, plus a teeny-weeny governmen-tal presence. The segments aired Friedman's views on govern-mental controls (get rid of them); the reason for the Great Depression (a benighted Federal Reserve Board); the welfare system (scrap it); egalitarianism (it's dangerous); public educa-tion (overhaul it); consumer protection (don't trust Uncle Sam or Ralph Nader); worker protection (don't trust the unions); inflation (control the money supply); and individual freedom (battle bureaucratic bloat).

Viewers were treated to such sights as an animated, Disney-like explanation of no less a topic than the international economic role of gold, Friedman in shirtsleeves in an impoverished village in India and in white-tie-and-tails receiving his Nobel Prize, the country's last single-room schoolhouse in Vermont, a Boston school where students had to be frisked for weapons, a Japanese electronics factory, and the splendiferous boardroom of the New York Federal Reserve Bank. For viewers eager to learn more, Friedman also supplied a best-selling book bearing the same title as the television series. Co-authored with his devoted wife and researcher Rose, the book ran to 338 pages, its 10 chapters neatly coinciding with the 10 television segments. Among its messages:

- Social Security—"It is a tax on work which discourages employers from hiring workers and discourages people from seeking work. . . . The winding down of Social Security [would mean a] more rapid rate of growth of income [and so] add to the security of many workers."
- The Interstate Commerce Commission—"If the ICC had never been established and market forces had been permitted to operate, the United States would today have a far more satisfactory transportation system."
- Pollution—"In fact, the people responsible for pollution are consumers, not producers. They create, as it were, demand for pollution. People who use electricity are responsible for the smoke that comes out of the stacks of generating plants."
- Department stores—"The chief economic function of a department store . . . is to monitor quality on our behalf."
- The American Medical Association—"For decades it [has] kept down the number of physicians [and] kept up the costs of medical care . . . all, of course, in the name of helping the patient."
- Advertising—"Government . . . advertising is more misleading than anything put out by private enterprise."

- The press—"Reporters and TV commentators seem especially resistant to the elementary principles they supposedly imbibed in freshman economics."[15]

Near the end of their book, the Friedmans made clear their hope that, as they phrased it, the tide was "turning" in America, promising at long last a laissez-faire revival. However unrealistic that hope may have been, the very success of such a book containing such advice was convincing evidence that Keynesianism no longer could straddle the nation's economic landscape. New ideas on how best to manage the economy were emerging and making converts, and advocates such as Milton Friedman were by no means shy about putting forward their beliefs, all too often in oversimplified and overly optimistic fashion designed to attract even the most benighted reporter, reader, or television viewer.

Ken Galbraith, a long-time champion of Keynes and big government, in the mid-1970s had hosted a similarly staged public-television series plus an accompanying book. Like the Friedman book it was a best-seller. Unintentionally, I am sure, the title that Galbraith applied to both—"The Age of Uncertainty"—might as well have referred to uncertainty over the outlook for Keynesianism as to uncertainty over the nation's general situation, which was clearly Galbraith's intention. In contrast, there was nothing at all uncertain about the conviction of Friedman's presentation. Indeed, his series and the accompanying book might well have been dubbed "The Age of Certainty"—which in fact, it was in jest by the soon-to-be chairman of the Fed, Paul Volcker, while he was enjoying a couple of late-night beers with some friends at a New Hampshire inn shortly before the Friedman show first aired.

However cocksure Friedman may have been in the early and middle postwar years about the efficacy of his economic prescriptions, the title of Galbraith's series would prove to be a far more appropriate label for the confusion and self-doubt that soon engulfed the economics profession—including the monetarists. In an arresting debate that he had with Friedman at New York University in November 1968, Walter Heller, who as a Keynesian believed in considerable governmental intervention in the economy, confessed that the Chicago professor's concepts seemed wonderful. But unlike his own prescriptions, Heller went on, Friedman's would surely work only in heaven. By and large, Heller turned out to be right about Friedman's concepts and wrong about his own, for in an increasingly uncertain era, the emerging truth was that nothing seemed to work very well, at least as far as strategies for sustaining the American economy were concerned.

3

Keynes Redux

From time to time through the postwar decades, economists have gained such authority that, out of overly optimistic natures or mere ignorance of economic history, they have managed to convince themselves and others that the economy's cyclical behavior has somehow become outdated, that healthy economic growth can be sustained indefinitely through diligent policy making, and that nasty, recurrent recessionary periods are readily avoidable. I can well recall in this regard an encounter in the mid-1960s with Otto Eckstein, a young Harvard economics professor who was on leave in Washington where he was serving as a member of President Johnson's CEA.

The meeting occurred in New York City just after Eckstein had addressed a large conference of business executives, a well-heeled audience that appeared delighted with the economist's highly optimistic appraisal of the short- and long-term prospects for business. A recession had ended in early 1961, and the overall economy had been expanding for several years. Recession memories, understandably, were growing distant and dim. Indeed, some economists in policy-making positions in Washington, including Mr. Eckstein, were starting to talk boldly about a new era in which the economic course could—and would—be made smoothly expansionary year after year after year. Recessions, to these sanguine economists, were now a mere memory from a benighted pre-1961 past.

Unconvinced, I had recently written a piece in *The Wall Street Journal*, where I served as economic news editor, suggesting that anyone, from President Johnson on down, who believed that the business cycle was dead and buried, and recessions along with it, might be in for some rude surprises in the years to come. The piece apparently attracted the attention of Eckstein, a particularly enthusiastic member of President Johnson's economic team. Accordingly, when we happened to meet in New York, the presidential adviser turned to me and, fixing me in his bespectacled gaze, inquired loudly: "You don't really believe that stuff you wrote the other day about a recession coming along, do you?" Rather than engage in public debate with a high-ranking White House economist, I chose the cowardly path and, mumbling an unintelligible response, quietly removed myself from the circle of business executives who were mingling around the professor to express their admiration for his cheerful, recession-free appraisal of the outlook.

As Eckstein and I soon found out, the business cycle was still very much alive. The expansion phase that was well under way when he gave his optimistic address persisted only until 1969, when a new recession set in that lasted for one year. Since then, of course, the ups and downs have kept coming. Before the long expansion of the 1960s ended, however, the hubris of the Washington policy makers assumed remarkable proportions. I recall, particularly, an incident involving a monthly publication of the Commerce Department which for years had been called *Business Cycle Developments*. This was a most appropriate appellation because the periodical not only reported all sorts of business data but also took the extra, crucial step of relating the data back over the decades to the varying phases of the business cycle. The publication's title—in accordance with the prevailing idea that the business cycle had been eliminated through adroit policy making—was changed to *Business Conditions Digest*, thus retaining only the *BCD* abbreviation and eliminating what appeared to Eckstein and his colleagues to be an anachronistic reference to the business cycle.

Notwithstanding the change, the economy, as perverse as ever, soon entered the 1969 recession. The new name for the publication stayed, I should add, until the arrival of George Bush at the White House in 1989, when the publication was foolishly shut down altogether. At the time of its demise, the economy had been expanding for an unusually long time. Shortly after, however, as happened in 1969, the economy fell into yet another recession, the slump of 1990–1991.

I should note that Eckstein, before his untimely death in 1984, did become convinced of the cycle's inevitability. We appeared as fellow panelists on a number of occasions—the final time, shortly before his death, was at an annual convention of the nation's textile manufacturers—and we found that we had come to agree on many economic matters. By that time, Eckstein had returned from Washington to teach at Harvard, where he was much admired by his students and his lectures, with their frequent references to the economy's cyclical uncertainties, were a far cry from the hubris that he and his White House colleagues had evinced in the 1960s.

OLD MYTHS AND NEW ONES

When he assumed the presidency in January 1961, John F. Kennedy had had only one elementary course in economics. His level of economic expertise can be glimpsed in a conversation that he had with Arthur Okun, the Yale professor who later became the chairman of the CEA under Lyndon Johnson. As Okun recalled years later, Kennedy telephoned the professor at his home on a Sunday afternoon seeking an explanation of an exceedingly fundamental economic matter: the difference between monetary and fiscal policy. After a half hour or so of Okun's instruction about the former, Kennedy declared, "I think I've got it: M stands for money; it also stands for monetary policy, which is mainly concerned with the money supply, and that means M also stands for Martin," a reference to William McChesney Martin, Jr., the chairman of the Federal Reserve Board at the time.

Kennedy had taken his single economics course as an undergraduate at Harvard, where the influence of Keynes was strong in Kennedy's time there and remained so as the postwar decades passed. Perhaps for this reason, the young chief of state tended to lean toward concepts that espoused considerable governmental intervention in the economy when he entered the White House. But his thinking, after his single Harvard course, was by no means set, and thus he offered fertile ground for a persuasive teacher. There was no shortage of applicants for this assignment, and all of them, for all their differences over specific points of policy, reflected aspects of the Keynesian approach to economic management.

First and foremost was Paul Samuelson, the distinguished economics professor at MIT whose textbook, *Economics: An Introductory Analysis*, and its subsequent revised editions have dominated the introductory field since the original printing in 1948. Samuelson earned his economics doctorate at Harvard, where he studied under, and was deeply influenced by, Alvin Hansen, who, at the time, was perhaps the leading American proponent of Keynesian economics. Samuelson was at Harvard in 1936 when Keynes published his *General Theory*. Samuelson gained his Ph.D. in 1941 for a dissertation titled *Foundations of Economic Analysis*, which delved into such arcane matters as how individuals make economic choices in a highly mathematical fashion. As a result of this and similar endeavors, Samuelson was recognized early on as a brilliant economist. His dissertation won him the Wells Prize at Harvard.

Such was his early academic success that Samuelson seemed a worthy successor to the elderly Hansen. Yet, on account of anti-Semitism at the time within the Harvard economics department, he was offered only an instructorship. Meanwhile, neighboring MIT dangled an assistant professorship before him. He readily accepted the latter and thereafter taught at MIT; along the way, he collected the Nobel Prize in economics. Otto Eckstein, a devout admirer of Samuelson, confided to me shortly before his death that "Harvard will never live down losing the leading American economist of his generation to the local competition."

In any case, Kennedy turned first to Samuelson for economic

counsel as he prepared to take the presidential reins from Eisenhower. To his credit, Kennedy attempted to enlist those individuals who seemed the ablest and brightest in their respective fields. In the 1950s, Samuelson had appeared repeatedly as an expert on the economy before various congressional committees. Much of his testimony was sharply critical of the Eisenhower team's economic management. He claimed that the Republicans had kept too tight a rein on the economy, with the unfortunate result that potential growth had been lost in the name of fighting a greatly overblown threat of inflation. Samuelson characterized the Eisenhower administration's economic policies during Burn's CEA tenure as experiments in sadism. Urging a new strategy, the MIT professor told one congressional hearing that the economic reins should be loosened so that "our economy can have full employment and whatever rate of capital formation and growth it wants." And he went on to assert that "a community can have full employment, can at the same time have a rate of capital formation it wants, and can accomplish all of this compatibility with the degree of income distribution it ethically desires."

Not surprisingly, such utopian assertions appealed to a president-elect eager to expand his political constituency and still sufficiently naive in economic matters to believe in free lunches. Accordingly, Kennedy asked the professor to lead an economic task force for the new administration. Accepting the assignment, Samuelson presented the president-elect with a paper titled *"Prospects and Policies for the 1961 American Economy"* that urged, in the finest Keynesian tradition, governmental steps to spur the economy. The emphasis, as one would expect from the Keynesian camp, was on fiscal measures, especially new spending for foreign aid, the military, and education. Looking to the longer term, however, Samuelson went on with a suggestion that placed him somewhat at odds with such other prominent Keynesians as Galbraith and Keyserling: he indicated that "temporary" reductions in tax rates might be desirable if the economy behaved too sluggishly.

Much impressed with his advice, Kennedy offered Samuelson the chairmanship of the CEA, a position occupied during Ei-

senhower's last months in the White House by Raymond Saulnier. Samuelson considered the offer at some length but finally
turned it down, choosing to continue an enjoyable, stimulating
academic life on the banks of the Charles River at MIT. He
knew that his views would continue to be heard in Washington,
and he had no burning desire for a share of the political spotlight. A year after Kennedy's inauguration, Samuelson supplied
the administration with a paper titled *"Economic Policies for
1962,"* in which he lamented the economy's sluggish behavior
and urged greater fiscal stimulation, even at the risk of a mounting deficit in the federal budget. His prescription, predictably,
included increased federal spending and tax breaks.

After Samuelson's decision to remain in Cambridge, Kennedy
turned to Walter Heller who shared many of the MIT professor's convictions. Their backgrounds, however, could hardly
have been more different, which proved a political convenience
for Kennedy who had become concerned that his team might
be seen as too heavily represented by prominent academicians
from his native Boston area. This was not a worry with Heller.
Before catching Kennedy's attention, Heller was merely "a col-
onel in the Keynesian army," Robert Sobel recalls, and "hadn't
much chance of reaching the rank of general," a rank already
held by such luminaries as Galbraith at Harvard and Samuelson
at MIT.[1] In 1960, Heller was comfortably ensconced far from
Cambridge, teaching economics at the University of Minnesota.
A 1935 graduate of Oberlin College, he had gained his doctorate
at the University of Wisconsin, where he studied under Harold
Groves, an outspoken Keynesian and an expert in the linkages
between various tax policies and overall business activity. Under Groves, Heller was drawn to study taxation and made this
the subject of his dissertation.

Kennedy might never have offered Heller a place within his
administration had not the president-to-be attended a political
dinner in Minneapolis in October 1960 with Democratic leaders
from Minnesota. The most powerful of these, Senator Hubert
Humphrey, knew and admired the University of Minnesota
economist and arranged for him to meet briefly with Kennedy.

The two men hit it off, and Kennedy was particularly impressed by Heller's forceful advocacy of governmental measures to spur economic growth. Heller followed up the meeting with a written report providing more detailed policy suggestions. After the election, Kennedy asked Heller to come East for further talks. Impressed with Heller's concepts, the president-elect then offered him the chairmanship of the CEA. This offer was accepted.

It is difficult to underestimate the influence that Heller exercised during the brief Kennedy presidency. By instinct, the newly installed president was fiscally conservative. He seemed very concerned with maintaining budgetary balance. He was hesitant, for example, to reduce taxes or greatly increase spending—even in the name of brisker economic growth. However, this instinctive reluctance gradually diminished, largely as a result of Heller's persuasiveness and support from Samuelson back at MIT. Heller "had the knack of composing breezy memoranda on economic problems—some hundreds in three years—and Kennedy read them faithfully," recalls Arthur M. Schlesinger, Jr., who remembers Heller as an "urbane and articulate" presidential adviser who proffered much of his counsel "in the President's presence."[2]

The recession, which had very possibly cost Nixon the 1960 election, dragged into the early weeks of the Kennedy administration, but by March 1961, the economy was beginning, ever so gingerly, to revive. Still, the numbers spewing from Washington's relentless statistics mills hardly constituted cheery news. As often happens in the early stages of a recovery, the public mood was excessively glum. The recovery, as usual, was slow to manifest itself clearly in the economic data. An index of consumer expectations, compiled by the University of Michigan's Survey Research Center, was lower in November 1961 than in May. Initial claims for unemployment insurance actually increased between March and April 1961. The average duration of unemployment was 17.3 weeks in July, up from 14.1 weeks in March. The average number of hours put in by production workers each week in September, at 39.5, was lower than the

June reading of 39.9. The inflation-adjusted value of contracts and orders for new plant and equipment was less in May than at the recessionary nadir in February.

Under such circumstances, patience is not a characteristic commonly displayed by Washington's policy makers. Accordingly, there was little disagreement at the White House and in Congress when Heller, as early as the spring of 1961, began urging tax reductions and increased spending to close what he saw as a "performance gap" of some $40 billion—the difference between what he calculated the economy appeared able to produce without undue strain and what it was in fact turning out. Heller asserted that his program would so invigorate the economy that the federal budget—buttressed by rising incomes and therefore swelling revenues as the economy expanded—would move into increasing surplus. This happy situation, he theorized, would ultimately set the stage for still more tax reductions and spending increases. "It was the kind of vision few politicians could resist—if only they could be made to believe it possible," remarks Robert Sobel, adding that "the inculcation of this belief was Heller's major task as CEA chairman."[3]

Ironically, the culmination of Heller's educational effort at the White House occurred on the campus of Harvard's long-time rival—Yale—in June 1962. By then, the economy was on the road to recovery, but the recovery seemed exceedingly sluggish and, most worrisomely, the stock market had fallen sharply. On May 28, a Monday, the stock market suffered its biggest single-day decline, up to that time, since the crash of October 1929. This stirred fears that the recession might soon resume. Noting that the ups and downs of the stock market often have foreshadowed the economy's ups and downs, some Cassandras even talked of a new depression.

Also feeding the general pessimism about the economic outlook was a recent clash between the Kennedy administration and the steel industry. In September 1961, Kennedy had urged the industry's corporate leaders to forgo a price increase. He had also urged the leaders of the United Steelworkers to hold their wage demands within the limits of gains in worker productivity, which they had indicated they would do. This was all part of a so-called guidepost program for wages and prices that had been mapped in large measure by Heller. The plan was first put forward in the CEA's *Annual Report* of January 1962. Designed to prevent inflation and induce swifter economic growth in major industries such as steel, the plan called for wage increases to be limited to productivity gains. This arrangement would serve to stabilize per-unit labor costs, which periodically had been edging higher to cause what economists labeled "cost-push inflation"—the upward push of rising costs on the general price level.

The plan, Heller hoped, would inspire workers to achieve swifter productivity advances as an avenue to heftier pay gains. If the hourly output of widgets could be made to rise 4%, for example, then the hourly wages of widget workers also could climb 4% without an increase in the labor cost involved in the production of a single widget.

Even though the steel union had expressed willingness to limit its pay demands to the guideposts established by the plan, in mid-April 1962, Roger Blough, the chairman of U.S. Steel, called at the White House to inform Kennedy of his company's decision to boost its basic price for steel by $6 a ton. Kennedy's reaction was immediate. He was outraged and excoriated Blough and the several other steel-industry chieftains who followed Blough's lead. The White House promptly threatened a number of moves against the offenders, including antitrust investigations. During the showdown, in a much-quoted remark, Kennedy declared: "My father always told me that all businessmen were sons-of-bitches, but I never believed it till now." The upshot was that several other steel companies, led by Inland Steel in Chicago, reluctantly chose not to raise their prices, and a few days later, the original increases were rescinded.

Clearly, Kennedy had won, and Heller's plan remained intact. However, while the price of steel did not rise and inflation remained dormant for a considerable time, there was also a less agreeable aftermath to the confrontation. It produced a nasty souring of relationships between the new administration and corporate leaders across a broad range of industries. And this cast an additional pall over the general economic outlook.

It was this glum atmosphere that formed the economic back-drop for Kennedy's appearance at Yale. In his memoir of the period, Heller recalls the Yale speech as "justly famous" since it constituted Kennedy's "own declaration of economic independence" from the "economic mythology" of the past. This, of course, was the economist's thinly disguised criticism of the long-standing idea, prevalent especially within the Eisenhower White House, that the federal budget should be made to balance over the course of the business cycle, with recession-fighting deficits offset by expansion-throttling surpluses. With Kennedy's new "economic independence," Heller claimed, this "myth" would be cast aside. Henceforth, it would be acceptable for the government to run budgetary deficits even during long, strong expansions of the business cycle as long as the economy exhibited a significant "performance gap," wherein the level of overall business activity remained below a rate of operations that would fully utilize the nation's resources of labor, production facilities, and materials.

"As his economic advisers, we were confident that this [Yale] speech marked a new era in American economic policy," Heller states, adding that it laid the foundation for Kennedy's "decision two months later to call for a massive tax cut early in 1963." The speech, in Heller's highly partial view, was "the most literate and sophisticated dissertation on economics ever delivered by a President, and he wrote most of it himself."[4] In the address, which Heller and Arthur M. Schlesinger, Jr., in fact, had helped to draft, Kennedy asserted that "the great enemy of truth is very often not the lie—deliberate, contrived and dishonest—but the myth, persistent, persuasive and unrealistic." Too often, he claimed in elegant fashion, "we hold fast to the cliches of our forebears. We subject all fact to a prefabricated set of interpretations. We enjoy the comfort of opinion without the discomfort of thought." In 1962, he continued, "The myth persists that federal deficits create inflation and budget surpluses prevent them." Yet, he noted, "Sizable budget surpluses after the war did not prevent inflation, and persistent deficits for the past several years have not upset our basic price stability."

Notwithstanding Heller's admiration for it, in retrospect Kennedy's Yale speech seems to have added a new myth to the economic catalog more than to have expurgated any old ones. It is true that the federal budget, after the massive deficits run up in World War II, was in surplus briefly in the very early postwar years—1946, 1947, and 1948—before falling into deficit again in 1949. It is also true that the general price level rose substantially before leveling off in those surplus years. But the primary forces underlying this pattern, despite the budgetary swing from surplus to deficit, reflected the settling-in of peace. Wartime price controls were ending and the pent-up demand of consumers flush with the savings that had accumulated during the war years was released. Accordingly, it can be argued that the early postwar price climb would have been still sharper had not the budget been in surplus and that the subsequent easing of inflation would have come sooner and would have been more pronounced had the budget not slipped back into deficit at the decade's end.

BUDGETARY BAFFLEMENT

To suggest, as the Yale speech did, that the Eisenhower administration's esteem for balanced budgets amounted to worshipping economic myths was, to say the least, a questionable assertion. The relationship between the economy's behavior and the state of the federal budget was not so easily defined in Kennedy's time, nor has the matter grown easier for economics in the years since Kennedy.

To illustrate, let me briefly skip ahead two decades to recount a conference, unintentionally hilarious, that I attended in 1983. It was hosted by the Federal Reserve Bank of Boston and held at the Bald Peak Colony Club in Melvin Village, New Hampshire, overlooking the magnificent northern shore of Lake Winnipesaukee. The conference was designed to address a straightforward question: Just how much should Americans worry about the rising sea of red ink engulfing the federal budget? In 1983, some officials of the Reagan administration—Treasury Secretary Donald T. Regan springs to mind—were giving the impression that the perennial budget deficits weren't all that worrisome and that the public was perhaps overly concerned about the issue. However, other White House officials, such as Martin Feldstein, President Reagan's chief economic adviser, were warning that the outlook would be dark indeed if the red ink kept rising.

To try to gain insight into the issue, I went to the conference to study the scholarly papers presented there and attend the assorted discussions. During the three-day affair I learned various things. I discovered what an earthquake feels like; a tremor registering 5.2 on the Richter scale shook me awake at my assigned lakeside cottage at 6:21 on the third morning of the conference. (Initially, I believed that the furnace in the cottage was seriously malfunctioning on a surprisingly cold mid-October morning.) I also learned that the leaves in the area were at least a week behind in their annual color change on account of an extraordinarily hot summer. And I discovered (from the bumper sticker on his car) that Robert M. Solow, the MIT economist who was soon to win the Nobel Prize, believed that Harold (Pee Wee) Reese, the stellar shortstop of the old Brooklyn Dodgers, deserved a place in the baseball Hall of Fame (which Reese was eventually awarded, to his—and Solow's—delight).

For all of these discoveries, I was unable to determine just how much attention the budget deficit warranted. For a brief while, I thought I had glimpsed the truth. Among the early speakers was Benjamin M. Friedman, a Harvard economics professor and a director of the National Bureau of Economic Research. His message was unequivocal. Discussing the deficit's "implications" for capital formation, he stressed, with extensive use of charts and tables, that there was "indeed cause for concern." In fact, he warned repeatedly that "deficits of the magnitude now projected for the balance of the 1980s" would probably impede capital formation.

No sooner was Friedman seated, however, than Albert M. Wojnilower, the chief economist of First Boston was on his feet with a different view of things. Known as a relative pessimist on economic prospects, Wojnilower provided a surprisingly san-

Seldom have economists been accorded the power and importance that Harry Dexter White (left) and John Maynard Keynes (right)— with their shared faith in government intervention— enjoyed over their long careers.

Arthur Burns: with his focus on the business cycle, he worried that "the rules of economics are not working in quite the way they used to."

John Kenneth Galbraith: an admirer of Keynes, he worried that President Kennedy's policies were insufficiently liberal.

Gardner Ackley: his party
loyalty may occasionally have
clashed with his instincts as an
economist.

Walter Heller (middle)
and Gardner Ackley (left):
reluctantly, Heller remained on
after Kennedy's death as CEA
chairman until late 1964, when
Ackley, a like-minded
Democrat, replaced him.

Arthur Okun: he tutored
President Kennedy about the
various forms of money and
counseled President Johnson
about the economy.

Milton Friedman: for his own
monetarist reasons, he lent
respectability to the supply–side
cause while oversimplifying his
monetarist message.

Otto Eckstein: with President Johnson in Washington, he talked of a recession–free era that never materialized and went on to become the nation's most successful private economic consultant.

Paul Volcker: though wary of the monetarists, he brought their operating procedures into the Federal Reserve's policy making with painful consequences.

Arthur Laffer: preaching that supply creates its own demand, he kept in shape on long flights between speaking engagements by doing lots of deep–knee bends.

Martin Feldstein: an unhappy
adviser to the Great
Communicator, he found
"absolutely no indication that
Laffer's ideas will work."

Paul Samuelson: an adviser to
President Kennedy, he
preferred the banks of the
Charles River to Washington
and viewed supply–side
economics as "kind of
scatterbrained."

Alan Greenspan: no monetarist, he worried in the fall of 1992 that the Federal Reserve's techniques for analyzing the economy were "simply failing."

Geoffrey Moore: an arbiter of when recessions end, he believed that "we waited much too long" to proclaim an end to the "Bush " recession.

guine appraisal, suitably titled "Don't Blame the Deficit." He suggested, for example, that "government deficits may well promote rather than deter investment" and even declared that "it is hard to visualize realistic circumstances in which a larger deficit would not be associated with larger profits and investment."

Wojnilower concluded, "In sum, I question whether federal debt has been or threatens to be inimical to business borrowing or investment. . . . The budget is like the weather: Everybody complains about it but nobody does anything about it, and no one is expected to." (Ben Friedman's reaction to this line of thought did little to relieve my confusion. His main complaint about the Wojnilower commentary bore not on the central question of how such disparate opinion could arise but on a passing Wojnilower remark that the Harvard economist was "a self-proclaimed Keynesian." Radiating more than a little heat, Friedman denied the allegation.)

Subsequent speakers served only to increase my perplexity. Henry C. Wallich, a Federal Reserve Board governor, seemed moderately concerned that the budget was too deeply in deficit and wondered whether the red ink might best be controlled by "some rule of thumb that is understandable to politicians." He gave no hint of what that rule might be however, and the next speaker, Otto Eckstein, offered no suggestions. Instead, Eckstein urged no less than four rules of thumb, explaining that "there are so many angles that you can't have just one."

An intriguing concept was put forward by Robert Eisner, an economics professor at Northwestern University. He argued that the budget deficit was in large measure an illusion, caused by what he deemed inappropriate accounting methods at the federal level. Some years later, Eisner spelled out his position in a book titled *How Real Is the Federal Deficit?* "A deficit which finances construction of our roads, bridges, harbors and airports is an investment in the future," he maintained. "So are expenditures to preserve and enhance our natural resources or to educate our people and keep them healthy." Yet, he noted, under federal accounting procedures such investment is regarded as additional red ink, driving up the yearly budget deficits. As intriguing as this theory seemed at the time, it did not appear to account for the progressive deepening of the deficits in a period of largely unchanging accounting procedures. Moreover, a pattern of increasing red ink was evident even using budgetary data adjusted to take Eisner's objections into account.

My bewilderment reached a new high on the final day of the conference, with a paper—or rather a pair of papers—prepared by Richard W. Kopcke, a vice president and economist at the Boston Federal Reserve Bank. His topic was "Will Big Deficits Spoil the Recovery?" and his initial presentation—distributed for perusal shortly before the meeting—left no question about his conviction that deficits were not a major worry.

"Big deficits need not spoil the recovery," the Kopcke paper stated, adding that "the deficit is a nuisance statistic capable of spoiling the recovery only if policy makers allow it to divert their deliberations from the important issues. . . ." Indeed, the analysis went on, "it is not meaningful to speak of the link between budget deficits and inflation or interest rates" and, far from "crowding out" economic progress, deficits tend to "crowd in business profits."

When Kopcke rose to speak, however, he had in hand a "revised" version of his presentation. The greatly shortened rendition, I discovered, was stripped of its earlier enthusiasm for deficits. In fact, its nearest approach to endorsing any red ink at all was a cautious suggestion that "there are periods when fiscal policy runs deficits as it restores . . . production." Was this the real Kopcke speaking, or were we listening to words forced into his mouth, most likely by our host and his boss Frank Morris, the president of the Boston Fed? When the conference finally ended, I wasn't sure with whom I agreed or disagreed, or about what–except that Bob Solow was clearly right: Pee Wee did belong in the Hall of Fame.

A WATERSHED

In 1962, when Kennedy delivered his speech, the federal budget was in deficit to the tune of $4.2 billion, which even in those relatively frugal years did not seem a worrisome amount. However, the 1962 deficit did exceed the $3.9 billion budgetary shortfall of the previous year, Kennedy's first in office, and it followed a $3 billion surplus in 1960, Eisenhower's final year in the White House. With the economy clearly on the recovery road, the budget returned to a surplus position in 1963, but the black ink totaled only $300 million, a trifling amount by Washington standards. This, of course, was also the year of Kennedy's assassination, and Lyndon Johnson's abrupt elevation to the presidency.

On the economic front, Kennedy's legacy to Johnson was the speech at Yale and its legislative aftermath: the 1964 tax reductions. Though Johnson was occupying the White House when the tax cuts occurred, there is no question that their origins can be traced to Kennedy's Yale speech. When Kennedy made that speech, the top federal rate on income was 91%; with the 1964 tax act, this was reduced to 70%, and further reductions in subsequent years brought the rate to as low as 28%. It should be added that Kennedy had championed a cut in business taxes as early as 1962. A 7% investment tax credit was introduced, and the depreciation lives for new plant facilities and equipment were shortened by as much as 40%. These moves eventually constituted about one-third of the full Kennedy-Johnson tax package. The reductions under Johnson also included excise-tax cuts on an array of items from dishwashers to telephone service. By 1966, the amount of personal reductions totaled more than $12 billion, and the corporate cuts amounted to about $6.5 billion.

In a follow-up speech before the economic Club of New York in the fall of 1962, Kennedy had elaborated on his theme at Yale. He stressed the importance of keeping a close rein on federal spending as a way to keep the budget close to balance. At Heller's urging, he once again placed great emphasis on the role of lower tax rates. Indeed, he pronounced tax cuts "the soundest way to raise revenues in the long run." This, not surprisingly, upset the fiscally conservative Eisenhower, who labeled his successor's approach "fiscal recklessness." Meanwhile, on the political left, Keyserling and Galbraith grumbled at what they regarded as a retrogressive, insufficiently liberal policy. Kennedy, however, seemed well satisfied, declaring that "I gave them straight Keynes and Heller and they loved it."[5]

Whether or not the general public "loved it" is a matter for historians to assess, but there is no question about Walter Heller's admiration for the economic direction that Kennedy was moving in. The president continued in this direction until his assassination in Dallas. Wishing to see the tax-cut proposal through the legislative process, Heller remained on as CEA chairman for President Johnson until mid-November 1964, when Gardner Ackley, a like-minded economist from the University of Michigan who had served as a CEA member since August 1962, replaced him. Before his return to Minnesota, Heller repeatedly stressed the benefits that would flow from his economic strategy: a briskly expanding, vigorous economy as well as healthy, perennial surpluses in the federal budget. With his chief economist exuding such optimism, it is little wonder that Johnson had no inhibitions about launching Brobdingnagian spending programs for what he promised would soon become a "great society" in America. He urged Heller to help pave the way for his War on Poverty, and the economist responded by joining other members of the Johnson team in recommending the addition of a new antipoverty agency to the ranks of Washington's expanding bureaucracy.

Keynesianism was in full sway. On December 31, 1965, the dead economist's visage appeared, in fact, on the cover of *Time*. "Today," the cover story stated, "some 20 years after his death, his theories are a prime influence on the world's free economies, especially on America's." In the capital, the piece went on, "the men who formulate the nation's economic policies have used Keynesian principles not only to avoid the violent cycles of prewar days but to produce a phenomenal economic growth and to achieve remarkably stable prices." Keynes and his ideas, *Time* conceded, may "still make some people nervous [but] they have been so widely accepted that they constitute both the new orthodoxy in the universities and the touchstone of economic management in Washington." The Englishman's concepts, the piece concluded, "are so original and persuasive that Keynes now ranks with Adam Smith and Karl Marx as one of history's most significant economists."

Time cover subjects often have encountered misfortune soon after appearing on the front of the magazine, and Keynes' legacy, if not the man himself, proved no exception to this rule. In the same issue of *Time* there was an article about the growing number of wounded troops in Vietnam. This was an omen of sorts, as W. Carl Biven, an economics professor at the Georgia Institute of Technology, has noted. "The imbalances caused by the war broke the rhythm of the Keynesian experiment," he recalls. "More was demanded than the economy could deliver."[6]

Even so, the Heller strategy seemed at first glance to have proved a success. Years later, in fact, some analysts continued to argue that there had been a close linkage between reduced tax rates and ensuing economic growth. Robert L. Bartley, the editor of *The Wall Street Journal*'s editorial page, as recently as 1992 wrote, "The Kennedy tax cuts, passed after the martyred president's death, cut the top rate to 70% [and] the 1960s expansion ensued."[7] In the late 1970s and early 1980s, advocates of further tax reductions—the so-called supply-siders, whose ranks included Bartley—repeatedly pointed to the Kennedy cuts and their economic aftermath as proof that such policies were highly beneficial.

However, such analyses fall short in a number of ways. For one thing, the long economic expansion that we remember today as the Soaring Sixties had been under way for almost four years before the Kennedy tax cuts became law. The record makes it clear that much of the healthiest growth occurred before—and not after—the cuts were enacted. In his famous 1968 debate with Heller at New York University, Milton Friedman declared bluntly that "so far as I know, there has been no empirical demonstration that the tax cuts had any effect on the total flow of income" in the years after the legislation. In retrospect, income is only one of many facets of the economic scene that appear to have benefited little, if at all, from the tax cuts.

Corporate profits, for instance, rose briskly from the start of the expansion in early 1961 until mid-decade, but then they stagnated. In December 1969, when the 106-month expansion

finally ended, the profit total was actually slightly lower than it
had been in 1965, soon after the Kennedy cuts. In similar fashion, the stock market rose sharply in the first half of the decade
and then floundered. The volume of new private housing units
fell by about one-third in the two years that followed the tax
cuts. After climbing steeply in the early 1960s, nonresidential
investment for new production facilities and structures—essential for sustained economic growth—showed virtually no further
gain. Industrial production rose far faster in the early 1960s
than thereafter. The average workweek lengthened appreciably
in 1961–1965 but then shortened again. The unemployment rate,
which dropped steadily before 1965, showed little further decline. Although reasonably stable until mid-decade, labor costs
per unit of output then climbed sharply. The nation's foreign-
trade account, in healthy surplus in the early 1960s, barely
remained in surplus in the late 1960s. Labor productivity, surging at annual rates of 5% and higher in the early 1960s, hardly
advanced near the decade's end.

It is true that the expansion of the 1960s was extraordinarily
long. In fact, at 106 months, it remains the longest expansion
on record, according to business-cycle historians at the National
Bureau of Economic Research, which has data on the economy's
ups and downs since the middle of the nineteenth century. But
to attribute this longevity to Heller's Keynesian strategy of
fiscal stimulus, particularly through tax reductions, overlooks
another possible explanation put forward by economists less
wedded to Keynesian ideology: that the expansion's duration
was a legacy of years of fiscal restraint during Eisenhower's
tenure in the White House. Many analysts have raised this
possibility, including even Paul Samuelson who, in a debate
with Arthur Burns in 1967, conceded that Eisenhower, by heed-
ing Burns' counsel to be patient when the economy seemed in
need of stimulus, had probably created conditions conducive to
the long expansion of the 1960s.

Wherever the truth may reside, from the vantage point of
some three decades later there seems little question that—
whatever their impact may have been on exposing economic
"myths"—the Kennedy tax cuts were a sort of watershed. Fig-

ure 3-1 shows this. In the years before the tax cuts, the federal budget was in or reasonably close to balance. But in the years after the cuts, far deeper deficits have been the rule with the exception of 1969, the lone surplus year. This was hardly the picture drawn by Heller when he held out the prospect of an economy so invigorated by reduced tax rates that there would be increasing surpluses in the federal budget.

If Kennedy had been right in what he said at Yale, the perennial red ink of the post–Kennedy years would not have injured the economy. Instead, it would be reasonable to look for more vigorous growth, with longer, stronger expansions and shorter, milder recessions than in the Eisenhower years, and even balanced budgets. But this has hardly been the situation. In the early 1970s, from November 1973 to March 1975, the economy suffered its longest, most severe downturn since the 1930s. Less than a decade later, in mid-1981, an even harsher downturn struck; when the sinking economy finally hit bottom near the end of 1982, 11% of the labor force was unemployed, and many economists, for the first time since the 1930s, were using the term *depression* to describe the business landscape.

Though relatively long expansions have occurred, they have been marked by relatively high levels of inflation and interest rates and, by no coincidence, widespread joblessness and sluggish growth. The 12-month cyclical upswing of 1980–1981 remains the shortest ever recorded by the National Bureau of Economic Research. And the economy's initial recovery phase in the wake of the 1990–1991 recession remains the feeblest on record, resembling more a recession than the start of a new cyclical upswing.

Apart from the business cycle, there is abundant evidence that the economy's performance before the Kennedy tax cuts exceeded its performance thereafter. Gross domestic product (GDP), adjusted for price changes, is the broadest gauge of overall economic activity. In the first half of the 1960s, before the tax reductions took hold, real GDP rose at an average annual rate of 4.6%. In the first five post-cut years, this average fell to 3.1% annually. In the second five, from 1970 to 1975, it fell to 2.3%, and since then it has never again in a five-year

Figure 3–1

FEDERAL BUDGET

Surpluses vs. Deficits

(in billions by fiscal years)

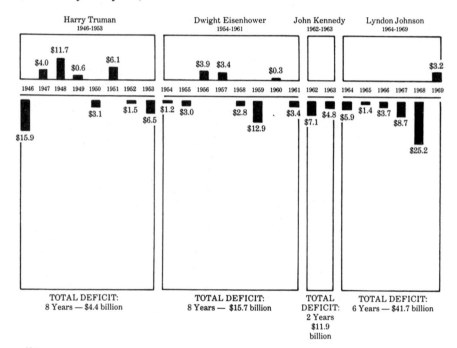

Harry Truman	Dwight Eisenhower	John Kennedy	Lyndon Johnson
1946-1953	1954-1961	1962-1963	1964-1969

TOTAL DEFICIT:
8 Years — $4.4 billion

TOTAL DEFICIT:
8 Years — $15.7 billion

TOTAL
DEFICIT:
2 Years
$11.9
billion

TOTAL DEFICIT:
6 Years — $41.7 billion

<u>Note:</u>
Fiscal years end on 30 June through 1976. From
1977 on, years end on 30 September.
—Each president is listed for the approximate fiscal
years and estimated "Total Deficit" figure while he was in
office.
—Not shown in these budget deficit totals are certain
other federal obligations amounting to trillions of dollars
including unfunded pension plans, unfunded social security
accounts, loan and credit guarantees, and other short- and
long-term commitments.

<u>Sources:</u> National Taxpayers Union, U.S. Department of the Treasury,
and the Office of Management and Budget.

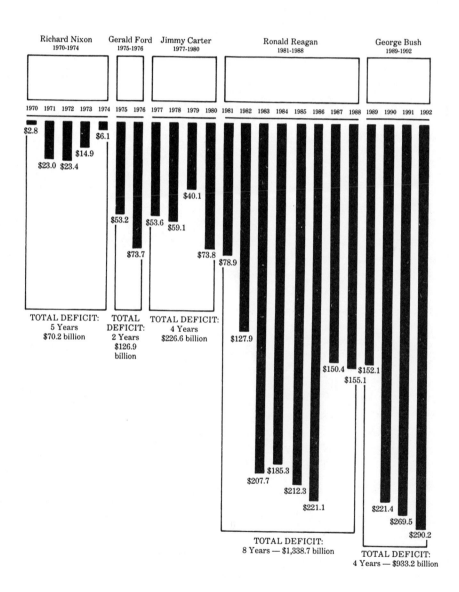

Richard Nixon
1970-1974

Gerald Ford
1975-1976

Jimmy Carter
1977-1980

Ronald Reagan
1981-1988

George Bush
1989-1992

1970 1971 1972 1973 1974   1975 1976   1977 1978 1979 1980   1981 1982 1983 1984 1985 1986 1987 1988   1989 1990 1991 1992

$2.8

$6.1

$14.9

$23.0 $23.4

$40.1

$53.2 $53.6 $59.1

$73.7 $73.8 $78.9

TOTAL DEFICIT:
5 Years
$70.2 billion

TOTAL
DEFICIT:
2 Years
$126.9
billion

TOTAL DEFICIT:
4 Years
$226.6 billion

$127.9

$150.4 $152.1

$155.1

$185.3

$207.7

$212.3

$221.1

$221.4

$269.5

$290.2

TOTAL DEFICIT:
8 Years — $1,338.7 billion

TOTAL DEFICIT:
4 Years — $933.2 billion

stretch approached the early-1960's rate of gain. Similar patterns are evident for such other gauges of the economy's health
as productivity, investment spending on new production facilities, and industrial output.

Jean de La Bruyere, the seventeenth century French mor-
alist, wrote that truth is often "the exact contrary of what is
generally believed." Anyone attempting to appraise the decade
of the 1960s would do well to keep the Frenchman's comment
in mind. Although the economy was in an expansion phase for
nearly all of the decade, in retrospect the truth appears to be
that, by some measures, the expansion almost stopped soon
after taxes were cut during Johnson's presidency. In conventional terms, using the inflation-adjusted GNP, the economy
was some 5% larger in 1968 than in 1967, some 2% larger in
1967 than in 1966, and some 5% larger in 1966 than in 1965. All
the while, the unemployment rate was dropping. This hardly
sounds like the profile of a recession.

However, there are other, less conventional ways of assessing
the decade. It is possible, for instance, to focus on the average
American's "standard of living" in those critical years. Absolute
definitions of general living standards do not exist, but statistics
published monthly, then as well as now, show what is left of
the average weekly income of nonsupervisory workers after
inflation and federal tax payments have been taken into account.
What remains is a reasonably close reflection of the typical
worker's living standard: the actual purchasing power of his or
her weekly paycheck. Viewed in this manner, the economy
appears to have entered a recession in 1965, not in 1969 as
National Bureau historians maintain. In October of that year,
the weekly purchasing power of the average worker stood at
$72.72, a record. Near the end of the decade, when the 1969–
1970 recession officially began, the purchasing-power figure was
nearly $2 below the 1965 high point.

The year of 1965, it should be noted, was also when inflation
began to pose a serious economic problem for the United States.
Before 1965, the consumer price index had been climbing for
many years at annual rates just over 1%. But after 1965—and
the Kennedy tax cutting—the yearly increases were 3% and

higher. It may be no coincidence that stock prices, adjusted for inflation, also peaked in mid-decade and then entered a decline lasting not just for years but for decades.

THE "GRATE SOCIETY"

In the two decades beginning near the end of the Eisenhower presidency, the size of what has been called the Washington Economic Industry grew mightily. Indeed, this expansion stands as "one of the arresting features of the recent history of the United States government," says William J. Barber, a Wesleyan University professor who specializes in the history of economic thought. It is beyond dispute, according to Barber, that "the growth in numbers of economists in federal employ has expanded at a faster rate than the overall expansion in federal employment of professionals and that economists have been increasingly spread over an ever-widening range of agencies, bureaus and Congressional staffs."[8]

It is difficult to pinpoint this growth of economists in Washington. As Barber notes, attempts to do so are frustrated by "ambiguities in the official assignment of the title economist." Many federal employees classified as economists are actually engaged in statistical and administrative work, rather than in any sort of economic analysis or in providing economic advice or policy guidance. Moreover, presidential appointments are not included. Still, an indication of the trend can be seen in data supplied by the Office of Personnel Management. Between 1958 and 1978, the number of federal workers classified as economists rose 91% while total federal employment of white-collar professionals climbed at less than half that rate: a relatively low 45%.

With such growth in the number of economists within the federal bureaucracy, it is hardly surprising that there was a concurrent rise in self-esteem. Changing the name of *Business Cycle Developments* to *Business Conditions Digest* was but one small illustration of the overconfidence consuming not only such White House economists as Otto Eckstein but economists all across the federal bureaucracy. The state of economic knowledge, it was supposed, had advanced so impressively that at

last it was possible to manage the economy's progress much as
a body builder might proceed: carefully regulated ingestion of
foods and liquids best designed to reduce fat and encourage
muscle, augmented by a program of exercises deemed suitable.

Ensconced in the White House, Lyndon Johnson was not one
to discourage this rising self-esteem. On the contrary, he was
delighted with their message that sustainable economic growth
was no longer a highly uncertain matter but could be readily
managed. If Johnson needed an additional spur to go forward
with his Great Society plan beyond the perceived social necessity for such an undertaking, he had it in his economists' prop-
osition that recession-free growth was possible and, in fact, in
prospect.

Ironically, Walter Heller, the economist perhaps most responsible for the administration's perilously high confidence
level, was only briefly involved in Johnson's policy making.
Heller clearly was in full accord when Johnson, in his first State
of the Union address in early 1964, proclaimed, "This administration today, here and now, declares unconditional war on
poverty in America." Heller saw this promise as a logical con-
tinuation and amplification of Kennedy's own inclinations. However, it was soon apparent that there were limits to the CEA
chairman's role in carrying forward the Great Society plan.
Increasingly, Johnson felt that he could make his own judg-
ments about how to implement his Great Society. More and
more, in his view, Heller seemed overly cautious, even conservative. For instance, Heller repeatedly urged that pilot projects
be established before a full throttle was applied to new spending
programs, but Johnson paid little heed. Gradually, one historian
recalls, as the president's "grip on the presidency tightened and
he became more secure in his office, Heller and the few remaining [Kennedy] New Frontiersmen lost much of their remaining influence."[9]

In Gardner Ackley, Johnson acquired a chief economist whose
economic convictions, solidly Keynesian, were similar to Heller's. But Ackley appeared readier than Heller to implement the
president's ambitious spending proposals. And while Ackley
shared Heller's political views, there remained a difference be-

tween the two economists that was significant and surely pleasing to Johnson: the president enjoyed compliance in his advisers and Ackley appeared a good deal readier to comply with Johnson's wishes than Heller might have been had he remained at the CEA helm. Ackley was more loyal than Heller to Johnson's—and the Democratic party's—advocacy of heavy federal spending as the way to achieve a sounder economy.

Ackley's party loyalty in fact may have occasionally clashed with his instincts as an economist. Soon after Ackley had left the CEA, I was talking with a friend who headed a successful Wall Street firm about the economy, which was slowly pulling out of the 1969–1970 recession. At the time, Ackley was still linked to the Democratic party through the Washington-based Americans for Democratic Action (ADA). As an ADA spokesman, he was publicly lambasting Nixon for what he claimed was a lack of stimulative policies to get the economy moving. Without stronger action, he warned, the recession would probably resume. But I knew that Ackley also served as a consultant to my friend's brokerage firm, and my friend seemed reasonably optimistic—correctly, as matters turned out—about the economic outlook. I asked how this optimism squared with the gloom voiced by the firm's economic consultant. "We know that in his public statements he has been sharply critical of Nixon's economic performance, charging that the president isn't doing nearly enough to pull the economy out of the recession," my friend explained, "but his private advice, for which we pay him a considerable retainer, has been that the Nixon team has done a good job of getting inflation under control without letting the recession get too deep, and the business outlook is very good."

It was during Ackley's chairmanship at the CEA—from November 1964 until Arthur Okun replaced him in February 1968—that Johnson's Great Society gained momentum. Unrestrained by his economic team, the headstrong president pressed forward with his programs at an awesome pace, as a few statistics suggest. Transfer payments to individuals—money that the government pays people, such as the unemployed, for which no work is performed—amounted to $25 billion in 1961, a recession year. As the Great Society programs took hold, this total rose sharply, even though the economy was in an expansion phase. This should have led to reduced transfer payments, since much of this money traditionally goes to the unemployed, and unemployment fell sharply during Johnson's presidency. With the array of new spending programs, however, transfer payments climbed to $30.3 billion in 1965, $33.5 billion in 1966, $40.1 billion in 1967, and to $46 billion in 1968. In 1969, the year that Johnson turned over the presidential reins to Nixon, the total crossed $50 billion, nearly double the sum paid when Johnson replaced Kennedy. With the Great Society programs in place, the amount continued to rise steeply, reaching $80.5 billion in 1972 and $158.8 billion—a near-doubling—four years later.

Transfer payments were only one of many categories of federal spending that soared during Johnson's presidency. Even sharper than the rise in transfer payments was the jump, for instance, in federal grants-in-aid to the states and localities. After rising less than $2 billion between 1961 and 1963—from $7.2 billion to $9.1 billion—these federal handouts more than doubled to $18.6 billion in 1968. These surging federal outlays, it should be stressed, reflected programs quite apart from the well-publicized buildup in the military budget as Johnson doggedly pursued the Vietnam War. At $50.3 billion in 1963, federal spending on military goods and services reached a peak of $76.9 billion in 1968.

With this fiscal explosion on the heels of the 1964 tax cuts, it is hardly surprising that the level of budgetary red ink mounted steeply. The budget was $300 million in surplus when the 1960s began. The deepest deficit under Kennedy had been the 1962 shortfall of $7.1 billion. The next year's total fell to $4.8 billion, and by mid-decade, the red ink was down to $1.4 billion. However, as the Great Society programs expanded and the Vietnam War intensified, this budgetary improvement was reversed. By 1968, Johnson's last full year in office, the shortfall was $25.2 billion, dwarfing any deficit since the World War II years.

As these fiscal excesses began to cause dislocations within the economy, the society that Johnson envisioned increasingly took on the features not of a Great Society but of a society that grated, which is what I called it in a *Journal* column, "The Grate Society." More and more, things seemed to grate. An immensely unpopular war, of course, was much to blame for a souring national mood. But so was the increasingly shaky notion of the White House economists that the economy could be spurred indefinitely along a painless, recession-free course.

AN END TO HUBRIS

Even the implementation of President Roosevelt's New Deal in the 1930s, with its burst of legislation in the first 100 days, pales when compared with Johnson's launching of the Great Society. A brief chronology suggests the scope of the endeavor. On December 16, 1963, less than a month after he assumed the presidency, Johnson signed a bill setting up a $1.2-billion construction program for college classrooms, libraries, and laboratories. Two weeks later, on December 30, Congress enacted a $3 billion foreign-aid bill that allowed Johnson to channel more money to Communist-bloc nations that seemed relatively friendly. On March 16, 1964, the drive moved into higher gear as Johnson sent his antipoverty program to Congress. On August 20, he signed an antipoverty bill calling for nearly $1 billion.

Then, on January 4, 1965, Johnson delivered the memorable State of the Union message in which he formally proposed the building of a great society in America. "A president's hardest task," he said, "is not to do what is right but to know what is right." Less than two months later, on March 3, Congress enacted a $1.1 billion aid bill for the impoverished Appalachian region. On April 11, Johnson signed a $1.3 billion bill providing additional funds for elementary and secondary schools. On July 30, he signed a bill that established Medicare and a short five weeks later, a bill funneling $7.5 billion into low-income housing. On October 6, the president signed a bill appropriating $300 million to combat heart disease, cancer, and stroke, and three days later he signed a bill providing an additional $1.8 billion in antipoverty funds, which approximately doubled an earlier appropriation. On September 19, 1966, Johnson signed a foreign-aid bill totaling $3.5 billion and six weeks later, a $3.9 billion bill for controlling water pollution.

As spending mounted, so did the size of the bureaucracy that would oversee this unprecedented outpouring of federal largesse. On August 31, 1965, a new cabinet post—Housing and Urban Affairs—was created. On October 15, 1966, another new cabinet office—the Department of Transportation—was established.

All the while, spending for the Vietnam War kept mounting. On May 18, 1964, Johnson asked Congress for an additional $125 million in aid for South Vietnam. On May 6, 1965, Congress appropriated another $700 million to support the expanding Vietnam War effort. On June 13, 1967, the House of Representatives approved a massive $70 billion defense bill, the largest single appropriations bill ever passed in Congress.

As the red ink continued to rise along with the unbridled spending, Johnson's economic advisers gradually became concerned about the budgetary situation and urged the president to revert to a more restrictive fiscal course.

Near the end of 1965, as the Johnson historian Doris Kearns recalls, Gardner Ackley cautioned the president that unless federal outlays were reined in, a "significant" tax increase might be required to avert "an intolerable degree of inflationary pressure" down the road.[10] But Ackley was not a forceful advocate of restraint, and even if he had been, it is doubtful that the president would have heeded the advice. America, in Johnson's view, could afford both guns and butter. The president felt that the Tax Reduction Act of 1964 was already spurring economic activity, and this only served to increase his general optimism and his appetite to spend freely in pursuit of what he expected to be still greater prosperity.

As the force-fed economy came under increasing strain and dislocation, however, Johnson reluctantly began to heed the calls for a more restrained fiscal policy. At length, on January 10, 1967, he asked Congress to enact a 6% surcharge on income taxes to help finance both the war effort and the various Great Society programs. He also urged the suspension of a business tax credit for new plant and equipment. Congress was slow to accommodate the president's new conservatism, however, and the surcharge proposal remained mired within the House Ways and Means Committee for 18 months. Indeed, its passage was delayed until after Johnson had dropped out of the 1968 presidential race, frustrated not only by developments in Vietnam but, also by an increasingly stormy economic climate. Even so, as late as 1968, Arthur Okun, who replaced Ackley as Johnson's chief economic adviser, was still maintaining that "when recessions were a regular feature of the economic environment, they were often viewed as inevitable [but they] are now generally considered fundamentally preventable, like airplane crashes and unlike hurricanes."[11]

Before his withdrawal from the race, Johnson at last acknowledged that the economy appeared to be woefully overburdened. Declining confidence abroad in the dollar's value only added to his concern and increased his belief that a tax surcharge was needed. "The specter of 1929 haunted him daily," Kearns recalls, but the president "was convinced the Republicans in Congress would stall the surtax, so they could campaign in the fall against 'Johnson's inflation' as well as 'Johnson's war.'"[12]

The mounting economic strain was plainly visible in the nation's credit markets, as well as in the deepening budget deficits. In early 1965, at the start of Johnson's full presidential term, the average yield on long-term Treasury bonds, for example, was just over 4%, which was roughly the same rate that had prevailed through the first half of the decade. But this stability soon disappeared. By August 1965, a rate climb was unmistakably under way, and within a year, the average for the long-term Treasuries was 4.8%. By the following fall, the average reached 5.44%. Soon after Johnson turned over the presidency to Nixon, the 6% level was breached, and the rate was close to 7% when the 1969–1970 recession began in December 1969. Most other interest rates climbed even more sharply in the period. The average yield on highly rated corporate bonds roughly doubled. The so-called federal funds rates that banks charge one another on very short-term loans approximately tripled, as did the average yield on three-month Treasury bills.

Inflation, not surprisingly, followed a similar course. The consumer price index, for example, was rising at an annual rate of only 1.7% when Johnson took the oath of office in January 1965. Within a year, the annual rate of increase had accelerated to 4%, and by early 1969, it was 6.3%. Such a speedup can greatly affect the dollar's value. With inflation running at 1.7%, the dollar would lose half its buying power in about 42 years. With inflation at 6.3%, however, half the buying power would disappear in just over 11 years. As inflation worsened, therefore, it is not surprising that interest rates rose. Lenders grew increasingly concerned about the value of the dollars in which their loans would be repaid. For protection, they began to demand higher and higher interest rates from borrowers.

As the economy came under more strain, investment spending for new plant and equipment, which early in the decade had been rising briskly, virtually stopped. Such spending, of course, is essential to healthy productivity gains, which in turn provide a foundation for a competitive, expanding economy and, ultimately, pave the way for higher living standards.

Lamentably, Johnson and his economic team seemed not to recognize a fundamental truth: the more Washington borrows, the lower national savings will tend to be, and low savings inevitably portend a low level of investments. Low investments, in turn, will lead to slow economic growth and stagnant or declining living standards. The link between savings and investments involves a concept that economists call net national savings. This is simply the sum of business and personal savings, minus the federal budget deficit. What remains is money available for private-sector investment. When Johnson left the White House, net national savings averaged roughly 7% of the GDP. But after a vigorous rise, the rate was beginning to drop, and this decline, a part of Johnson's legacy, would persist. Within a couple of decades, net national savings amounted to less than 3% of the GDP, which was substantially less than the comparable reading for any other major industrial nation.

As economic dislocations worsened during the Johnson years, the high confidence of his Keynesian economists began to erode. Gone was the hubris that had presumed an unending period of recession-free growth perpetuated through skillfully applied fiscal and monetary policies. If Keynesianism was not in full retreat as the decade neared a close, it was at least an exceedingly battle-weary doctrine. For all the push and shove of governmental authorities, the economy was grinding toward yet another recession. Inflation and interest rates were on the rise, the budget was in deepening deficit, and—a most disheartening development—the unemployment rate, for all the stimulative policies, was stuck near 4% of the labor force, about where it had been since the middle of the decade and a level that, in later, troubled years, seemed almost enviable.

There is a happy sequel to Otto Eckstein's realization, long after he had left his post at the Johnson White House, that the business cycle was still alive. Data Resources, which he founded after resuming his teaching duties at Harvard, became enormously successful—so much so that he was eventually able to sell it to McGraw-Hill. The publishing giant handed him a check for some $20 million for his stake, which he promptly invested, he later told me, in banker's acceptances. I suggested to him that in all likelihood—up to that time, at least—he had become the richest economist in the history of the United States, and possibly the world. I further suggested that perhaps *The Wall Street Journal* should profile his remarkable success in a front-page article. Eckstein pleaded against this, explaining he continued to reside in the same middle-class neighborhood where he had lived for years and that he felt such an article, focusing as it surely would on his considerable wealth, would not be conducive to good neighborly relations. With two young children, he also feared that the publicity would pose a kidnapping threat.

So the article was never written, and when Eckstein died several years later, he was still enjoying the middle-class lifestyle that belied his well-earned riches—riches that surely never would have materialized had the Johnson White House really managed to vanquish the business cycle. After all, the main attraction of Data Resources was—and still is—its ability to keep its clients abreast of the economy's latest ups and downs and its likely direction, up or down, in the future.

4

The New Confusion

Easy money means lower interest rates. Or does it mean higher interest rates? Tight money means higher interest rates. Or does it mean lower interest rates? A tax increase will stem inflation. Or will it worsen inflation?

The new economics of the Soaring Sixties gave way to a new uncertainty as the decade drew toward a close. Although this new uncertainty was most apparent, perhaps, in academic circles, it was not unnoticed within the perplexed ranks of public and private policy makers.

Skeptics had long questioned the new economics of Messrs. Heller, Ackley, et al. whose tenets included the conviction that deft fiscal and monetary maneuvering could produce sustained business growth and prevent recessions. ("I do not believe recessions are inevitable," declared President Johnson in his 1965 economic report to Congress.) The new uncertainty, however, extended well beyond a sense that the new economics was unmindful of such political realities as congressional abhorrence of tax increases. The new uncertainty reflected a larger doubt: Even if political hurdles could be overcome somehow, would the economic maneuvering achieve the intended results?

Previously, for example, it had been presumed that policies sharply increasing the nation's money supply would reduce interest rates. The logic seemed plain enough: as more money became available, its cost to borrowers would diminish—a simple case of supply and demand. As the Johnson presidency went along, however, this did not prove to be the situation. In some months in 1967, for instance, the M1 version of the money supply (checking accounts plus currency) increased at annual rates of 12% and 13%. This was a faster pace than at any time since World War II and came on the heels of an earlier tightening of the monetary reins by the Federal Reserve Board. The January-through-October increase worked out to about 8%, nearly four times the average yearly rise of 2.1% during 1950–1960. By late 1967, the amount of money sloshing around in the economy exceeded $180 billion, an increase of more than $20 billion in only three years.

So where were interest rates? Long-term rates, so important for business planning, were at the highest levels since the post–Civil War era. So high was the cost of borrowing for even the nation's largest corporations in the fall of 1967 that U.S. Steel, for example, was forced to postpone a $225 million debenture offering.

Did the high interest rates prevailing at the time mean that the fast-growing money supply wasn't growing fast enough? Or had a swiftly growing money supply somehow brought on the high interest rates?

A STRANGE COLLOQUY

In the latter years of the Soaring Sixties, most economic planners in the Johnson White House and in Washington's other power centers still adhered to the view that easy money tended to reduce interest rates, while tight money served to raise them. During a visit to New York City in mid-1967, Federal Reserve Governor Andrew F. Brimmer provided a sample of the prevailing sentiment. "Where the heck would interest rates be now if we hadn't been easy?" he asked me over a morning cup of coffee at the Waldorf-Astoria Hotel. With the next breath, he proceeded to answer his own question: "Through the roof, that's where."

Away from the nation's capital, however, an increasing number of economists, some in private businesses and some on campuses, were voicing different views. Consider, for instance, the opinion of A. James Meigs, an ardent disciple of Milton Friedman's and, at the time, a vice president in the economics department of New York's First National City Bank, now known as Citibank. "An increase in the money supply does tend to reduce interest rates at first, but then it tends to raise them," he claimed. His argument, he said, stemmed from the Friedmanite belief that a rapidly rising money supply ultimately will increase the amount that people will earn and spend. This in turn will tend to drive up prices in general—including the price of credit, which is the rate of interest. The reason, according to Meigs, was that rising demand for goods and services would eventually place excessive pressure on the economy's resources of labor, production facilities, and materials.

There was a corollary to this argument which held that an inflationary psychology develops and erodes resistance to higher prices and interest charges. Borrowers, for instance balk less and less at paying high rates because they feel repayments will be made in much cheaper dollars. "I guess you could call it the banana republic psychology," Ira T. Ellis, the chief economist for DuPont, told me in 1967. "In effect," he said, "money can never get easy enough." He hastened to add, however, that the situation developing in the United States under the Johnson administration was hardly akin to those prevailing in such countries as Brazil, where the money supply routinely grew at annual rates of 33% or more and interest rates ranged above 60% on loans extending over no more than a single year.

An occasional note of concern over the emerging economic predicament could be heard even at the distant outposts of officialdom. At a conference in Phoenix, Arizona, in 1969, Homer Jones, a vice president of the somewhat maverick St. Louis Federal Reserve Bank, told economists from academia and private businesses that the recent growth of the money supply could be fairly characterized as "out of hand, and maybe even wild." Milton Friedman, then teaching at the University of Chicago, expressed similar concern in a subsequent address to the same group.

But a more typical sample of officialdom's position was expressed to me a short while later by another Federal Reserve official, George W. Mitchell, a governor of the Federal Reserve Board. "Friedman," Mitchell asserted, "has everybody mesmerized—economists, the press, us." He went on to deny that the Federal Reserve's policy had been too easy.

There were no statistics to pinpoint just how prevalent this alleged mesmerization may have been. But Paul W. McCracken, who had returned to teaching at the University of Michigan in 1967 after a brief tenure as a member of Eisenhower's CEA and before becoming chairman of Nixon's CEA, conceded that "more of us are becoming Friedmanites." At the Phoenix conference, Homer Jones estimated that perhaps one of every three economists in mid-1967 adhered to "Friedman-style monetary ideas."

This division of opinion over what policies would best guide the economy was by no means limited to the monetary arena. In 1967, most economists still believed that a tax increase, such as the 10% surcharge proposed by Johnson, would help curtail inflation and reduce interest rates. However, this stand was questioned by a number of other people. Thomas B. Curtis, a Republican congressman from Missouri and a member of the powerful House Ways and Means Committee, which was holding up the surcharge proposal, predicted that the Johnson plan would "intensify inflation" rather than reduce it. He stressed that the current inflation was essentially a reflection of fast-rising costs. In such a situation, Curtis maintained, the proposed tax increase would merely add to the general cost pressure—and ultimately to inflation as companies (through price increases) and individuals (through higher wages) attempted to pass on any new tax "cost."

Some economists, meanwhile, argued that the tax proposal would tend simply to reduce what had been a relatively high rate of personal savings rather than trim consumer spending as Johnson and Ackley hoped. In the middle months of 1967, consumers' savings averaged almost 7% of their after-tax earnings, up from an earlier rate of less than 5%. Several economists attributed this rise to a widespread anticipation that the proposed surcharge would become law and should be prepared for in advance.

Whatever the explanation, it was argued that a cut in savings to pay for higher taxes would tend to drain investment funds from thrift institutions. Such a development, in this view, would only add to the inflationary strains already evident in the nation's financial markets. These markets would come under still more strain, it was feared, if a tax boost also prompted corporations to borrow heavily for capital expenditures that otherwise would be financed out of higher earnings.

Clearly, managing the economy was becoming a most uncertain undertaking. This uncertainty became almost comically apparent at repeated intervals during the 1967 hearings of the Ways and Means Committee. Consider, for example, the following exchange between Committee Chairman Wilbur D. Mills, an Arkansas Democrat, and Chairman William McChesney Martin, Jr. Martin appeared as a Johnson administration witness in favor of a tax increase to stem inflation, but that position hardly emerged from the colloquy, which may seem almost fictional but was all too real:

> Mills: All right. We enact this tax bill. We are going to take more money away from [corporations]. How are they going to compensate for that? They are going right back to the market demanding more credit, aren't they?
>
> Martin: I think that there will be some increase in demand for credit.
>
> Mills: There is bound to be.
>
> (Chairman Mills then asked Chairman Martin whether increased taxes and continued high interest rates would not intensify cost-push inflation.)
>
> Mills: If I know anything about business, those are costs, are they not?
>
> Martin: They are.
>
> Mills: Do they then not make a contribution to the cost-push inflation that we are fearful of?

Martin: A modest one.
Mills: Modest.
Martin: A very modest one, yes.[1]

At about the same time that Martin was testifying, another official, Governor Sherman J. Maisel, was in San Francisco telling a meeting of the U.S. Savings and Loan League that there wasn't much the Federal Reserve Board could do to control interest rates. Most forecasts, he said, were that interest rates would be "far lower" by the end of the decade than at present. But this assumed, he went on, that the economy would show "normal growth" and that the federal government's fiscal policy would become "more balanced."

A proper mix of fiscal and monetary policies probably would be the primary factor influencing interest rates in the years just ahead, Maisel added, stressing as well that the Federal Reserve, for all its reputation, really had little power to hold down interest rates single-handedly. If a central bank such as the Fed determined to create money at a faster pace than the output of goods and services could comfortably expand to, he explained, it would serve merely to generate higher prices.

By 1967, as Martin's responses to Congressman Mills suggest, the Fed was coming under increasing pressure in Washington, not so much for any clear mismanagement of monetary policy but rather as a ready target of blame—as well as a possible source of salvation—for an increasingly troubled economy. In late 1966, monetary policy was tightened: short-term interest rates jumped, and as credit grew scarce, new-home starts plunged to a rate of barely 850,000, down from 1.4 million early in the year.

It is worth noting, however, that short-term rates had once again started to ebb by the middle of 1967, suggesting that a tight monetary policy would eventually bring lower rates. Inflation also eased, while joblessness edged up and overall economic growth slowed slightly but not enough to rekindle fears of a recession. "The decline in the money supply which began in July 1966 caused interest rates to start to fall by December" of the same year, recalls Michael K. Evans, a Washington-based economic consultant to major banks and corporations. Thus, he maintains, *"tight* money led to a *decline* in interest rates and inflation within a year"* of the tightening.[2]

That would seem to settle matters. However, as Evans himself concedes, a new round of Fed tightening in 1968 produced a very different result. This time, instead of declining, short-term rates *rose.* The prime rate that banks charge their most credit-worthy customers, for instance, jumped to 8.5% from 6%. Moreover, inflation began to worsen, rising from 3% in 1967 to nearly 5% in 1968 and crossing above 6% in 1969. Meanwhile, the rate of income saved by individuals eroded sharply with the arrival of Johnson's tax surcharge. Near the end of 1969, a full-scale recession, lasting about a year, set in.

What had worked in 1966–1967 failed in 1968–1969. In the end, the familiar questions remained unanswered: easy money means lower interest rates. Or does it mean higher interest rates? Tight money means higher interest rates. Or does it mean lower interest rates? A tax increase will stem inflation. Or will it worsen inflation?

MORE DATA, LESS CERTAINTY

For a while in the early Johnson years, it seemed that the "dismal science" was not really so dismal after all. A glamorous young president had talked about inherited economic "myths" and held out the dazzling prospect of a "new frontier" on which business would grow and grow, at last free from the age-old curse of recession. Across the country, the word went out from executive suites: hire more economists. DuPont had roughly doubled its corps of economists in a decade, to more than a dozen.

And yet there was a troubling paradox. There were more economists than ever before in U.S. history. They were more in demand than ever before (the median income of economists employed by private businesses stood at about $19,000, a respectable income in those years and roughly twice the average for economists a decade earlier). They were even receiving more publicity than ever before: presidential adviser Gardner Ackley made the cover of *Newsweek* in 1966. And they were better informed because more information about business poured from Washington's well-staffed statistical mills daily. Yet, seldom had there been such confusion, such abiding uncertainty, over what might lie ahead for the American economy.

William H. Peterson, at the time the chief economist of U.S. Steel, recalls, borrowing from *A Tale of Two Cities*: "It was the best of times, it was the worst of times, it was the age of wisdom, it was the age of foolishness, it was the epoch of incredulity. . . ." Pierre Rinfret, an outspoken economic consultant based in New York, responded that "nobody knows" when I asked, in November 1966, for his assessment of the economic outlook. The uncertainties surrounding the outlook, he said, were greater "than at any time in the last 20 years—at least."

Why? The explanation appeared to reside within the nature of the beast. Never had economic forecasters been so inundated by such a flood of economic information. For example, the daily volume of sales for all U.S. retailers was now supplied to economists every Thursday, for the week ended the previous Saturday. A few years earlier, only sales of department stores had been available weekly, and the reporting had been less prompt. Similarly, a highly regarded leading indicator of what overall business activity will probably do next—new orders for durable goods—was now available within three weeks of the end of each month, some two weeks sooner than in the early 1960s.

Altogether, the government now published each month a grand total of 30 leading indicators, 15 "roughly coincident" indicators, 7 "lagging" indicators, 28 "other selected series," and 7 "international comparisons." Included were such esoteric tidbits as "vendor performance, percent reporting slower deliveries," one of the leaders; "unemployment rate, married males, spouse present," a coincidental series; "index of labor cost per dollar of real corporate gross national product," a laggard; "secondary market yields on FHA mortgages," among the "other selected" group, and "Japan's index of industrial production," among the international measures.

By Johnson's second year in office, the quantity of economic data had become "more than a little overwhelming and bewildering," recalls a forecaster then employed at Chemical Bank New York Trust. "We were all better informed, I suppose, but also increasingly uncertain about things. I guess it all went to prove, once again, that the more one knows, the less, you realize, you really know." A glance at the 30 leading indicators suggests how such a profusion of statistics could be perplexing. In November 1966, roughly half of the leaders were moving ahead. However, roughly half seemed in a downtrend, including such stellar, far-seeing precursors as new-home starts, which had plunged.

The contradictory performance of the leading indicators was not the sole reason for the uncertainty that was frustrating practitioners of the dismal science. Rinfret put the situation well: "Economics as an abstraction came to an end in 1966." He asserted that military and political decisions, particularly about the war in Vietnam, had assumed such importance in the overall economic picture that economic forecasters could no longer rely on the familiar statistics—even if they could properly interpret them. "The action," Rinfret recalled, "had moved to the political level."

The government's growing influence was readily apparent. In the first quarter of 1966, the nation's GNP climbed, at a seasonally adjusted annual rate, by about $17 billion, and federal spending, mainly for defense, accounted for less than one-quarter of the increase. In the second quarter, the GNP increase amounted to $11 billion, and about one-third of the rise came from federal expenditures. In the quarter ended September 30, the GNP increase was approximately $14 billion, and the government accounted for very nearly half of the increase. The situation was such that it was possible for forecasters to claim the economy was headed into a recession—or was rolling along at a fairly healthy clip. It all depended on whether one was talking about the civilian side of the economy or all of it. In any event, was it really possible to separate the two?

An added complication was the inscrutability of the Defense Department. There was a distressing dichotomy between Defense Secretary Robert McNamara's forecasts of what Vietnam would cost and the eventual figures. A year earlier McNamara had predicted that the defense bill would climb by some $2 billion in 12 months. That prediction proved to be about one-fifth of the actual rise.

Even government economists were having trouble ascertaining the Defense Department's plans. One corporate economist remembers spending a disquieting evening in Washington in the fall of 1966 with a former colleague who had joined the Johnson team as a high-level economic adviser. "My friend spent half the time complaining about the trouble he was having trying to get information out of Defense Department planners," the corporate economist recalls, adding, "It was not a very happy situation when some of the economists responsible for advising the president and Congress couldn't get information they needed" to make sound policy recommendations.

Contributing to the confusion was the fact that the Johnson administration undertook to fight a war without imposing strict controls on sensitive elements of the economy, such as wages and prices. "If we get controls—and who can say definitely that won't ever happen?—it's a new ball game," was the comment of Alan Greenspan, who was then president of Townsend-Greenspan, a New York-based economic consulting firm, and who later became the chairman of the CEA and eventually the chairman of the Federal Reserve Board.

Yet another imponderable in those years was the soundness of the Bretton Woods system. Would the pound sterling finally be devalued? If the devaluation was substantial, would the dollar run into severe difficulty? Would French central bankers continue to be uncooperative? An increasing worry was the apparent similarity of the Bretton Woods system to the international monetary arrangements that had collapsed in the early 1930s. Economists in France had long argued that the Bretton Woods system was inherently unsound and should be scrapped for a system tied more tightly to gold. Trouble in the dollar and the pound, it was increasingly feared, could lead to a loss of confidence among international investors and traders. This, in turn, could bring a drastic contraction of the international movement of capital and goods—worth hundreds of billions of dollars—and ultimately deep economic trouble, not only in the United States but around the globe.

If sheer manpower could have cleared away much of the uncertainty that pervaded the forecasting business in the Johnson years, the economists' crystal balls would have soon grown much less murky. The NABE boasted more than 1,000 members by late 1966, a doubling in half a decade. The executive suite's growing interest in economics was also evident in the activities of the National Industrial Conference Board (NICB), the New York-based nonprofit economic research group now known as the Conference Board. In 1966, the NICB held conferences for business executives to bring them up to date on economic topics, ranging from the international monetary situation to the outlook for capital investments. In the course of the year, some 10,000 executives signed up for these conferences, up from a yearly rate of about 6,500 at the decade's start.

By the fall of 1967, the forecasting game had become so hard to play, in fact, that Manufacturers Hanover Trust in New York titled the fall issue of its business review "The Schizophrenic Economic Outlook," and Wisconsin Telephone dubbed its review, in keeping with the spirit of the times, "The Psychedelic Economy." To dramatize the confusion, the telephone company went so far as to color its pages in a swirling array of blues, greens, and yellows and suggested to its readers that many economists, after peering into their crystal balls that fall, would come away feeling they had been on an LSD "trip."

As an economics reporter who had recently attended a variety of forecasting conferences, I certainly felt a bit that way. Many of the business prophets were warning their audiences that dangerously rapid inflation and chaotic financial conditions loomed; the trouble ahead would be exceedingly dire if taxes were not raised and federal spending were not reined in to avert a threatening inflationary boom. Other forecasters, however, were sounding a different sort of warning. They cautioned that the economy still had worrisome soft spots. Accordingly, they argued that a tax increase would unnecessarily depress a none-too-buoyant economy.

No one knew, of course, who was right—the forecasters who feared dangerous inflation and urged restrictive measures, or those who maintained that business activity was generally weak with soft spots and needed no curbing. Obviously, much would depend on developments in Vietnam, where the war was intensifying, and on negotiations with the Soviet Union over limiting the costly arms race.

Compounding the confusion was the fact that seemingly sound logic was embodied in entirely different appraisals of the economic outlook. Consider, for example, the seemingly sensible reasoning that was at the center of what I would call the soft-spots school of forecasters. The after-tax profits of U.S. corporations—no small force in an economy such as America's—had been running substantially below levels a year earlier. Moreover, the almost unanimous (though strangely little-noticed) view of forecasters was that after-tax profits would not perk up significantly in the months ahead; in fact, the consensus held that the 1968 profit total very possibly would fall below 1967's reduced level if taxes were raised.

As the soft-spotters also noted, a considerable amount of plant capacity—more than 15%—remained idle. This was at least five percentage points below the so-called preferred operating rate that most manufacturers deemed most efficient and profitable. In the past, this idle capacity had tended to preclude rapid price inflation, the soft-spotters argued. They claimed, quite logically, that price increases were not likely to last when so many production facilities were not in use. Moreover, they argued, companies were much less likely to spend heavily for new plant and equipment when they were not utilizing a high proportion of their existing facilities and, at the same time, faced a discouraging profits outlook. Flat or declining outlays for new facilities, of course, were hardly the customary ingredients for an inflationary boom.

Altogether, the soft-spotters contended, there was plenty of reason to doubt that business was on the verge of any boom. The recent performance of the much-publicized leading indicators of economic activity raised further doubts, according to them. In the fall of 1967, only half of the 12 most widely followed indicators—the list at that time included such familiar gauges as corporate profits and stock prices—pointed upward. The other six were moving sideway or were pointing down toward a recession. The soft-spotters argued that all, or nearly all, of these barometers would be pointing upward if a boom were just around the corner.

What I would call the boom-and-gloom school of forecasters was warning, in contrast, that wrenching inflation threatened. The boom-and-gloomers did not dispute the facts put forward by the soft-spotters. Rather, they contended that the facts were largely irrelevant. The thing to look at, they said, was the federal budget. They estimated that a $30 billion deficit—enormous by 1967 standards—was possible in fiscal year 1968 unless restrictive measures were applied. Such a deficit, they warned, would bring on an inflationary boom of the worst sort.

Paul McCracken was a typical proponent of the restrictive approach, which by 1990s standards seems almost quaint. "A budget with a $30 billion deficit is in a state of fundamental disequilibrium and corrective action is essential," he cautioned. "Failure to narrow the deficit exposes us to the risk of severe inflationary pressures and disorderly credit markets."

The boom-and-gloom school argued that such a deficit ultimately would pump so much money into the economy that inflationary strains would set in, notwithstanding the relatively low rate of factory operations, the disappointing level of profits, or the dichotomous behavior of the leading indicators. They warned that booming demand, fueled by too much money flowing through the economy, would severely strain the nation's labor force and trigger inordinate pay—and then price—increases. It would strain production facilities and disrupt credit facilities, and with inflation rampant, the nation's already ailing balance of payments would swiftly worsen, jeopardizing the international value of the American dollar.

Though the boom-and-gloomers appeared to be in the majority in the fall of 1967, Congress showed little appetite for higher taxes; President Johnson's proposal for a tax boost languished

on Capitol Hill. If it languished long enough, perhaps the worst
fears of inflation would be realized—or perhaps they wouldn't.
Economics may or may not be a dismal science, but as the
Soaring Sixties moved along it clearly had become an exceedingly muddled one.

DREADFUL FORECASTS

The Soaring Sixties ceased soaring at the very end of the
decade. In December 1969, a new recession set in. It proved to
be a rather average setback for the economy, not exceptionally
long and not exceptionally short, bringing painful but by no
means unprecedented levels of joblessness as the months wore
on. In all, the 1969–1970 recession lasted 11 months, and over
its dreary course, unemployment rose from slightly over 3% of
the labor force to about 6%, a near doubling.

A major task for economists, particularly for those who work
for private businesses or policy-setting agencies in Washington,
is, of course, to anticipate just when a new recession is likely
to arrive. How accurately did the various forecasters predict
the 1969–1970 recession? Not very accurately at all, the record
shows—despite the considerable increase in their ranks. According to a survey that I took in July 1968 for *The Wall Street
Journal*, the long expansion of the 1960s had already ended or
would surely do so by the fall of that year. The finding was
based on interviews with several dozen of the nation's most
prominent economists. These forecasters cited the drag on economic activity that would be caused by the Johnson administration's package of fiscal restrains—the tax surcharge and a
planned slowdown in the growth of federal outlays—as a major
cause for the end of the expansion.

Reasonably typical was an assessment given me by the chief
economist for a large insurance company who declined to be
identified in my article because "the firm wouldn't want to see
this in print." He unambiguously predicted that the economy
would enter a recession by the end of 1968. Based on such
appraisal, I concluded that 1968 looks "like the year in which
the country's record-smashing economic expansion will finally

end. That's the view of a broad range of business analysts interviewed in recent days."[3] In fact, the economy continued to expand for another year and a half, generating some 2.5 million additional jobs before the recession finally settled in.

If the majority of economists jumped the gun in 1968, what happened in 1969 was even more embarrassing for them—if indeed it is possible for people to be embarrassed who must try to make a living forecasting the economy's ups and downs. In late September 1969, a bare three months before the recession actually did begin, I conducted another survey for the *Journal*, again asking my stable of forecasters what was in their crystal balls. The headline on my article carrying the survey results read: "Most Economists Doubt Recession Will Occur." The consensus forecast for the year ahead was that overall economic activity would rise "slightly more than 5%." A typical forecast came from Thomas V. D'Allessandro, an economist for General Foods, who assured me that the inflation-adjusted GNP would "continue to rise" right through 1970 and beyond, and he added, "I don't expect a recession or even a mini-recession."[4]

In fact, the GNP gauge fell at an annual rate of more than 4% in the final quarter of 1969, the three months immediately after the survey was taken. The measure continued to drop through much of 1970; for the year in full, the GNP decline slightly exceeded 3%, and for the last three months of 1970, the gauge fell at a fairly precipitous annual rate of nearly 8%. The upshot was that most forecasters, having incorrectly signaled the start of a recession in 1968, now compounded their error by predicting recession-free growth at the very time a recession was setting in.

Credentials, I should add, seemed to matter little. Most economists, then as now, were degree-laden, typically sporting a doctorate as well as a master's degree in economics. But there was little relationship between the accuracy of individual forecasts and the academic backgrounds of particular forecasters. Few economists could match the credentials of Milton Friedman, even before the outspoken professor captured the Nobel Prize. Yet, his performance as a forecaster was abysmal. I recall an interview with him in the summer of 1969 in which he predicted that the consumer price index would rise at an annual rate of only 4% by year's end and would increase at an even milder pace in 1970. It was a bold prediction, based on his assessment of the "lagged effects" of recent Federal Reserve policy. At the time of the interview, the consumer price index was climbing at an annual rate of 6.4%, up from 4.6% in the final half of 1968. In June 1969, the rate of increase reached 7.2% annually, a pace that, were it to persist, would halve the dollar's value in a decade.

Friedman's optimistic scenario proved utterly wrong. Instead of rising at a 4% rate at year's end, consumer prices accelerated sharply to rates of well over 6%, and faster gains persisted through much of 1970. In retrospect, it seems clear that his forecast placed too much weight on Fed policy, which he deemed restrictive, and too little on such other factors as labor costs and fiscal policy. Louis Stone, the chief economist of Hayden, Stone and, incidentally, the father of Oliver Stone, the noted film director, lacked Friedman's academic credentials. Stone, however, proved a far better forecaster than the professor. Skeptical about the possibility of abating inflation, Stone worried about the power of labor to win big wage increases and the power of big corporations to impose pay increases. "It is plain nonsense," Stone told me, "to talk about controlling inflation through monetary restraint alone."[5]

Indeed, occasionally there seemed to be an inverse relationship between forecasting accuracy and credentials. I recall, for instance, predictions made in 1973 by two widely followed economists with remarkably disparate resumes. One of the forecasters was Robert H. Parks, who now heads his own economics consulting firm and teaches economics at Pace University in New York in his spare time. In 1973, Parks was the chief economist for Blyth Eastman Dillon, a large and highly respected New York securities firm. The other forecaster was Harry D. Schultz, then, as now, publisher of an expensive, successful economic newsletter that boasts thousands of devout subscribers and makes Schultz a rich man.

The two men's credentials could hardly be more different. Bob Parks' were, to say the least, impressive. The "doctor" that he used before his name in 1973 was well earned. His academic training included a doctorate and a master's degree from the University of Pennsylvania, a bachelor's degree from Swarthmore, and professorships at two universities. Harry Schultz, on the other hand, once told a *Wall Street Journal* reporter—who unfortunately accepted it as fact—that the "doctor" he used before his name in his newsletter and on the lecture circuit reflected a doctorate he had received from St. Lawrence University in New York State. However, I discovered that his name was totally unknown to officials at St. Lawrence. "We find no indication that one Mr. Harry Schultz ever attended St. Lawrence University at any time or that he ever received an honorary degree from this university," an official of the Canton, New York, institution told me. Schultz did spend a couple of years at City College of Los Angeles, where he majored not in economics or finance, but journalism. (Schultz' unhappiness over my report prompted him to seek my dismissal from *The Wall Street Journal*, but Fred Taylor, the paper's managing editor in those years, backed me up, much to Schultz' disgust.)

And so the question: Which man's view of the economic future would you tend to heed—that of Dr. Parks or that of "Dr." Schultz? In mid-1973, if you had been listening to Bob Parks over the preceding year or so, you probably would have kept much of your money invested in the U.S. stock market—and taken your lumps along with most investors and, by no coincidence, most economic forecasters. If you had listened to "Dr." Schultz, however, your investments would have fared far better. His letters of investment advice had dripped gloom about the outlook. One suggested portfolio, consisting wholly of South African gold-mining shares, had appreciated more than 200% since the beginning of 1972. Another, made up largely of securities from such nations as France and Switzerland and without a single share of U.S. stock, had climbed about 20% just since the start of 1973, a period in which the prices of most U.S. stocks dropped sharply, correctly anticipating the start of the severe 1973–1975 recession.

Looking ahead in mid-1973, Bob Parks remained relatively optimistic. One Parks appraisal of economic prospects, for instance, voiced the conviction that "this expansion [of business activity] will turn out to be one of the longest in U.S. history." He was dead wrong, of course; the expansion came to an end in November of that very year. Parks also opined that President Nixon's actions on the price front—to initiate a series of price-control moves in August 1971—had "visibly and believably" strengthened the nation's "attack on inflation." In fact, inflation worsened severely in the year or so after Parks' forecast.

Harry Schultz, in contrast, saw the outlook in mid-1973 as dark indeed. One Schultz report, almost comical in the extent of its pessimism, began: "Civilization as we know it, is crumbling." He went on to advise "short positions" in the U.S. stock market, adding that "even in 1930 there were rallies." He appeared confident that the price of gold—his favorite metal and a traditional haven for economic pessimists—would head upward in the near future, as it most certainly did.

Whatever Schultz may have lacked in credentials, he more than made up for in showmanship. I was fortunate enough in the fall of 1971 to attend a seminar that he held at the Hamilton Princess Hotel in Bermuda for several hundred wealthy investors, primarily subscribers to his newsletter. It afforded me a fascinating glimpse of a very special breed of investors, derisively called "gold bugs" by the more conventional, more numerous investors who were taking their lead from the likes of Bob Parks. The advice dispensed by Schultz and several other speakers was, as usual, exceedingly downbeat. "America," Schultz warned, "like a child pop singer who dies of drugs, became far too wealthy too young in her history as a country. And like the pop singer, she became drunk with power while not knowing how to take the responsibility that goes with it." Looking ahead, Schultz declared, "What I foresee is a U.S. depression and a global recession." His recommended portfolio to protect investors against such a future included major positions in gold, gold shares, various foreign securities, and time deposits, designated in a variety of "stronger" foreign currencies. (For advice tailored to individual requirements, Schultz claimed to command what may have been the highest consultation fee in the world at the time—$700 per hour; this claim,

I should note, was corroborated by an elderly, wealthy investor who consulted privately with Schultz during the Bermuda weekend.)

Perhaps the most extraordinary event of the Bermuda meeting involved the appearance of John Exter, a leading economist at New York's First National City Bank. In the prelude to Exter's appearance, Schultz' showmanship was at its best. Exter's devotion to gold was a long-standing, well-known fact that had been noted repeatedly in such widely circulated newspapers as *The Wall Street Journal* and the *New York Times*. Even so, Schultz warned me and Dana Thomas of *Barron's* magazine, the only other journalist in attendance, that Exter's speech would contain such radical advice that his status at his bank might be jeopardized "if the word gets out." Schultz urged us to write nothing, a request that only Thomas honored.

Exter then proceeded to express precisely the same views that he had been expressing for years: big economic trouble lay ahead, and investors should buy gold and Swiss francs and steer clear of the U.S. stock market and the U.S. dollar. For 13 years Exter, whose background included a string of important Federal Reserve posts, had been speaking his pessimistic mind on economic matters. And for 13 years his superiors and colleagues at the bank had tolerated, but with growing dismay, his extraordinarily grim assessments of the economic outlook. Soon after I reported his remarks at the Bermuda meeting, the gulf between Exter and his associates at the bank become so great that he decided to accept, at age 61, early retirement. "I caught a lot of static over" the speech in Bermuda, he told me with no apparent resentment at me for the publicity or at the bank. "It was the last time, until leaving the bank, that I really spoke my mind in public." (For the record, advice dispensed in that speech, would have yielded large investment profits—largely in South African gold-mining stocks—for anyone bold enough to have followed it.)

After leaving First National City in May 1972, Exter became a private economic consultant and investment counselor, working from his home in Mountain Lakes, New Jersey. There, he made himself available to anyone, bull or bear, willing to pay for his advice. His clients ranged from wealthy individuals to the pension fund for state employees of Alaska. His yearly earnings from such clients and occasional lecture engagements amounted to approximately triple what he estimated he would have earned had he remained at the bank.

Fully as arresting as the dire predictions contained in Exter's Bermuda speech were the rumors, often generated by Schultz, that swept the conference. The U.S. government had contingency plans to invade Canada in the event that nation decided, as it well might, to cut off its natural resources (including gold) from Uncle Sam. U.S. government coffers actually contained only $3 billion of gold, rather than the $10 billion reported to the public. Washington had plans to halt the transfer of any funds out of the United States. A critical shortage of bank vault space had developed because so many Americans were hoarding gold and silver coins. Uncle Sam had already printed up new, tri-colored paper money that eventually would be dispensed at the rate of one tri-colored dollar for each two dollars turned in. The new bills were said to have been stored "in the Chicago area" after a recent, mysterious transfer from "a bank in Kansas City."

As the 1960s drew toward a close and confusion over the outlook mounted within the economics profession, a new problem arose for forecasters. The supply of data available for gauging the economy's health and prospects was cut back, reversing the long postwar proliferation of such statistics. However valid the reasons for it, the new trend only worked to worsen the already sorry state of economic forecasting. In the 12 months prior to June 30, 1968, the federal government had spent more than $140 million to provide statistics. This was a record, nearly $20 million more than in the previous 12 months. In the fall of 1968, however, for both political and budgetary reasons, there was a drive in Washington to reduce the supply of data. By that fall as many as 40 bills had been introduced in Congress to limit the number of questions that citizens were required to answer for census takers. Under law, a person who refused to respond to a census taker's questions could be sentenced to 60 days in jail and fined $100. This had prompted mounting congressional concern that many citizens were being subjected to flagrant violations of their privacy. A deeper worry was that compulsory answers could lead eventually to a *1984* scenario in which the government, as a sort of Orwellian "Big Brother," would know everything about everyone.

One congressional proposal, for instance, limited answers to only 7 of the 70-odd questions planned for the decennial census, which was scheduled to begin in April 1970. The legislation went forward even though many economists warned that such changes would seriously reduce the usefulness of the census and thus adversely affect all sorts of statistical series based on it.

At the same time, federal budget-cutters were stepping up their efforts to trim spending in areas least likely to antagonize voters. Spurring this drive was a rising tide of budgetary red ink—$25 billion in the fiscal 1969 budget alone. High on the list of candidates for spending cuts was money used to support Washington's statistics mills—a move unlikely to anger or even concern most voters. The effort was highly ironic inasmuch as accurate economic statistics help planners avoid budgetary problems, among other economic difficulties. Yet, it was hardly surprising, as William H. Chartener, the assistant secretary of Commerce, put it, that "in a time of general budgetary restraint statisticians should be treated with less solicitude by budget officers and appropriations committees than postal employees or air-traffic controllers."

Early in 1968, the White House had sought $158.4 million to support statistical programs during fiscal year 1969. But this plan was abandoned by the middle of the year, and the eventual sum provided fell short of the amount provided even a year earlier. This marked the end of a long string of spending boosts to gain broader and better data. One casualty was a plan to improve the quality of construction statistics. The government had hoped to initiate periodic checks on the progress of new residential construction projects which was then only estimated. Among other things, the checks would have given economists a far better idea of the impact on home building of such factors as bad weather. Other casualties of the budget-cutters included improved measurement of quality changes in the government's consumer price index; the use of transaction prices, rather than list prices, in the government's wholesale price index; reports on inventories that manufacturers maintained at locations away from the factory; increased coverage of such institutions as banks and insurance companies in government surveys of capital spending plans.

Although the budget-trimming campaign in the fall of 1968 did not scrap any major statistical series, during the next few years several key measures were abandoned. These included the rate at which workers were changing jobs or quitting jobs as well as the number of jobs needing workers, a statistical series predictably detested by labor union leaders. Geoffrey Moore, whose long career as an economist in academia and in Washington included a stint as President Nixon's commissioner of Labor Statistics, regarded the so-called quit rate as the best possible gauge of consumer confidence, far better than any of the widely publicized, privately conducted consumer surveys. "What could possibly constitute a surer indication of a person's confidence level than the decision to quit a job?" Moore says. The job vacancy series, of course, provided policy makers with a more balanced view of supply-and-demand forces in the labor market than could be provided by simply observing changes in the unemployment rate or in the number of people at work.

For all of this, it should be noted that Washington's statistics mills remained, by and large, the best in the world. Consider, for example, the consumer price index, the most widely followed measure of inflation. It continued to be published monthly on the basis of samples taken from coast to coast in 58 cities, drawing on reports from 1,775 food stores, 40,000 tenants, and 16,000 other sources ranging from lawyers to psychiatrists. By comparison, Brazil's consumer price index in 1968 was based on spotty sampling done only in the city of Rio de Janeiro. In 1967, shortly before Brazil's political leaders removed some rent controls in Rio, housing was quietly removed from the index. This prompted an economist at the U.S. Commerce Department to remark wistfully to me: "Wouldn't it be nice if we could do something like that once in a while, when the complaints about inflation come pouring in?"

THE INFLATION PUZZLE

Economics, like most fields of study, depends in large measure on the exercise of logic. Certain things will happen in the economy, and as a result, there will be certain consequences—depending, of course, on a countless variety of interrelated developments that the practicing economist must carefully weigh. Indeed, a responsible forecaster's major task is to pull the many threads together in logical fashion and to come up with some assessment, presumably valuable, of what the future may hold. This procedure formed the basis of what in the Soaring Sixties was the nascent practice of econometrics—the careful blending of increasingly sophisticated computer technology with old-fashioned economic analysis. No matter the level of sophistication, however, the fact remains: garbage in, garbage out. And one way in which forecasters of the Soaring Sixties attempted to protect against this danger was through the assiduous application of logic, whether by way of a Keynesian focus on the likely ramifications of fiscal developments, or through a Friedmanite focus on the money supply, or through some happy combination of the different theories.

Whatever the approach, however, it was becoming increasingly clear by the end of the decade that logic was not necessarily a reliable tool for dealing with the various facets of the economy's behavior. This seemed especially true with regard to inflation, the economic matter of greatest public concern. The course of inflation kept confounding the forecasting community. Milton Friedman was only the most prominent economist to fall victim to its vagaries. Inflation persistently defied the sort of logical analysis that reasonable forecasters would normally employ.

If logic were applied, an effort to appraise the economic implications of a general rise in prices, for example, might run something like this: consumers expect prices to go up and up, so quite sensibly they hurry out to buy new suits, new coffee tables, or whatever else they may need before such items get any costlier.

Pointing to this line of behavior was the experience of Germany in the early 1920s, when it endured a horrendous bout of inflation. Prices rose at an awesome, accelerating pace—faster than the German central bank could increase the money supply. Most Germans, fearful that their currency would be worth far less within a day or two, hurried out to buy things before the next price hike. By no coincidence, the German economy performed remarkably well through the early stages of this inflationary spiral. Unemployment, for instance, was comfortably below 4% of the labor force until well past the middle of 1923.

This was only months before the rapidly depreciating German mark became totally worthless. A year earlier, the German money supply had stood at 252 billion marks: by January 1923, it approximated 2 trillion marks; and by September 1923, it was up to 28 quadrillion marks. A short two months later, it reached 497 quintillion—the number 497 followed by 18 zeroes. By late 1923, just prior to the total collapse of the mark, some German enterprises were forced to pay their employees in special scrip that could be used only to buy a particular company's products or services. Borrowing, not surprisingly, became virtually impossible as more and more lenders feared they would be repaid in worthless notes. Food riots broke out in various German cities as prices changed—quite literally—by the hour.

Yet, it was only when the country's currency had lost its entire value that the German economy finally nosedived. Until the very end of the price spiral, fear of imminently higher prices spurred extensive hedge buying by consumers and corporations alike. In July 1923, only 3.5% of Germany's trade union members were without jobs; only three years before, the jobless rate had been as high as 6%. As things deteriorated near the end of 1923, however, and as barter replaced the mark as the primary means of carrying on trade, the unemployment rate began to leap, reaching 9.9% in September 1923. By year's end, the jobless rate was at 28.2%, higher even than the U.S. unemployment level at the worst of the Great Depression.

But in the United States in 1971, simple logic, as well as

Germany's painful precedent, failed most forecasters miserably. As the year unfolded, a very different situation developed: people expected prices to go up and up—but instead of hurrying out to buy something, people hurried over to the nearest bank to sock away some more cash.

Few economists had expected that consumers, with memories of the 1969–1970 recession still fresh, would undertake a wild spending spree, but almost no one looked for the frugality and caution that prevailed. As a result, the young recovery in 1971 turned out to be far less vigorous than many forecasters had anticipated. In fact, this lackluster showing was a major reason why President Nixon turned abruptly to wage-and-price controls in mid-August and abandoned America's assigned responsibilities within the Bretton Woods system.

In the second quarter of 1971, consumers saved at an annual rate of $62 billion, a record up to that time; this amounted to 8.4% of after-tax earnings, up from an already hefty 8.1% in the first quarter and 7.9% in the recessionary quarter a year earlier. The economic impact of this propensity to save can be measured. If, for example, consumers had suddenly reduced their rate of saving in the second quarter of 1971 from 8.4% to 6.3%, the average for the previous two decades, it would have freed some $15 billion for spending—approximately enough to double the rate of growth in consumer outlays, which accounted for roughly two-thirds of overall economic activity. "Consumer income—buttressed both last year and this by a series of government actions, including increased Social Security benefits, federal pay hikes and the end of the income tax surcharge—has been sufficient to fuel a more vigorous expansion in retail activity than has actually occurred," an economist at Morgan Guaranty Trust remarked to me at the time. "What's been lacking," he added, "is not the means but the will to spend."

But why weren't consumers in a buying mood, especially with worry over unemployment waning as the economy continued to recover from the 1969–1970 recession? The answer, as illogical as it may seem, was fear of worsening inflation. In August 1971, Albert Sindlinger, an economist heading a consulting firm specializing in consumer studies, offered me this decidedly non-

academic and seemingly illogical explanation: "Money is going
to stay in the bank until the consumer is convinced that the
value of the dollar will stabilize. People have finally become
scared by inflation; I believe they rather enjoyed it for a few
years, but now they are reacting to this new fear by wanting
to save." A few statistics bear Sindlinger out. In 1946, consumers saved 9.6% of their after-tax earnings—and consumer prices
rose 8.5%, an increase that made even 1971 inflation seem moderate; in June 1971, consumer prices rose at a 6% annual rate.
In 1951, the saving rate averaged 7.6%—and consumer prices
climbed 7.9%. But in 1955, savings came to only 5.7% of earnings—and consumer prices actually declined slightly. And in
1963, the saving rate stood at 4.9%—and the consumer price
index rose only 1.2%.

Altogether, it is apparent, if illogical, that through much of
post–World War II period—unlike Germany in the early
1920s—high rates of inflation were usually accompanied by relatively high rates of saving, and conversely, the low inflation
rates of the mid-1950s and early 1960s were associated with
relatively low saving rates.

Another reason for high savings during periods of high inflation was the interest rates that accompanied the rise in prices.
Lenders, concerned about being paid back with cheaper dollars,
sought to hedge against this threat by demanding more for the
use of their money. In the process, the sharp rise in interest
rates both discouraged consumer borrowing and encouraged
consumer saving. The upshot was ironic as well as perplexing
for forecasters. While it was clear that worry over inflation was
prompting Americans to save rather than spend, it also was
evident that this illogical propensity might eventually work to
curb inflation—inasmuch as the act of saving tended to hold
down demand for goods and services and thus, at least in the
short term, slow overall economic activity.

The complexity of the issue did not end there. Sluggish demand for goods and services tended, of course, to hurt corporate
profits. This, in turn, depressed the level of stock prices. And
a depressed stock market naturally prompted many sharehold-
ers, stung by their paper loses, to hang on to more cash. A

further complication involved the placement of savings. If savers deposited their funds in thrift institutions, such as savings banks, which served as sources of funds for home construction, it clearly benefited the housing industry. It was no coincidence that home building was one of the most rapidly expanding sectors of the economy during much of 1971.

The extent to which unionization was responsible for rising prices in this period was also widely misunderstood by forecasters. In much of the Johnson presidency, the prevailing belief was that the nation's worsening inflation was fueled by union demands for ever higher wages. However, this argument missed the fact that the largest price increases were in areas in which unions were weak or labor costs were not a major consideration. For instance, few businesses were more strongly unionized than the auto industry. Yet, despite the annual hubbub when prices of new models were announced, the government's consumer price index showed that the average price of new cars in the late 1960s was no higher than in the late 1950s. On the other hand, few fields were so little unionized in those years as medicine. Yet, physicians' fees, on the average, were almost 40% higher in the late 1960s than a decade earlier. The idea that big unions commanded big pay increases simply does not square with the facts. Instead, the record shows that the largest pay increases were in fields in which highly skilled professionals were needed to meet sharply rising demand or in which it had grown difficult to offset higher wage rates through the use of automated equipment. The first table lists some items that were leading the climb of consumer prices in the fall of 1968; the increases are for the preceding 10 years, a decade in which the consumer price index as a whole rose about 20%.

Only about 10% of workers in the broad category including maids, medical personnel, movie-house attendants, and barbers, were union members, and only 2% of insurance company employees were unionized.

The second table lists some items for which prices actually declined in the same 10 years. The statistics, it should be added, take quality improvements into account. For instance, if a car's price happened to stay the same throughout the 10-year period,

	Price increase in decade (%)
Daily Hospital Service	101
Movie Admissions	70
Maid Service	48
Auto Insurance Rates	44
Postal Charges	42
Physicians' Fees	38
Men's Haircuts	37
Property Insurance Rates	36

but its quality was deemed by Labor Department statisticians to have improved, it would be counted in the consumer price index as a price reduction. The buyer, in effect, was getting more for the money.

	Price decline in decade (%)
Radios	23
Television Sets	20
Vacuum Cleaners	20
Refrigerators	17
Washing Machines	14
Home Permanent Refills	11
Drugs	3
New Autos	2

The industries that made the items listed in the second table were highly unionized. About 70% of the people turning out transportation equipment, a major component of which was autos, belonged to unions in 1968. About half of the people employed in appliance production were in unions. More than one-third of those employed in the drug and chemical industry were union members. All these percentages, it should be noted, were substantially higher than the comparable figures of 24% for the unionization of the entire U.S. labor force in 1968.

A closer look at the record shows, moreover, that there was no particularly close connection between the magnitude of pay boosts and price developments. The third table shows how much average weekly earnings increased in the same 10 years for workers in various occupations.

	Pay increase in decade (%)
Registered Nurses	75
Auto Workers	65
Drug Industry Workers	49
Appliance Workers	45
Insurance Company Employees	29

Auto workers' salaries rose sharply in the 10 years, but not auto prices. Salaries for those employed in appliance production climbed substantially, but appliance prices declined markedly. Pay for insurance workers increased relatively slowly, but insurance rates rose steeply. On the other hand, nursing was an area in which both salaries and the cost to customers soared. One pattern that emerges in such numbers is that the pay of highly skilled, essential personnel was climbing sharply, whether they were union members or not. Unionization was relatively low in both nursing and insurance, but in the late 1960s, the nation needed about 150,000 more registered nurses than the 659,000 it had. There was no such shortage in the insurance field. Another pattern that emerged was the extent to which mechanization and automation offset higher pay in some industries. While auto pay climbed sharply, so did the hourly output of auto workers, thanks in large measure to the introduction of increasingly efficient equipment and work methods. The same situation prevailed for most other production employees, whether they made appliances, TV sets, drugs, or chemicals for home permanent sets.

In all, the record shows that inflation in those years, to a remarkable extent, reflected factors that had little direct connection with labor costs—though for many economists, as well as editorialists and politicians, labor costs continued to be a major culprit in the price spiral. In the insurance business, for example, pay had risen relatively slowly, but rates were up sharply because of increased rioting and vandalism, more auto accidents, and a general trend toward larger claims and settlements. Similarly, admission prices in movie houses were up 70% in 10 years, primarily because of such factors as sharply climbing real-estate prices, attempts to fight the competition of television by offering reserved-seat showings of big-budget films, and the increased ability of movie producers to command large sums for films from theater owners, whose bargaining power had ebbed since the early postwar years. As for labor costs, the average pay of ushers in movie houses in New York City, for example, was about $30 for a 24-hour week—and that lowly amount was higher than in many cities around the nation.

Among the fastest-rising items in the consumer price index were mortgage interest rates, property taxes, auto registrations, and golf-green fees, and in each instance, the influence of labor costs was, at best, indirect. Even homeownership costs, up more than 20% in a decade, reflected rising land prices more than rising construction costs. The average land cost for a new home soared more than 70% between 1958 and 1968, and yet the average weekly earnings of workers who were building new homes increased roughly 50%.

Through much of this period, I should add, the rise of U.S. wages was less than in most other industrial countries. To be sure, the U.S. wage level in absolute terms continued to be appreciably higher than elsewhere. However, if the patterns shown in the table below were to persist, the U.S. competitive position was bound to improve, which eventually happened. The table pinpoints the annual rates at which hourly wages rose during the first half of 1968, 1969, and 1970.

	1968	1969	1970
Belgium	4.2%	7.8%	10.8%
France	5.9%	7.0%	10.6%
Germany	6.0%	8.0%	16.7%
Italy	3.9%	8.0%	30.6%
Netherlands	7.8%	12.8%	10.1%
Japan	16.3%	14.1%	11.1%
Britain	7.9%	7.2%	6.1%
United States	7.4%	5.6%	4.3%

The wage increase for the United States in 1970 was the smallest of the eight. Moreover, the *trend* of wage boosts in these three years was downward in the United States but upward in most of the other countries.

For all of this, many economists in the late 1960s continued to argue blindly that if inflation was to slow, the impetus would have to come from industries in which prices had, in fact, been relatively stable or had declined. The reasoning, however faulty, was that such industries—prominent examples included autos and appliances—were the only areas in which further major productivity advances seemed feasible.

Far more sensible than the claims of many economists that outsized pay increases were responsible for a worsening price spiral was an editorial that appeared in *The Advance*, a union newspaper, near the end of 1970. Labor costs, it stated, "aren't the Frankenstein monster they're often cracked up to be." The roots of inflation, the article correctly stated, are to be found elsewhere than in workers' pay rates.[6]

SPREADING BEWILDERMENT

The increasing confusion among business forecasters, as the early certainty of the Soaring Sixties eroded, had repercussions that lasted long after the Sixties were history and extended far beyond the ranks of economists. I recall, for instance, two incidents during the relatively prosperous middle part of the Reagan presidency. One involved a New York investment banking firm and its well-heeled clients and the other, a powerful Washington politician; both encounters illustrate the extent to which the long-standing uncertainty on the economic front had led to great bewilderment elsewhere.

The New York encounter occurred when a friend employed at the investment banking firm of Morgan Stanley invited me to attend a day-long seminar at Morgan Stanley's mid-Manhattan headquarters. As a result of the seminar, I came to realize that investment heavy-hitters were just as confused as the rest of us about the economy's prospects—the likely course of inflation, interest rates, the dollar, the trade deficit, and so on. My hosts, I should emphasize, owned one of the most respected names in the investment field and managed enormous sums for giant institutions, as well as for rich individuals.

Other than myself, a journalist with no Morgan Stanley account, no millions to manage, and no clear idea of why I had been invited, the several dozen guests were plainly deep-pocketed—on my right was the overseer of a multibillion-dollar pension fund, on my left the head of a well-known management consulting firm.

Our session began at 9 A.M. sharp with a presentation on "investment strategy" by Barton Biggs, a Morgan Stanley managing director. In shirt sleeves, speaking with considerable aplomb, Biggs presented a positively radiant picture of investment prospects over the near term. He talked—presciently as matters turned out—of a "synchronized world-wide expansion," with economic growth in the industrialized nations probably averaging more than 4%. He went on to discuss the likelihood of a "world stock market surge" on top of the appreciable gains that had taken place in recent weeks. Powered by rising profits, the U.S. stock market could well climb another 20% or so in the next six to eight months, Biggs said. He projected a similar rise—even sharper, if anticipated currency changes were taken into account—in some overseas markets. He produced a chart showing that, in terms of "real" rather than reported profits, U.S. share prices seemed "exceptionally low."

But then, as euphoria began to flood the conference room, Biggs trotted out another chart, suggesting that in the longer term–perhaps a couple of years down the road—the economy and the stock market might well collapse. "We are really laying the groundwork for one hell of a market bust," he said, blaming among other things "too much use of highly leveraged" financial transactions. "We're doing this stuff too," he added, pointing toward the sprawling Morgan Stanley securities-trading room just down the hall. "You ought to see the sort of deals going on in there. Everybody's gonna get carried out when the junk-bond market goes."

When might Morgan Stanley clients begin to prepare for this bad time ahead? Biggs was asked by an elderly attendee. "At some point in the next couple of years." Biggs said, "we're gonna come to you and say we want to raise a considerable amount of cash in your accounts." And how sharply might the market fall? "I see a decline on the order of 1973-74," he replied. At that time, the Dow Jones industrial average plummeted from a high of 1051.70 to a low of 577.60.

By now, any euphoria among the clients had given way to a rising nervousness that was broken only by the arrival of Biggs' special guest, Jack Kemp, the former Buffalo Bills quarterback who, at the time, was a Republican member of the House from New York State. Introduced by Biggs as his number one choice for the White House, Kemp soon eased whatever fears had been stirred by the talk of a coming bust. The strapping, beaming congressman painted an economic picture in which such nagging worries as a multibillion-dollar budget deficit would simply fade away amid swift—indeed "unlimited"—economic growth. Kemp did interject a worrisome remark about a tax "reform" plan of the House Ways and Means Committee, saying that tax rates had not been cut nearly enough. But he added cheerily that before any new tax bill was passed "we can get the right reform out of Congress."

The prevailing mood at the coffee break, after Kemp's sanguine talk, seemed once again upbeat. However, this was not to last for long. The third speaker was another Morgan Stanley managing director, John Paulus, the firm's chief economist. His message was decidedly downbeat. "We are entering phase two of a growth recession," he began. For the short run, he warned, consumer savings were seriously depleted. "The chairman of a big retail company thinks it's disaster," Paulus confided. The longer term, he added, was also highly worrisome. Among his many concerns was that the dollar "will go right through the floor if we continue to try to outgrow the rest of the world." The luncheon speaker was a former governor of the Bank of England, Lord Richardson, who recounted the history of international monetary arrangements and eschewed forecasting the economy or the stock market, near term or long term. Anyone who wanted to hear more about the outlook, however, could remain for the afternoon session with still other Morgan Stanley speakers. I did not feel that I could handle any more forecasts, so I slipped away, ever so briefly happy that I had no millions to invest.[7]

My Washington encounter with confusion over the economy's behavior occurred a few weeks after my visit to Morgan Stanley. It began, I must confess, in a most flattering way. However much journalists may enjoy gathering and reporting the news, many of us occasionally wish we could actually partake in making things happen; this urge has touched me on more than one occasion. But such opportunities rarely arise, and when they do, they may be missed. Indeed, when such an opportunity arose in the fall of 1985, I failed miserably to seize it.

I was in my New York office savoring a second cup of company-cafeteria coffee when the phone rang. The legislative assistant to a powerful Democratic member of the House of Representatives—Illinois' Marty Russo—informed me that her boss and some of his congressional colleagues were attempting to fashion a House version of a Senate plan—known as the Gramm-Rudman-Hollings amendment—to balance the federal budget by 1991. "We need your help," the caller said. She explained that one of the plan's provisions would, in effect, suspend the deficit paring if a recession were imminent. "We're calling you," she went on, "because you've written a lot about the various economic indicators that show when a recession is coming, and we want to know which ones should be used for this legislation." She added that the Senate version depended only on estimates by the Office of Management and Budget and the Congressional Budget Office, and the members would prefer something less subjective, like a few solid statistical measures of the economy's future course.

"Which ones do you think we should use?" the caller asked. I responded that there were many statistics—daily, weekly, monthly, and even quarterly—that often presaged the economy's broad ups and downs. The most widely known, I added, was probably the Commerce Department's monthly index of leading economic indicators, a composite then embracing such diverse data as the Standard & Poor's index of 500 common stocks and the Labor Department's index of average weekly hours worked in manufacturing. I further explained, however, that no single statistic, or for that matter any group of statistics, could ensure an accurate forecast of precisely when a recession might develop. In early 1984, I noted, the Commerce composite fell sharply, and yet no recession ensued. Conversely, the Standard & Poor's stock index was rising when the 1980 recession struck.

"Much as I would like to be of help," I said, "you're asking the impossible. There's no way of telling just when a recession will strike." She persisted, however. "Well," she said, "could you at least suggest what you think are the best statistics to watch, even if they're not infallible? We need some yardstick to know when the deficit-reduction process should be temporarily suspended."

"Listen," I replied, "it's entirely possible that the next recession will have been under way several months or more before its arrival is widely recognized." I recalled that as late as August 1974, with the 1973–1975 slump already nine months old, no less an economist than Arthur Burns, then chairman of the Federal Reserve Board, assured a congressional committee that the "economy's movements do not have . . . the characteristics" of a recession. Several months before that, I neglected to add, the president's CEA proclaimed that "a number of factors . . . support the expansion of the economy" in coming months.

I also neglected to explain just how it's decided that a recession is upon us. The arrangement was the same then as it is now. The official arbiter is the National Bureau of Economic Research. A committee made up of NBER economists, all prominent academicians attached to major universities, convenes every six months or so to discuss the overall condition of the economy. The committee, appropriately called the Business Cycle Dating Group, never attempts to forecast a recession but instead decides well after the fact, when all the final numbers are in, that a recession began back in such and such a month. This decisional lag has usually exceeded six months and has been longer than a year.

I would have explained all this to the caller, but I sensed a rising impatience with my inability to be more definite. She was polite enough but clearly had other calls to make and a bill to help write. I regretted having failed to deliver, of course, but I did appreciate having had the chance to observe close up the confusion prevailing among the people who make things happen in the Congress.

As confusion spread within the forecasting ranks, so, by no coincidence, did the practice of group forecasting. Increasingly, economists banded together to issue consensus estimates of the economy's prospects. The economy's perverse behavior, as we have seen, had caught many forecasters way off target time after time. One or another of them did manage by luck or skill to be on the mark for a year or two—only to miss badly later on. As the 1960s ended, it seemed that consensus forecasts, while rarely exactly right, were less likely than individual forecasts to go horribly wrong. A study by the National Bureau of Economic Research supported this. It concluded that group averages over an 11-year stretch tracked changes in the economy better than the typical individual forecaster. Only about one-fourth of the individual forecasts studies were found to be superior to the group average.

"In times of widespread uncertainty about what's ahead for business, most forecasters don't want to get too far out on a limb," notes Victor Zarnowitz, a University of Chicago economist who directed the study. "If they're going to err one way or another, they want lots of company." So, in the increasingly troubled economics profession, as in so many other fields of endeavor, there appeared to be some degree of safety in numbers, as the saying goes.

5

The Monetarists, Rising and Falling

Among the early stories in the big-circulation press about the rise of monetarism was a page-one piece, full of unquestioning praise, that I wrote for *The Wall Street Journal* in the late 1960s. Looking back on that story now, I am forced to say that it seems distressingly one-dimensional. In part, I blame my inexperience as an economics reporter for this. I mistakenly presented monetarism to *Journal* readers through rose-colored lenses and as virtually dictated to me by Milton Friedman. I remember spending the better part of two days with the monetarist high priest in Ely, Vermont, and never once hearing mention, for example, of *velocity*—the rate at which money turns over or, more simply, changes hands.

Neglect of the importance of this turnover rate proved to be a crucial error, as we will see, in the monetarists' description of the link between the money supply and the economy's performance. And this omission was but one instance, sadly, of Friedman's tendency to oversimplify his monetarist ideas particularly in his dealings with the press. This tactic, I would later find, was also employed by his disciples during the early years of monetarism's ascendancy.

Why did Friedman and his followers do this? Did they really think that their concepts were as straightforward and problem free as they advertised them to be? I doubt it. To be sure, the monetarists were sincere when they stressed their belief in the money supply's overriding role in influencing the economy's performance. And it cannot be said that they were hatching a devious plot to mislead naive reporters about the virtues of monetarism as the key to greater prosperity. Still they were frustrated by what they regarded as a woeful lack of attention to a crucial matter: the movements of the money supply. They felt that their views were not being transmitted adequately by the press to the public at large as well as to policy makers.

The monetarists' frustration, I should add, was not without some justification. The short shrift that monetarism often received in the press in the late 1960s was evident in the *Journal*, among other places. For example, in its coverage of the Federal Reserve's weekly press conference, the paper rarely discussed changes in the money supply, however defined. Instead, the weekly story, which I was assigned to write, rambled on about such obscure statistical barometers as banks' vault cash and float. (Eventually, money-supply data were included regularly in the report, but only after repeated complaints about the omission by various monetarists including particularly A. James Meigs, a close and demanding reader.)

Friedman and his disciples were convinced—as it turned out, quite correctly—that wider dissemination of their views and a sharper press focus on the money supply would position the monetarist doctrine for a major role in steering the economy. If monetarism could be made simple enough and its alleged benefits could be spelled out in plain English, they reasoned, it would increase chances for the adoption of their economic prescriptions in Washington. To gain this broader recognition, they frequently oversimplified their ideas.

The tactic was remarkably successful, and monetarism did indeed gain considerable influence in monetary policy making toward the end of Jimmy Carter's presidency—and surely contributed to his defeat in 1980, inasmuch as the economy's woes were largely due to monetarist procedures implemented in 1979 at the Federal Reserve. But was it right for Friedman and his disciples to have oversimplified the monetarist message so blatantly? I, for one, feel misled, and I regret that through my naiveté I may also have misled many *Journal* readers.

A BEGUILING CONCEPT

Through the years of monetarism's ascendancy, a period stretching roughly from the late 1960s until the early 1980s, Milton Friedman was regarded by most people as a conservative economist, though he challenges that appellation to this day. On the international front, his skepticism about the workability of the Bretton Woods system was proving warranted. On the domestic front, he urged keeping a tight lid on the growth of the money supply, tailoring its expansion to the economy's own capacity to expand easily, which in turn depended on the amount of resources available—people, plant, and materials, all measurable items. If this is done, Friedman preached, the benign forces of the free market will converge to ensure sustainable prosperity.

Friedman estimated that the American economy's capacity to expand, based on the nation's readily available resources, was somewhere between 2% and 3% a year in the late 1960s. Accordingly, he urged, the Federal Reserve, through buying and selling government securities, to limit the growth of the money supply to about the same rate. If this strategy were adopted and maintained, Friedman asserted, the economy would remain reasonably healthy—provided, of course, that the government did not meddle too much, as might happen for instance under the sort "industrial policy" approach advocated by such diehard Keynesians as John Kenneth Galbraith and Wassily Leontief, a winner of the Nobel Prize in economics in 1973.

Not every economist, to be sure, regarded Friedman's brand of economics as all that conservative. One prominent skeptic on the right was Friedrich A. von Hayek of the University of Vienna, who won the Nobel Prize in economics a year after Leontief. Hayek and his colleagues within the so-called Austrian school of free-market economics were dismayed at Friedman's espousal of so rigid and important a monetary role for the government. Hayek viewed it as undue governmental interference in the marketplace. Moreover, he questioned the ability of the Federal Reserve to maintain such precise control over the money supply—a concern that would prove prophetic. And, while Hayek realized that to do so would be politically impossible, he nonetheless advocated that money once again become a private matter, created by individual banks. This, in fact, was the situation before the advent of the Federal Reserve System in 1913. In the years before the Federal Reserve System, banks often issued promissory notes based on nothing more than their own faith and credit. These bank notes functioned much as Federal Reserve notes, such as a dollar bill, function now.

So, it could be argued, the monetarism that Friedman and his followers were preaching was not quite as conservative as advertised. In fact, the University of Chicago professor was treading not far from the middle of the economic road, flanked on the left by the likes of Galbraith and Leontief and on the right by Hayek, along with such other Austrian-school luminaries as Hans Sennholz, chairman of the economics department at Grove City College in western Pennsylvania, and Ludwig von Mises, transplanted from Austria and finishing out a distinguished academic and writing career at New York University.

For myself, I would rather think of Friedman and his monetarist colleagues as super salespeople, successfully merchandising, after much frustration, an economic medicine that promised far more than it could possibly deliver. And if there is a single document that epitomizes this salesmanship, it may be a column that Friedman wrote for *Newsweek* in early 1972. In the article, Friedman lays out his case for strict control of the expansion of the money supply—month after month and year after year. It has been "established," he writes, that "there is a close, regular and predictable relation between the quantity of money, national income and prices over any considerable number of years." This being so, he goes on, "an announced, and adhered to, policy of steady monetary growth would provide the business community with a firm basis for confidence in monetary stability," which in turn would promote "economic stability."[1]

In his column Friedman anticipates questions that may arise about the efficacy of this prescription. "Is the rule that we have proposed technically feasible?" he asks. "Can the Fed control the quantity of money?" In the unhesitating fashion of monetarism's most successful salespeople, Friedman answers his own questions: "No serious student of money—whatever his policy views—denies that the Fed can, if it wishes, control the quantity of money. It cannot, of course, achieve a precise rate of growth from day to day or week to week. But it can come very close month to month and quarter to quarter."

Though Friedman would later deny it, his argument in the *Newsweek* column came close to guaranteeing recession-free growth—if only Washington would follow his recommendations. (When I suggested this in a column of my own years later in *The Wall Street Journal*, Friedman wrote me a testy note, objecting "strenuously" to my suggestion and claiming that I had exaggerated his faith in the power of money.) The *Newsweek* column also made crystal clear the economist's conviction that the Fed was perfectly capable of controlling with great precision the growth of the money supply on at least a monthly basis, though Friedman carefully does not specify which particular version of the money supply he is talking about.

With the benefit of hindsight more than two troubled decades later, these claims seem wildly utopian. In 1972, however, they sounded to many of us remarkably credible and highly desirable. In February 1972, when Friedman wrote his *Newsweek* column, the U.S. economy had been expanding for nearly a year and a half. However, it was hardly a time of worry-free growth. The Bretton Woods system was unraveling. Interest rates, which had been falling, were beginning to climb, and the unemployment rate seemed stuck near 6% of the labor force, almost as high as it had been at the end of the 1970–1971 recession. Early in 1972, surveys showed a slight rise in consumer optimism, but around midyear, the public's mood began to sour, and this continued through 1973.

At the same time, inflation began to worsen markedly. The consumer price index, which had been rising at a reasonably moderate annual rate of 2.6% in the late spring of 1972, was climbing at 6%-plus rates by year's end, and the speedup continued in 1973. By the fall of that year, the price spiral was in double digits. By mid-1974, it was near 13%, a rate that would halve the dollar's purchasing power, were it to persist, in less than six years. In November 1973, the economy entered yet another recession, the sixth since 1945, and it proved to be long and harsh, enduring for a full 16 months and pushing unemployment to 9% of the labor force, a level not previously seen in the postwar era.

In such an economic environment, it is easy to understand the eagerness for new formulas that promise, as monetarism did, a healthier, happier business climate. The monetarist gospel was simple enough: all will be well—if the monetary authorities stop their erratic behavior, first pumping too much money into the economy and then, when this begins to cause economic overheating and dislocations, reining in the money supply too tightly. In the beguiling monetarist prescription, the economy would prosper—not spectacularly but certainly well enough—as a direct result of a Federal Reserve policy geared to produce slow, steady expansion of the money supply, year after year, through times of economic strain and of economic slack. The advent of the 1973–1975 recession, according to Friedman and his colleagues, was but one more painful consequence of mindless policy at the Fed. Surely, the monetarists argued, Washington's policy makers could no longer afford to ignore their counsel.

The monetarist view, it should be noted, paid remarkably little attention to such concerns as the state of the federal budget, federal spending levels, tax trends, and government-guided industrial planning—all matters near the top of most Keynesian economists' priority lists. This disregard for such Keynesian concerns flowed naturally from monetarism's conviction that the money supply was the overriding force dictating the economy's behavior. A favorite comment of the monetarists in those early years—heard less and less as the 1980s unfolded—was not simply that money mattered, but that it mattered most, and in conversations with such ardent monetarists as Jim Meigs, I gained the impression that money mattered *entirely.* In an interview that took place just as the federal budget deficit was deepening, I asked Meigs whether or not the rising red ink was cause for concern about inflation. He virtually dismissed the question, indicating that the state of the federal budget was a wholly unimportant consideration in any effort to ascertain the course of inflation or, for that matter, the course of the economy in general. If inflation were to worsen, he asserted, the reason would be, pure and simple, the money supply's excessive rate of growth, regardless of the federal budget's condition.

Such assertions, in retrospect, appear exceedingly dubious. Between mid-1966 and mid-1967, for example, there was a marked acceleration in the growth of the M1 money supply, which was the focus of most monetarists in the early years of their doctrine's rise. This M1 acceleration, in the monetarist view, portended steeper inflation down the road; some monetarists placed the lag at roughly a year and a half while others, including Friedman, claimed simply that the lag would be long and variable. In any case, inflation actually began to ease around the end of 1969, precisely a year and a half after the M1 speed-up. Near the end of 1969, the consumer price index, for instance, was climbing at an annual rate of about 7%, and within two years, this rise was cut in half.

None of this was readily apparent, however, as monetarism continued to gain support. What did attract increasing notice was the evident failure of Keynesian tactics to produce a more robust economy. An 11-month recession in December 1969 and a 16-month recession in November 1973 did not help the Keynesian cause. Each of these economic downturns developed, I should add, even though the federal budget showed narrowing surpluses and, in fact, ran up large deficits as the two recessions deepened. The problem for the Keynesians, enunciated by Arthur Burns, was that "fiscalist ideas of economic management aren't viable policy for our country."[2] Moreover, Keynesian theory held that high interest rates will preclude robust economic growth, and yet the long economic expansion that began in November 1982 endured in the face of extraordinarily high rate levels. This was an embarrassing turn of events for the many Keynesian economists who, when the 1981–1982 recession was nearing an end, were grimly warning that the ensuing recovery would be short and weak.

In fact, by Keynesian standards, the record-setting deficits that have marked the federal budget in recent decades should have spurred the economy and brought down unemployment. But joblessness has been higher as the deficits have mounted than in the early years of the post–World War II era when the budget was more nearly in balance. Furthermore, according to Keynesian theory, federal spending, which has expanded far more rapidly in recent decades than in the early postwar years, should have brought vigorous economic growth, but this has not occurred. Growth has slowed, and the economy has been staggered by repeated, long recessions.

There is no easy explanation of why the Keynesians have been so wrong. In theory, the federal budget should have shifted into healthy surplus once recessions ended, and the economy and, most crucially, federal revenues were again on the increase. But the budget remained stubbornly in deep deficit through times of expansion as well as times of recession. Perhaps by the 1980s the economy was so severely out of kilter that neither the Keynesian prescription nor any other economic strategy could readily set things right. Federal borrowing had become so extensive that it threatened to swamp the nation's credit markets. Interest payments on the federal debt—a persistently mounting expense item in the federal budget—had grown so large that any sharp boost in federal spending, intended to hasten economic growth, merely unnerved the credit markets and thus deterred new business activity.

SPREADING THE WORD

Sam I. Nakagama is a name seldom mentioned now in discussions of the economists who did the most to spread the monetarist gospel in the early years of its ascendancy. When I first met Nakagama in the mid–1960s, he was an editor of First National City Bank's monthly economic review. Although he had studied under Friedman at the University of Chicago, much of his early career was spent as an economic journalist. Before becoming editor of the bank's monthly review, he helped cover the economic beat at *Business Week*. The crucial lift that Nakagama supplied to the monetarist doctrine occurred as a result of his move in 1965 from First National to Argus Research, a small but well-respected investment advisory firm based in the Wall Street area and headed by Harold Dorsey, who had founded the firm in 1934. Dorsey's faith in the monetarist solution to the nation's economic ills predated Nakagama's arrival as the firm's economist. Dorsey's monetarism was largely the result of his own economic homework rather than the influence of Friedman or any college professor.

In the fall of 1969, Dorsey decided that the time was right to celebrate his firm's 35 years in business. His failing health may have been an added spur; he died in 1970. In any case, Dorsey instructed Nakagama to arrange an economic conference that would turn the spotlight on monetarism and not to worry much about the expense. Nakagama selected the plush Arizona Biltmore in Phoenix for the three-day event, which began on November 21. He invited some 200 influential individuals from various fields, including the government, academia, private business at home and overseas, and most important, the press.

Among the governmental officials were Charls E. Walker, the influential undersecretary of the Treasury Department, several of his top aides, and Darryl R. Francis, the president of the St. Louis Federal Reserve Bank and a member of FOMC, the Fed's key policy-setting arm. Prominent academics included most of the leading monetarists, such as David Fand of Wayne State University, David Meiselman of Macalester College, who had done extensive research work with Friedman, Allan Meltzer of Carnegie-Mellon University, and of course Friedman himself. As the top-billed speaker of the conference, Friedman was flown to Phoenix on the last day—much like a modern-day *deus ex machina*—on a private jet, supplied by Argus. (Karl Brunner, another prominent monetarist who taught for many years at

the University of Rochester, did not attend the Argus conference. Although Nakagama remains mum on the matter, I suspect that he wished to keep the spotlight on his former professor
and perhaps believed that Brunner's presence would steal some
attention from the Chicagoan. Lindley Clark of *The Wall Street
Journal* also did not receive an invitation, though he too was a
former student of Friedman's at Chicago and was as enthusiastic a supporter of his theories as Nakagama. Clark's omission,
I later discovered, was simply a result of his anonymity at the
Journal, where he authored many of the "Review and Outlook"
editorial-page columns. A while after the Argus conference, I
introduced Clark—by then a signed *Journal* columnist—to
Nakagama over lunch, and the two remained in close touch for
many years, until Nakagama largely abandoned his monetarist
approach to dealing with the economy's difficulties.)

The business people assembled at the Arizona Biltmore were
also an impressive lot. They included, among many others,
James M. Lane, senior vice president of Chase Manhattan
Bank, Thomas C. Pryor, partner of White, Weld, Ernest B.
Kelly, president of Halsey, Stuart, David A. Leinbach, partner
of Lehman Brothers, and Beryl Sprinkel, senior vice president
of Harris Trust & Savings Bank. Later, during Reagan's presidency, Sprinkel served first at the Treasury Department and
then as chairman of Reagan's CEA.

Nakagama's lineup of press people included the economics
editors of *Time* magazine, *Business Week*, the *Chicago Tribune*,
and *The Wall Street Journal*, as well as the editor-in-chief of
Barron's financial magazine, the assistant managing editor of
Fortune, and senior economic correspondents from the *New
York Times* and the *Los Angeles Times*.

Speaker after speaker extolled the virtues of monetarism.
Sprinkel asserted that a close link ran between shifts in the
money supply and trends in the stock market. Leonall Ander-
sen, an officer of the St. Louis Federal Reserve Bank, attempted to explain the close relationship that he perceived
between changes in the money supply and changes in the economy as a whole. Allan Meltzer hammered home the theme that
money matters most. Friedman, not for the first time, lam-

basted what he claimed was Washington's misguided refusal to adopt a monetarist solution to America's economic ills.

The magnificent Arizona weather somehow made the monetarist doctrine seem even more enticing. The days were crisp and cloudless. Daytime temperatures rose to the low 70s, and the nights were clear and cool enough to warrant a second blanket. The food and accommodations at the Arizona Biltmore were a match for the weather. By the time the conference finished, even attendees initially skeptical seemed convinced that a far brighter economic future was indeed feasible—if only Washington's policy makers could be persuaded to cast aside their fiscalist proclivities and embrace the good sense of monetarism.

Throughout the conference, Nakagama performed as an expert master of ceremonies, introducing speakers and then heartily endorsing their pronouncements, mingling with audiences, jollying up the press people, ever gracious and seemingly ubiquitous. In a report for Argus, which had appeared just before the start of the conference and was widely distributed there, Nakagama warned that a new recession would begin soon because too many policy makers, including a good number of economists, were continuing to think "in old-fashioned Keynesian terms." He went on to warn, correctly as it turned out, about a "money squeeze, which has reduced the amount of mortgage and installment credit available to maintain the growth of household spending."[3]

Nakagama urged the Federal Reserve to "edge away from its ultra-tight policy" in order to avoid a "sizable recession" in the near future. And he gave short shrift to the belief of many Keynesian forecasters at the time that an anticipated "reduction—or abolition—of the [recently imposed] 10% tax surcharge at year-end and the 10% to 15% boost in Social Security benefits expected early in 1970 will forestall any adjustment greater than a mini-recession." Nakagama's report included an elaborate chart showing the highly erratic growth of the money supply from the mid-1950s onward and suggesting that this volatility had much to do with the economy's own stop-and-go record of recessions repeatedly punctuating periods of economic expansion.[4] In fact, a full-fledged recession developed the very next month, making Nakagama appear a prophet and Washington planners seem wedded to economic tactics that were not only outdated but also exceedingly dangerous.

In the wake of the Arizona Biltmore meeting, the attention paid to monetarism in the press increased sharply. Intrigued as much as any of my colleagues with the monetarists' simple-seeming solution to the economy's ills, I rushed into print on *The Wall Street Journal*'s front page on December 22 with an unskeptical account of monetarism's virtues. Only a week before, Milton Friedman's bespectacled visage had graced the cover of *Time* magazine, an achievement, at least in those years, that was the journalistic equivalent of scaling Mount Everest.

In my column, I noted that monetarism's "ranks have recently swelled in large part because of the publicity that Mr. Friedman and his ideas have been getting—not only in *Time*, but in *Newsweek*, where he writes a column, in this newspaper, on TV, in the *New York Times* and elsewhere." In the late 1950s, I went on to suggest, a seminar on the relevance of Friedmanite ideas to stock market activity would not have drawn much attention on Wall Street. However, I reported, a recent such seminar sponsored by Argus Research "drew dozens of Wall Streeters from such prestigious firms as Loeb Rhoades, Goodbody, Bear, Stearns, Lehman Brothers, Brown Brothers Harriman and White Weld."[5]

While I was trumpeting monetarism on the *Journal*'s news pages, Lindley H. Clark, Jr., at the time an associate editor of the paper, was singing its praises on the editorial page. In his editorials, moreover, he would occasionally refer to his readers, much to my delight, to newspage articles that I had recently written.

For example, when I produced a report for the news department explaining that excessive money-supply growth, rather than unionism, was mainly responsible for inflation, Clark followed up with an editorial essentially repeating and reemphasizing the report of "our man Malabre." I later discovered that Clark had gained his master's degree under Friedman at the University of Chicago in the early years after World War II.

Friedman had urged him to go on for his doctorate, but determined to become an ink-stained wretch, Clark made his way to New York and a job on the *Journal's* copy desk. An accomplished writer and a brilliant editor, he was soon in charge of editing the paper's showcase "leader" articles on page one. He carried out this demanding job with great success until the early 1960s, when he chose to join the paper's editorial page, where the pace was more leisurely and where he was freer to take a stand in praise of monetarism. His superior, Vermont Royster, was largely unschooled in economics and, while generally advocating a conservative approach in most matters, appeared happy to allow Clark to go his own monetarist way.

The monetarist approach to policy making was receiving wider notice at other major publications as well. This, in part, was a result of the increasing use of economist-columnists. The practice, now common, was relatively rare in the earlier years of the postwar era. Editors discovered, however, that many economists could write with reasonable clarity, or at least produce copy that could be whipped into readable condition by a good editor. The practice was somewhat like a baseball column by Mickey Mantle, though I suspect Mantle may have required more editing than, say, Milton Friedman. Friedman rotated the weekly turns at *Newsweek* with two nonmonetarist economists, Paul Samuelson and Henry Wallich, who was compelled to give up his space when he became a Federal Reserve Board governor. Meanwhile, Allan Meltzer took up the pen for the *Los Angeles Times*, and *Time* formed a so-called board of economists, which provided economic grist for the magazine. The board, though predominately Keynesian, did include monetarists. The *Journal* also formed a "board of contributors," made up largely of prominent economists, including some Friedman supporters.

The increased attention that investors were paying to the money supply in the late 1960s shows up in data assembled by the National Bureau of Economic Research and an analysis by Beryl Sprinkel, a speaker at the Argus conference. National Bureau records up to 1969 show that a major change in the growth of the money supply preceded a major change in the direction of the overall economy, on the average, by 14 months. Other National Bureau data for the same years show that a major change in the direction of share prices (measured by the Standard & Poor's index of 500 common stocks) preceded a change in the overall economy, on the average, by only four months. Thus, changes in monetary growth occurred an average of 10 months before changes in the direction of the stock market.

At the Argus seminar, Sprinkel produced charts, based on recent research by Friedman, that showed how the "lead" of money-supply changes over stock-price changes had recently shortened. At the start of 1952, money-supply growth began to drop, but stock prices didn't begin a prolonged decline until about the second quarter of 1953. Again, in early 1955, monetary growth began to decline, but stock prices continued to climb until mid-1956. However, the lead-time began to shorten in the late 1950s. Monetary growth started down near the end of 1958, and stock prices peaked about mid-1959. In the following years, as Sprinkel noted, the lead shriveled to nearly zero. In 1966, monetary growth began to drop at the beginning of the year, and stock prices headed down at almost the same time. Later the same year, monetary growth began to increase only about a month before stock prices began to climb. The shortening, Sprinkel told the audience, was the result of "greater recognition [by investors] of the effect of monetary policy on stock prices."

It was also, no doubt, due to the fact that good, timely statistics on the money supply had been available to investors for a relatively short period. By the late 1960s, the Federal Reserve Board released money-supply figures weekly. They were published only one week after the fact and were adjusted for seasonal variations.

In contrast, before 1965, the Fed issued only semimonthly money-supply data, and before 1955, it issued only monthly data based on much sketchier statistical material and not seasonally adjusted. Before 1948, the data were available only four times a year. As late as 1970, the money supply was still not a component of the Commerce Department's widely followed index of leading economic indicators. Even so, Geoffrey H. Moore, at the time in charge of research at the National Bureau, told me in December 1969 that he had come to regard the money supply as the *leading* leading indicator. The measure, broadly defined to include most savings deposits and adjusted for inflation, was finally included as a component of the index a few years later. (In the early 1960s, Friedman and Anna Schwartz, a National Bureau researcher, had painstakingly reconstructed money-supply data back nearly to the Civil War. This was done largely by studying old bank records; with evident bitterness, Friedman told me that they received little help from the Fed itself.)

W. Gordon Lyle, a highly successful investment adviser with the New York securities firm of Wood, Walker, was an early Wall Street user of money-supply trends as a precursor of stock prices. In a 1969 interview, he lamented, "I find I can no longer keep ahead of the stock market by watching statistics on the money supply—too many other guys have caught on to the idea." Lyle went on, "How delightful it once was to be so far ahead of the game. Those days, I'm afraid, are gone forever. Now that everybody has discovered the money supply, I don't know how to stay out in front." Soon after the interview, Lyle, not yet 50, left his brokerage firm to begin a comfortable early retirement in the Connecticut countryside and later in South Carolina.[6]

TOUCHING ALL THE BASES

Meanwhile, monetarism was gaining ground on campuses where Keynesian economics had long reigned supreme. At the University of Chicago, Friedman had turned out an impressive line of bright young economists, many of whom were to go on to eminent professorships at other universities and were to fill influential jobs in Washington and in the corporate sector. Besides Nakagama and Clark, high on this list were three men whom Friedman regarded as among his most brilliant protégés: Phillip Cagan, an economics professor at Columbia University and a senior research associate at the National Bureau's New York office; Michael Darby, a professor at the University of

California in Los Angeles and, during the Reagan and Bush administrations, a high official first in the Treasury Department and then in the Commerce Department; and Gary Becker of the University of Chicago, a widely read columnist at *Business Week* and the winner of the 1992 Nobel Prize in economics.

As Friedman's students moved on from Chicago, they took their monetarist beliefs with them. Moreover, another monetarist stronghold was developing at the University of Rochester in upstate New York. There, a remarkable Swiss scholar, Karl Brunner, was preaching his own brand of monetarism to a new generation of budding monetarists. Among his notable protégés from an earlier academic stint at University of California at Los Angeles were Jerry Jordan, who went on to occupy a seat on the CEA, the post of chief economist at First Interstate Bank in Los Angeles, and, later, the presidency of the Cleveland Federal Reserve Bank, and Anatol ("Ted") Balbach, for many years the senior vice president and research director of the St. Louis Federal Reserve Bank. Jordan laughingly recalls that "Karl terrified me" because, in times of stress, the professor would blow a bugle to summon his teaching assistants—who included the future president of the Cleveland Federal Reserve Bank.

After serving in the Swiss army's ski patrol during World War II, Brunner abandoned what he regarded as the "intellectual wasteland" of Swiss university life to take up a grant from the Rockefeller Foundation. The grant led to four months of study at Harvard University and another 18 months at the Cowles Commission at the University of Chicago. While there, he grew to know an array of brilliant scholars, four of whom would later win the Nobel Prize in economics: Kenneth Arrow, Lawrence Klein, Tjalling Koopmans, and, of course, Milton Friedman. From Chicago, Brunner moved in the late 1950s to UCLA where, according to Balbach, he "quite independently arrived at a set of hypotheses that are now described as monetarist thought and began publishing the results of his research."[7]

While at UCLA, Brunner started a long collaboration with Allan Meltzer, a student of his there. Each man stimulated the other's thought processes, which led to a stream of scholarly papers examining and promoting the importance of money in guiding the economy's general course. Lindley Clark, a close friend of both Brunner's and Meltzer's and a frequent visitor to Brunner's home in Rochester, recalls that the two would "fight a lot" and that things between them "didn't always go smoothly." He remembers that "Allan's smoking made Karl's wife want to throw open all the windows, but she didn't do it because it can be pretty cold up in Rochester and, more importantly, she didn't want the neighbors hearing Allan and her husband shouting at one another."

In 1969, the same year that Friedman received star treatment at the Argus conference, Brunner, an energetic and successful fund-raiser, began sponsoring an annual conference on monetary economics at Konstanz, a West German town on the Swiss border. Five years later, he launched yet another international conclave, this one at Interlaken and financed by the University of Rochester. As the years passed, the two conferences attracted an impressive list of leading economists and bankers from both Europe and the United States. Such was Brunner's influence in Britain that soon after Margaret Thatcher became prime minister, she sought him out, on the advice of Alan Walters, her economic assistant at 10 Downing Street. Much of Thatcher's economic policy in her early years in office, particularly her attempt to keep a stricter rein on Britain's money supply, was in large measure a result of Brunner's counsel.

Brunner's differences with Friedman were not large enough to divide the expanding monetarist camp. To Meltzer, for instance, Brunner complained only about such relatively trivial matters as some "missing equations and variables" in Friedman's case for the monetarist approach. Matters of wording also came under criticism: Brunner disputed Friedman's description of money as merely a "temporary abode" of buying power. "Defining money as a temporary abode of purchasing power," Brunner wrote, "does not distinguish between properties of assets or between a monetary and a barter economy in a manner independent of the medium of exchange function" of money.[8] This sort of quibbling was hardly sufficient to grab headlines, even on the business pages, or to produce fist-shaking debates between academicians or policy makers.

Meanwhile, many of Brunner's and Friedman's disciples were taking up teaching posts at other universities. Meltzer was fast becoming the brightest star within the highly respected economics department at Carnegie-Mellon University in Pittsburgh. Ensconced at Brown University was another astute young monetarist, William Poole, who in 1982 would begin a two-year stint as a member of President Reagan's CEA. At the University of Virginia in Charlottesville was Richard T. Selden, who in early 1970s was warning, in true monetarist fashion, that "expansion of the money supply at a faster rate than output growth" would bring worsening inflation. In blunt language that Friedman and Brunner surely endorsed, Selden blamed Federal Reserve officials for, as he put it, printing much too much money and thereby causing an "unfortunate 'greening' of America," which, he alleged, would bring not only a painful price spiral but also various other economic ills.[9]

As monetarism gained ground on campuses, so did its influence increase in policy-making circles. Perhaps the most striking instance of this new clout was within the Federal Reserve's regional bank at St. Louis. There, a band of young economists were working hard to promote monetarist theory within the Fed's sprawling, powerful network of regional banks and its board in Washington. Even the motto of the St. Louis Federal Reserve Bank had a monetarist slant, reading *In Hoc Signo Vinces*, or "In This Sign We Conquer," followed by the classic monetarist equation $MV=PT$, where M is the money supply, V is its rate of turnover or velocity, P is the average price level, and T is the volume of economic transactions.

Darryl Francis, a devout monetarist who attended the Argus conference in Phoenix, was president of the St. Louis bank. As the regional bank's president, Francis was entitled to sit on the FOMC and to vote one year out of every three. When he did exercise this privilege, in true monetarist fashion, he usually urged more attention to the money supply and less to interest rates. In the early 1970s, however, these suggestions, while duly noted, failed to alter the committee's consensus, which continued to focus on controlling rates.

Though Francis was its president, the driving force for a monetarist approach at the St. Louis bank was Homer Jones, the head of the regional bank's research department. Aided by young monetarist researchers, Jones conducted various studies that concluded the economy, with its natural tendency toward stability, should be managed largely through monetary rather than fiscal means. Much of this work was published in the bank's review, which had a circulation extending from New York to California and reached a wide assortment of private as well as public policy makers. Several *Wall Street Journal* editors, myself included, were among the recipients.

It may seem odd that this heresy was tolerated by William McChesney Martin, Jr., the Fed's chairman from 1951 to 1970. Martin, however, believed that the Federal Reserve was a system, not a bank or a single agency. Therefore, he said, "There is always room for differing views, as long as they don't keep the system from functioning. I never wanted to preside over a group where anyone was afraid to say what he thought."[10]

Paradoxically, the influence of the St. Louis Fed in the Martin years was perhaps greater with some economists at the White House than within the Federal Reserve System. Jerry Jordan, one of Jones' cadre of young economists, recalls that Otto Eckstein, then a member of Johnson's CEA, was one of a succession of prominent economists invited to be a scholar-in-residence at the bank. While there, as Jordan remembers, Eckstein was greatly impressed by the monetarist arguments presented to him and, as a result, urged his colleagues to pay more heed to monetary matters. "The strength and originality of their research is impressive," Eckstein told a friend after returning to Washington to resume his CEA duties.

In Washington a young monetarist economist named Robert Weintraub, a disciple of Friedman's, was trying to gain converts among the members of Congress. An able, well-liked administrator as well as a highly trained economist, Weintraub had secured a key staff position on the House Banking Committee. Among its members was a powerful black Democrat, Parren Mitchell, whose training in economics was as skimpy as his enthusiasm for helping disadvantaged blacks was great. Miraculously, under Weintraub's tutelage, Mitchell became an ardent monetarist, convinced that the economic doctrine, if properly implemented, would benefit not only the nation as a whole but its poor black citizens in particular.

The Full Employment and Balanced Growth Act of 1978, more commonly called the Humphrey-Hawkins Act after its congressional sponsors, was in large part a consequence of Weintraub's influence with Mitchell and other important legislators. The act was supposedly designed to help unemployed workers, but in fact its most important provision, which proved to be an early foothold for monetarism at the policy-making level, compelled the Federal Reserve to set and make public target ranges for the main monetary aggregates, M1, M2, and M3. Under the provision, which Milton Friedman himself could have authored, the Fed chairman would have to appear twice a year before the House and Senate banking committees to lay out the central bank's money-supply goals and to explain, if they were not met, why the targets had been missed.

Besides the inroads it had made in Washington and in academia, monetarism was gaining ground in many private businesses, where frustration with the economy's persistent difficulties was running high. The corporate counterpart to the St. Louis Federal Reserve Bank was First National City Bank in New York. The bank's espousal of a monetarist approach began in the 1960s under the chairmanship of George Moore, and his successor, Walter Wriston, continued this support through the 1970s. Indeed, as we will see, Wriston would play a crucial role in the Fed's historic adoption of monetarist operating procedures in 1979.

Moore, after his retirement to a Spanish golfing resort with a new young wife and family, became something of a chrysophile, promoting the virtues of gold and consulting with such other prominent gold bugs as Harry Schultz. Moore's fascination with the notion of a gold-based economic system—hardly a monetarist tenet—was, I suppose, a natural consequence of his essentially conservative nature. In his banking years in New York, however, he focused, in proper monetarist fashion, on the Fed's management of the money supply; this, of course, was also a conservative concept.

The bank promoted the monetarist cause in its monthly economic review, which had a circulation that reached a high of about 300,000 in the mid-1970s, higher than for many well-known commercial magazines. A subscription was free for the asking. Its readership included, among countless others, college students, journalists, politicians in Washington and in state and municipal governments, corporate chieftains, college professors, housewives, members of the White House staff, and foreign leaders. The review's editorial chief was also the bank's chief economist, Leif H. Olsen, whose early background included a stint as a financial and banking reporter at *The Wall Street Journal* where his immediate boss was none other than Lindley Clark. Joining the bank in 1962, Olsen, a fine journalist, was given a large budget to improve and expand the review, which had been published since 1904 and was already, hands down, the finest bank publication in the nation.

Olsen's most illustrious hire was Sam Nakagama. But other top-flight economic journalists were brought on board as well, lured by offers that their publications could not possibly match. The most notable of these, perhaps, was Peter Vanderwicken, whose credentials included outstanding work at *The Wall Street Journal*, *Time*, and *Fortune*. As a new employee working in the *Journal*'s Atlanta bureau in the early 1960s, Vanderwicken had conceived and then written a long, front-page article on bank drafts that showed a remarkable degree of sophistication for a young reporter stationed far from New York or Washington.

Olsen was also able to draw on the bank's enormous, expanding economics department. At the peak in the late 1970s, Olsen had 50 professional economists under him, as well as 30 support personnel. Prominent among these professionals was Jim Meigs, whose complaints were largely responsible, as we have seen, for the *Journal*'s greater attention to money-supply data.

Meigs, whose academic credentials were far superior to Olsen's, had begun his career as a practicing economist within the research department of the St. Louis Fed in 1953. After eight years there and a brief stint at the New York Stock Exchange, he joined the bank.

Meigs' influence with Olsen—and, through Olsen, with what was printed in the bank's monthly review—was substantial. His devotion to monetarist theory was carefully laid out in a 1972 book, which he titled, with a most appropriate double entendre, *Money Matters*. In it, Meigs expressed his conviction that a sort of monetarist "black box" existed by which the Federal Reserve, if it would only so choose, could, with remarkable accuracy and efficiency, steer the economy along a far more prosperous, stable path than it had recently traveled under Keynesian influence.

"There are strong and dependable linkages among money, income, and prices within the monetary black box," Meigs wrote, adding that "when a central bank changes the money supply, or allows it to change, changes in national income and prices will follow." With an array of charts and statistics, Meigs proceeded to drive home his contention that there existed "a strong relationship between changes in the money supply" and subsequent changes in such other, more discernible facets of the economic scene as "household expenditures for durable goods, apparel, and new housing."[11] Such assertions manifested monetarist doctrine in its clearest, most confident form. Reading them in 1972, when the book was published, one would hardly have imagined that within a decade much of what Meigs and his monetarist colleagues preached would, through dismal experience, be roundly discredited.

PAINFUL REALITY

The "money supply began to lose its significance as an economic and monetary indicator a dozen years ago, and the historical stability between it and the economy just about vanished in the 1980s."

This comment was made in the fall of 1991, in the September–

October issue of *Financial Market Perspectives*, a publication of the economics department of Goldman Sachs, the most successful and possibly most influential investment banking firm in the United States. The author is Robert Giordano, the New York-based Goldman Sachs partner in charge of the firm's economic research and, as a hard-charging Wall Streeter far from any ivory tower, an economist not overly concerned about pushing a particular ideology.

"In its modern form," Giordano further states, the "money supply (M2) times velocity (V) [was] supposed to equal nominal GNP." And, he continues, "monetarism's powerful simplicity easily and quickly won legions of converts, who were all especially hungry for new ideas. After all, orthodox Keynesian precepts, which guided the economy relatively well in the 1950s and much of the 1960s, could neither explain nor cure the complex disease of stagflation."

By "serving up this framework of monetary analysis," Giordano notes, monetarist "theorists skillfully persuaded a generation of students, journalists, practitioners, politicians and policy-makers to swallow three essential conclusions: money supply and the economy have a predictable and stable relationship; changes in the money supply cause changes in real economic activity when there is unused capacity; [and] movement and control of the money supply is the Federal Reserve's responsibility, and therefore it is the most reliable measure of the central bank's policy stance."[12]

What had happened "a dozen years ago" to prompt such a condemnatory assessment of monetarism? The answer is that monetarism was finally put into practice by Washington's policy makers, and the result, sadly, tarnished severely, if not demolished, the validity of its proponents' theories. A major casualty, of course, was Milton Friedman. As William Greider recalls in *Secrets of the Temple*, Friedman's forecasts in the early 1980s of, first, an inflationary surge and, next, a 1984 recession proved "spectacularly wrong." And both forecasts, of course, were based largely on the movement of the money supply. Friedman, to his credit, eventually admitted "I was wrong," and offered what must have been, for his monetarist disciples, a disquieting addendum: "And I have no good explanation as to why I was wrong."[13]

Indeed, the only economist whose reputation may have been enhanced by monetarism's unfortunate brush with the real world was that of a young Briton named Charles Goodhart, who served as the Bank of England's chief monetary adviser. Whatever else Goodhart may be good at, he sports a very good sense of irony, for, even before the advent of monetarism in Washington's policy making, he produced what has come to be known as Goodhart's Law: "Whatever definition of the money supply the Federal Reserve chooses to target and control as a policy instrument in guiding the economy inevitably will become meaningless."

This, essentially, is what happened in 1979, the year when the Federal Reserve, under Paul Volcker's dominating chairmanship, chose to change the central bank's so-called operating procedures from a Keynesian to a monetarist approach. In large measure, the move was as a result of relentless campaigning by the monetarists. Finally, on October 6, 1979, the Fed acted during a special, secret Saturday meeting of the FOMC. The FOMC members who were Fed regional bank presidents were summoned by wire to Washington as late as Friday, and when they arrived, they were carefully spread around the city, assigned to different hotels in order to avoid attracting any notice from an always-nosy Washington press corps.

William C. Melton, a former chief of the key monetary analysis division of the New York Federal Reserve Bank, recalls, "When the meeting got under way on Saturday morning, there was a great deal of discussion, but little dissension." And Lawrence K. Roos, then the president of the monetarist St. Louis Fed, later reported triumphantly, "All the people who had opposed monetary aggregate targeting before were now for it." After the meeting, Volcker called a press conference which, as Melton recalls, "hit the financial community like a bombshell."[14]

The press release that Volcker issued listed three specific actions that had been taken in order for the Fed to "assume better control over the expansion of money and bank credit, help curb speculative excesses in financial, foreign exchange and commodity markets and thereby dampen inflation." The first two measures were unremarkable: a 1-point increase—from 11% to 12%—in the discount rate that the Fed charges its member banks on loans and the establishment of an 8% marginal reserve requirement on bank liabilities used simply to finance a further rapid expansion in bank credit, rather than, for example, to help build a new factory. But the third measure was extraordinary and signaled the arrival at long last of monetarism at the seat of financial and economic power. It mandated a new method to be used in the conduct of monetary policy: to support the objective of containing growth in M1, M2, M3 to within ranges set by the Federal Reserve. These ranges, according to the announcement, were to be "consistent with moderate growth in the aggregates" and would entail "placing greater emphasis in day-to-day operations on the supply of bank reserves and less emphasis on confining short-term fluctuations in the federal funds rate." This turn to monetarist procedure, the release went on, "was approved unanimously by the Federal Open Market Committee."

In other words, the monetary managers intended to carry out policy without regard to interest rates, focusing instead on the level of money supply. For years, their policy had been to control the so-called federal funds rate that banks charge one another on very short-term loans. In practice, the FOMC would decide what seemed an appropriate rate for federal funds and then instruct the Fed's Open Market Desk in New York to buy and sell securities in a manner designed to reach and maintain that level. Thus, if interest rates were tending to climb above a level deemed appropriate by the FOMC, for example, the Open Market Desk might step up its buying of securities, thereby pumping money into the credit markets and, as a consequence, exerting a downward pressure on rates.

Under the post–October 6 procedure, an unwanted rise in the federal funds rate would not necessarily prompt a money-pumping reaction at the Open Market Desk. The action to be taken would depend on the level of money supply. If the money supply, for instance, happened to be growing faster than the range of growth the FOMC had designated, then the Open Market Desk might actually sell securities, draining funds from the marketplace and placing further upward pressure on rates, even though credit conditions appeared to be tightening. In brief, the focus for the Fed's new procedure became the annual growth targets for M1, M2, M3. Under the plan, M1 was the primary concern. Its target for a particular period might be set, for example, within a growth range of 4% to 8%. If its growth were tracking, say, only 2% annually, the FOMC might order more expansionary actions by the Open Market Desk, regardless of whether interest rates were moving up or down.

Friedman and other monetarists had advertised such adjustments as a wondrously simple, straightforward procedure. Friedman had even likened money creation to making steel. Control the production of steel, he said, and you will control the quantity of products that depend on steel; control the production of money and, by the same token, you will control the behavior of the entire economy, which relies on money just as an auto relies on steel. But the Fed's new operating procedure soon proved to be far from a simple, practical solution to managing a troubled economy.

THE DEBACLE

Before recounting the dismal reality of monetarism at the Fed, let us briefly examine the pressure that finally induced a reluctant and skeptical Paul Volcker and his fellow governors to call the October 6 meeting. In the spring of 1979, Volcker was still the president of the New York Federal Reserve Bank where, as a member of the FOMC, he had supported a tighter monetary policy through higher interest rates, a position opposite to the wishes of William Miller, the Fed chairman at the time. Later that year, when President Carter chose Miller to join his cabinet as Treasury secretary, Volcker was tapped for the chairmanship of the Federal Reserve Board. His qualifications included early experience as an economist at the New York Fed, the Chase Manhattan Bank in New York, and the Treasury Department in Washington. From 1969 to 1974, he had served as the Treasury undersecretary for monetary affairs. In his Senate confirmation hearings for the Fed chairmanship, Volcker described himself as a "pragmatic monetarist," a description a true Friedmanite would no doubt regard as oxymoronic. The monetarist faithful in those innocent years allowed little room for degrees of monetarism; a "pragmatic" approach to monetarism suggested fine tuning and was, in their eyes, not really monetarism of any sort.

In September 1979, soon after becoming chairman, Volcker flew to Belgrade to attend a meeting of the IMF and the World Bank. While there, foreign monetary officials repeatedly urged him to do something about a severe decline in the dollar's international value, caused in no small measure by steep inflation in the United States. A tougher monetary policy at the Fed was urgently required, Volcker was told. He returned to Washington on October 2 and promptly laid plans for the October 6 FOMC meeting. Strict control of the money supply, whatever the interest-rate consequences, seemed to him the best way to answer the complaints he had heard abroad. A monetarist approach hadn't been attempted, and Volcker realized, the fact that a new procedure was being tried would probably gain the Fed some sympathy just in case interest rates should happen to climb sharply in the process.

The monetarist die may have been cast even earlier, however, during a meeting between the Fed governors and a group called the Federal Advisory Council (FAC), a committee of a dozen prominent bankers chosen by the member banks within each Federal Reserve district. The committee meets once a quarter with the Federal Reserve Board, and one such meeting took place on September 7, 1979. A leading banker on the FAC at the time was Walter Wriston, the chairman of New York's First National City Bank, who had met Milton Friedman through Leif Olsen. At the meeting, the FAC urged the Fed governors to alter the FOMC's operating procedure in such a way that "monetary aggregates [would] take priority over concerns about further upward moves in domestic interest rates."[15]

Wriston and his FAC colleagues, in calling for a change in operating procedure, placed new pressure on Volcker who, with most other Fed governors, was suspicious of and unpersuaded by the strident monetarist calls of Friedman and others. Indeed, Volcker's disdain for Friedman is evident in the chairman's memoirs, written years later. "I know from Arthur Burns," he states, that "Milton Friedman and the extreme monetarists, who had long carried on an intellectual crusade against the Federal Reserve, would have like to have ended our independence, if not the institution itself." Burns, Volcker recalls, "was apoplectic about it. We were indeed fortunate that even in his retirement, his intellectual stature, his public standing, and his old friendships were brought to bear to keep the wilder views of some of his Republican friends at bay."[16]

When the Fed did at last switch to a monetarist procedure, the results were hardly what Friedman and his followers had advertised. I suspect even the ever-skeptical Volcker was taken aback by what ensued. During the first six months under the new operating procedure, the rate of growth in the money supply was cut roughly in half, which pleased many of Volcker's sternest critics abroad, as well as most monetarists at home. The international value of the dollar, which had been falling uninterruptedly for about two years, reversed direction. However, interest rates went through the roof. Already close to 10% in mid-1979, the federal funds rate was near 18% by early 1980.

Highly rated corporations, which had been paying less than 10% interest on long-term borrowing just prior to the swing to monetarism, were paying rates of more than 14% within a few months. An early, spectacular corporate casualty was a $1 billion offering of 7-year notes and 25-year bonds by International Business Machines (IBM). It was the largest public borrowing by a private corporation in the U.S. history up to that time. The underwriting syndicate was headed by Salomon Brothers and co-managed by Merrill Lynch, two Wall Street powerhouses, and 225 other investment banking houses also participated. The securities were offered to the public October 3, only three days before the Fed's memorable meeting. By October 10, only a week later, the syndicate disbanded with much of the IBM issue still unsold and its underwriters and early public buyers losing as much as $50 million as the entire corporate bond market sank.

Investor logic was plain enough: Why buy IBM bonds and notes when competing Treasury issues, with Uncle Sam behind them, would pay as much or possibly a bit more? Even on its short-term borrowing, the Treasury's costs soared, jumping from 9% to nearly 16% in early 1980. Other interest rates rose apace. Meanwhile, business failures, which had declined since the mid-1970s, began to increase sharply. Corporate profits, which had been edging down since the start of the year, plunged. Housing starts followed a similar downward path. And unemployment, below 6% of the labor force in the fall of 1979, was soon approaching 8%.

Particularly dismayed by the upward spiral in interest rates, the Carter administration in March 1980 pressured the Fed to implement, under the Credit Control Act of 1969, an obscure emergency regulation, credit controls on a broad range of institutions. Reluctantly, Volcker went along, and as people swiftly scaled back their borrowing, the dampening effect on overall economic activity was immediate and severe. The broadest economic gauge, the inflation-adjusted GNP declined at the extraordinary annual rate of nearly 10% in the second quarter of 1980. America was once again in a full-blown recession, the seventh of the postwar era.

By mid-May, only two months after the imposition of the new controls, the Fed began removing them. Alarmed at what seemed an economic free fall, it also began pumping money into the economy through the operations of the Open Market Desk. In a single month, the Fed's holdings of government securities jumped some $5.4 billion. Sharp but mercifully short, the recession was over by midyear. But not the Fed's experiment with monetarism. No sooner had the economy begun to stabilize than the policy makers again sought to bring money-supply growth back into a target range deemed consistent with the economy's long-term potential to expand. The growth of M1, for example, which had surged as the 1980 recession deepened, slowed precipitously after mid-1980 and continued to decelerate in 1981.

By then, Carter had been voted out of the White House, as much a casualty of the economy's troubles as a casualty of Ronald Reagan's indisputably superior skills as a communicator, preaching highly infectious optimism to a disgruntled electorate.

This monetary slowdown persisted through 1981 and the early months of 1982. In mid-1981, meanwhile, the economy entered yet another recession—illustrating once again the inability of any one administration, even a highly optimistic one, to propel the economy along an expansionary course. (Even an expanding economy may be insufficient help for a president seeking to remain in office. The economy was clearly on the rise in November 1976, when voters chose Jimmy Carter over incumbent Gerald Ford. But the long, severe recession of 1973–1975 had been over for barely more than a year, and unemployment, always slow to decline in the early stages of a recovery, was still near 8% of the labor force. This was less than in the spring of 1975, when the recession ended, but still high enough to put a final nail in the coffin of Ford's election hopes.) Far more severe than the 1980 recession, or even the 1973–1975 recession, the 1981–1982 slump eventually pushed the unemployment rate to 11%, a level that prompted some analysts to call the economic setback a depression instead of merely a recession. They had a point, for double-digit rates of joblessness— not seen in the United States in many decades—did seem more in keeping with the depressed 1930s than the supposedly prosperous 1980s.

As 1982 unfolded and the economic situation grew grimmer, the Federal Reserve's determination to use the monetarist approach—to hold monetary growth within a prescribed range, no matter what—began to dissolve. Finally, around midyear, Volcker and his increasingly worried policy-making colleagues had had enough. Monetarist caution was abandoned for a far sharper rate of money-supply growth. Between midyear and November 1982, when the long, harsh recession at last hit bottom, the rate of growth in M1 more than tripled and a similar surge was evident in M2, the somewhat larger monetary aggregate. The Fed's painful experiment with monetarism was near an end, and so, by and large, was the influence of the Friedmanites in Washington's policy-making circles.

What went wrong? Charlie Goodhart's law held much of the answer. M1, which the Fed had chosen as its primary target, had become an almost meaningless economic barometer. In practice, it turned out, the business of regulating M1 growth bore little resemblance to what such stalwart monetarists as Jim Meigs had claimed was possible. The black box by which the money supply, and thus the economy, could be deftly controlled, proved to be nothing more than an empty container. The Fed was unable to regulate even the growth of money, much less the growth of the economy. In some months when policy makers sought to slow M1, it grew more rapidly. In other months when they sought to speed it up, it slowed. Much of the time, the economy kept sinking even though M1, however erratically, kept rising. Sometimes, interest rates would rise along with the money supply. At other times, the situation was just the opposite. Lyle Gramley, a Fed governor, recalls, "I agonized over what to do with these goddamned money numbers. In fact, it was very hard to determine whether we were implementing a very tight monetary policy or a rather accommodative one."[17]

The factors skewing M1's behavior were many and impossible to pin down with a great deal of certainty. Money is a constantly changing medium, as the monetarists seemed to forget, and this applies to money in all its manifestations: M1, M2, M3, or M-whatever. In retrospect, it seems that M1's growth during the monetarist experiment, for example, may have been misleadingly inflated by an extraordinary influx of funds into new interest-bearing bank accounts from other monetary aggregates. In addition, M1's ability to fuel economic growth may have been subtly diminished by unusual growth in its least potent component—cash. All the while, by no coincidence, the velocity of M1—the rate at which M1 money was changing hands—kept dropping. According to monetarist theory, this debilitating pattern would be short-lived and, therefore, the Fed should stick to its monetary growth targets and not try to spur M1 on account of the slowdown in its turnover, however much it might weigh on economic activity. But the velocity slowdown turned out to be a protracted affair.

Other possible reasons that M1 proved in practice to be a useless policy tool are plentiful, but the lesson to be learned is short: the money supply, however defined, is an ever-changing thing that cannot be closely controlled.

Frank Morris, the former president of the Boston Fed, was among the first of the policy makers to urge the Fed abandon monetarism and return to a policy that would focus primarily on interest rates. Several years after the monetarist approach had been abandoned and the economy was once again expanding at a healthy pace, Morris told me, "We were placed in an impossible situation. The single thing that we were in a good position to control was bank reserves, and through them, M1. But, M1, as we quickly discovered, was not a meaningful target for monetary—or economic—policy making. If we hadn't made a policy switch in 1982, there's no telling how deep the economy might have sank, and I'm certainly glad we didn't wait around to find out."

Paul Volcker's tenure as Fed chairman ended, after his painful adventure with monetarism, on a relatively happy note. Replaced by Alan Greenspan in the summer of 1987, Volcker left the job amid the longest peacetime expansion in American history. Inflation was subdued, interest rates had fallen remarkably, and unemployment was back down at levels that, in the direst months of the 1981–1982 recession, had seemed unimaginable. The Fed, moreover, had turned away from Friedman's strict brand of monetarism and, as it had in earlier years, was again attempting to manage the economy through manipulating, however imprecisely, interest-rate levels; the policy key was once again the level of the federal funds rate. Monetarism's moment in the policy spotlight was over.

At First National City Bank in New York, the once-flourishing economic review, with its monetarist slant, was terminated in 1981. A few years later, Leif Olsen's impressive team of economists was disbanded. A few of these professionals—the lucky ones—remained at the bank but in jobs that had little to do with economics. Most were compelled to seek employment elsewhere. Some eventually found jobs as economists at other financial institutions, while others landed jobs as loan officers and took other work far removed from spreading the monetarist word. Olsen himself took early retirement and, from his home in Connecticut, continued to provide economic counsel, always with a close eye on the money supply, to a loyal list of clients.

Faith in monetarist policy faded even at the St. Louis Federal Reserve Bank. Benjamin Friedman, the Harvard economics professor unrelated by ideology or blood to Milton Friedman, recounts being invited to address a seminar sponsored by the St. Louis Fed in 1991. "I took my usual harsh position against any Federal Reserve effort to strictly target any particular category of the money supply," the Harvard economist says. At the end of the talk, he recalls saying: "Is there anybody in this room who's willing to make a case to steer Fed policy closely to some specific monetary aggregate and is he willing to specify which one?" He adds, "There were about 100 people in the room, perhaps 40 of them on the St. Louis Fed's staff and the rest invited guests, and not a single person raised a hand. I was encouraged; it shows that people learn."

My lasting memory of monetarism's passage, I should add, is not of the unfortunate fate of the Olsen team or of the grumbling of Milton Friedman and many of his hard-line academic disciples who, to this day, complain that the Fed failed to carry out their prescriptions properly. Rather, my lasting memory is of an afternoon tea party at *The Wall Street Journal*'s editorial offices in downtown Manhattan, where Beryl Sprinkel was the guest from Washington and Robert Bartley, in charge of the paper's decidedly nonmonetaristic editorial page, was the host.

At the time, the Reagan administration still had not decided on a replacement for Volcker, and Sprinkel, it developed, wanted the job. He used the meeting, which as I recall he sought, to boast about his credentials and plead his case. Clearly, he hoped that a strongly supportive *Journal* editorial, endorsing his qualifications, might impress the Reagan inner circle. The tactic failed of course, and Alan Greenspan, no monetarist and a protégé of Arthur Burns, was appointed.

During the tea, George Melloan, a *Journal* editorial writer, said in a disparaging way: "But Beryl, you're a monetarist." Reacting, Sprinkel seemed almost to grovel. "No, George," he said, "I'm not a monetarist. I've bailed out of monetarism. Honest I have."

Mercifully, Sprinkel's former mentor Milton Friedman was not present to witness this exhibition by an erstwhile disciple.

6

Supply-Side Economics: A Not-So-Free Lunch

Journalism is far less influential than its practitioners, or the public, tend to believe. There are, however, exceptions to this rule, and none perhaps is more notable than what occurred in the troubled period leading up to advent of Reaganomics, which is the label often applied with some derision to the sort of supply-side economic policy pursued during much of Ronald Reagan's presidency.

Through a series of seemingly unrelated events, the role of journalism—and particularly of *The Wall Street Journal*—appears, in retrospect, to have been a crucial element in Washington's adoption of supply-side economics.

Milton Friedman and his monetarist colleagues, as I have noted, managed to merchandise their particular prescriptions with considerable skill. The promoters of monetarism, however, rate as rank amateurs compared to the promoters of supply-side economics, many of whom were not bona fide economists at all but journalists or would-be journalists with the ability to turn a phrase. Their access to influential pulpits allowed them to spread the wonderful news that, conventional wisdom to the contrary, there really was such a thing as a free lunch.

This idea, as it turned out, was nonsense of the worst sort. The supply-side chorus notwithstanding, free lunches do not exist. Slow to develop, the painful consequences of supply-side

economics as practiced in the Reagan years have also been slow
to recede—as the one-term presidency of George Bush attests.
(Before he joined the Reagan team, it was Bush, ironically, who
first applied the label "voodoo economics" to the supply-side
idea; as he now must realize to his considerable regret, that
label was right on target.)

FROM EVANS TO LAFFER

Joseph Evans kept a low profile at *The Wall Street Journal*,
but his influence was considerable. With the promotion of Vermont Royster, the paper's long-time editor, to larger corpo-
ratewide duties, Evans was placed in charge of the paper's
highly influential editorial page. Of conservative bent, Evans,
like Royster, was ever on guard against red ink in the federal
budget and the subsequent inflation that he was sure such red
ink would bring.

Beyond this conviction, however, Evans exhibited little interest in particular economic theories—monetarism, Keynesianism, or any other doctrine. Rather, his interest tended to be in
political developments, which was hardly surprising since he
had served in the *Journal*'s Washington bureau as well as for
the paper overseas. As a result, the paper's editorials on economic policy were written usually by Evans' senior assistant,
Lindley Clark, whose monetarist leanings Evans tolerated more
through a lack of interest than through any shared admiration
for the prescriptions of Friedman, Brunner, et al.

The arrangement was a smooth one and seemed bound in the
early 1970s to continue for many years. Both men were in their
early fifties and vigorous. Each had served for many years with
high distinction in the paper's first-class news department, each
was a fine writer and, most important, each liked and admired
the other and was greatly respected by colleagues on the editorial page and elsewhere.

But the situation changed abruptly one evening in 1972 when
Joe Evans, en route home from the office, dropped dead from
a heart attack. The logical replacement for Evans, as well as
the popular one, was, of course, Lindley Clark. However, in a

remarkable decision, Royster tapped a relatively junior member of the editorial-page staff, Robert Bartley, to fill the void left by Evans' untimely death.

The surprising bypassing of Clark had little to do with Clark's admiration for the monetarists; like Evans, Royster had little interest in economic theories beyond the familiar conservative concerns about inflation and the budget. Rather, Royster felt that Bartley's writing contained a spark, a catchiness, that was missing in the smooth, well-reasoned copy that Clark turned out so easily. In addition, there had developed something of a mentor-protégé relationship between Royster, small of stature but large of ego, and Bartley, a quiet, self-effacing, and appreciative recipient of the older journalist's accumulated wisdom.

With the blessing of Warren Phillips, Royster's superior in the corporate hierarchy, Bartley, still in his thirties, was put in charge of perhaps the most influential editorial page in the United States, if not in the world. Clark chose to continue a signed column for the editorial page, but at his own request was transferred back to the news department where he could report to the managing editor and where, years earlier, he had starred in the important posts of page-one and banking editors.

Bartley's career at the *Journal* had begun with low-level reporting assignments in outlying bureaus where his reporting was, by and large, undistinguished. Then more than now, the fastest way for a young *Journal* reporter to gain the managing editor's notice and move swiftly through the news-department ranks was to produce well-written and well-reported front-page "leder" stories, the exhaustive, much-admired features that run along the two sides of the paper's front page every day. Bartley's output of these pieces was unremarkable, and as a result, his prospects in the news department, which boasted dozens of prolific, first-class reporters, seemed unexceptional.

The paper's editorial page, meanwhile, was short of first-rate writers in part because Royster, before he turned the reins over to Evans, had neglected to bring along talented young journalists. Therefore, the staff was small and, except for Evans and Clark, boasted few members with extensive journalistic credentials—from the *Journal* news department or any other

paper. This shortage was aggravated by the fact that the news
department's best reporters and writers were largely antipa-
thetic—particularly in the Vietnam War years—to the page's
conservative line.

In a belated effort to strengthen the page's staff near the end
of Royster's tenure, a talent search of sorts was launched, with
Clark serving as a chief talent scout. After being turned down
by a number of staffers, Clark managed to find a prospect in
the paper's Philadelphia bureau—Bob Bartley. Unlike more experienced news-department staffers previously approached,
Bartley seemed eager to write editorials. His academic background included little economics, but he appeared to have no
philosophical objections to the page's conservative slant. In
Clark's view, moreover, Bartley was a sprightly writer, an
opinion based largely on some book reviews that Bartley had
freelanced for the page.

Soon after Bartley joined the editorial page, Royster and
Evans, both former members of the paper's Washington bureau,
felt that the new arrival's training as an editorial writer required a brief turn in Washington—not as a member of the
news bureau there but as a Washington-based writer of editorials. It was decided that Bartley would continue to report to
Royster and Evans in New York rather than to the paper's
veteran Washington bureau chief, Alan Otten, who was generally unsympathetic to the conservative economic arguments
presented in the *Journal*'s editorials.

From a journalistic point of view, this seasoning in Washington was a valuable opportunity for young Bartley, affording him
a front-row look at the federal government in action. However,
it was also a somewhat difficult period for him as his presence
in the capital was a source of some aggravation to Otten and
others on his accomplished staff, which included many of the
news department's best-paid, most respected veterans.

Enter Jude Wanniski. Like Bartley, Wanniski was new to
Washington and something of a loner. Like Bartley, he had the
ability to turn a catchy phrase. But he was also a somewhat
cavalier writer who in a book dismissed Gibbons' view of the

fall of the Roman Empire in a single disparaging sentence, and who wrote an article about Jamaica for *The Wall Street Journal* that prompted more than a dozen factual corrections by the Jamaican ambassador to the United States. Wanniski had recently been hired to work in Washington for another Dow Jones newspaper, the now-defunct *National Observer*, a Sunday publication based in Silver Spring, Maryland; the Dow Jones corporate hierarchy mistakenly believed that a weekly newspaper could succeed with only a tiny reporting staff and a few talented editors, many of them transplanted from the *Journal*. Jack Bridge, who held the memorable title of vice editor at the *National Observer*, recalls that the recently hired Wanniski "arrived in town wearing a white snakeskin tie with a black shirt, in a fancy sports car from Las Vegas, where among other things he wrote about casinos for the local paper."

It is difficult to imagine less similar men than the circumspect, almost shy Bartley and Wanniski, a flamboyant refugee from Las Vegas who brimmed with self-confidence. (A sample of Wanniski's remarkable chutzpah was the title that he gave to his book in praise of supply-side economics: *The Way the World Works*.) But opposites do occasionally attract, and prowling the halls of government for journalistic grist, these dissimilar men inevitably crossed paths. Though neither was trained in economics, they shared an interest in the Washington political scene and its impact on the nation's economy.

After Joe Evans' death, Bartley hired Wanniski and brought him to New York as a writer of major *Journal* editorials. (Bartley's other primary hiring target, George Will, declined the offer and went on to fame and fortune as a syndicated columnist, best-selling author, and network television commentator.) In the corporate order of things, Wanniski was working for Bartley, but in fact Wanniski, with his extraordinary persuasiveness, eventually proved to be the more influential of the two editorialists. He was the leader in the promotion of supply-side economics, and Bartley happily followed along, enjoying a share of the limelight and the excitement of being able to exert an influence on the course of events in Washington.

While working in Washington for the *National Observer*, Wanniski met a young economist named Arthur B. Laffer. A tenured economics professor at the University of Chicago at the tender age of twenty-eight, Laffer took a leave in 1970 to join the Office of Management and Budget, which was headed then by another former Chicago economist, George Shultz, who later served as President Reagan's secretary of state, as well as in other high Washington posts.

Laffer, like Wanniski, was quick-witted, fast-talking, and exuded self-confidence, and the two men were soon close friends. (Laffer's confident style was immediately evident when I first met him in 1978 in Los Angeles, where he was teaching economics at the University of Southern California. To an easterner like me, the sun-filled campus seemed more like a country club than a place of learning. Laffer appeared thoroughly pleased with his growing fame and comfortable circumstances, which were due in considerable measure to the lucrative economic consulting business that he had developed as his ideas gained prominence on the *Journal*'s editorial page and elsewhere. He lived with his Scottish-born wife Patricia, since divorced, and their four young children. They occupied a four-bedroom house on a hillside near the Pacific; the home's value was a considerable amount for that time—about $225,000—and the value had nearly doubled in only 24 months. On the premises were a kidney-shaped pool, a guest cottage, a pet weasel, eight parrots, seven turtles, and about 300 kinds of cactus. "Biology is my hobby," Laffer told me during my visit to his home, and he then proceeded to reel off all sorts of detailed scientific facts about his various creatures and plants. A favorite parrot, a huge, colorful bird named Molly, perched on his shoulder while he worked or relaxed poolside.)

"Art was the only economist I knew who would answer silly questions about economics," Wanniski, a political science major, once remarked of his early Washington friendship with Laffer. One of Wanniski's first questions to the economist when they met was: "Who is the greatest economist alive today?" Laffer unhesitatingly named Robert Mundell, a Canadian then at the University of Chicago who was an early advocate of using tax

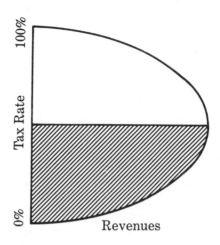

Figure 6-1   Laffer Curve

cuts and a tight monetary policy to spur economic growth and still keep inflation in check.

Laffer and Wanniski at a later time and then finally Bartley were deeply impressed by Mundell's argument. "It just set me off," Laffer told a *Journal* interviewer. Inspired, Laffer proceeded to construct a theory whereby a tax cut could set off such an explosion in productive effort that, in his view, any loss in revenue to the Treasury Department would be more than made up for.[1]

Laffer's basic concept can be glimpsed in Figure 6-1, the so-called Laffer curve. Essentially, it states that for every dollar of tax revenue collected by the government there exist, except at a single optimal point along the curve, two distinct tax rates, one high and one low. When the tax rate is zero, quite obviously, no revenues can be collected. However, a 100% tax rate also yields no revenues because, with all income confiscated, there is no incentive to work. The optimal point, that tax rate producing the most revenue, is at the extreme right edge of the curve. And, despite the appearance of the sketch, this optimal point is not necessarily at a 50% tax rate. Rather, it represents a rate above which—moving up the curve—further tax increases grow increasingly counterproductive. As the 100% level approaches, according to Laffer, incentives diminish, production declines, and tax revenues dwindle toward zero.

According to Laffer, taxation in America in the 1970s had moved appreciably above the optimal point on his curve.[2] Further increases in tax rates, he claimed, would only reduce tax revenues. Conversely, he argued, substantial tax reductions would increase incentives and thus production and revenues. Rising production and revenues, in turn, would help to ease inflation since, in this view, the supply of things to buy would expand and federal budget deficits would shrink.

Laffer stressed the importance of looking at tax rates in terms of their impact at progressively higher income levels. More than a country's overall level of taxation, it was the impact of higher and higher tax rates on higher and higher income levels, he argued, that eroded incentive. He cited, moreover, a widening "wedge" between what an employer paid a worker and what the worker actually brought home.

Implicit in much of what Laffer preached was the idea that supply creates its own demand. Little in the realm of economics is entirely new, of course, so it is not surprising that this view of supply and demand was first enunciated by a nineteenth-century French economist, Jean Baptiste Say. In fact, Say's Law, as it is known, was a part of the economic mainstream until the Great Depression when demand collapsed and seemingly unrelenting, painful surpluses of labor and material developed in the United States and abroad. Though Say's Law assumed that demand would rise to meet increases in supply, this was obviously not the case during much of the 1930s. As a result, the way was paved for Keynes and his concept that demand creates its own supply, precisely the reverse of Say's Law.

As evidence that his curve could work, Laffer cited the U. S. economy's sustained growth, with relatively little inflation and rising federal tax revenues, after a succession of federal tax cuts were initiated by the Kennedy administration in the early 1960s.

This view of Laffer's, however, was not shared by Walter

Heller, who, as we have seen, was one of the architects of the Kennedy tax cuts. Testifying on the supply-side proposals before the Senate Appropriations Committee in January 1981, Heller claimed that the plan "reverses the approach taken by the Kennedy administration, which . . . supply-siders say they are emulating." The Kennedy reductions were "carefully crafted and sharply focused [as] incentives to capital formation," the former Kennedy adviser recalled, adding that there was no such focus to the supply-side tax cutting. At the same hearings, Charles L. Schultze, the chairman of President Carter's CEA, cautioned along the same line, "It seems unwise to assume that the average productivity of the labor force will be improved by a personal tax cut [since] investment-oriented tax reductions for business are likely to increase saving, investment and productivity by a much more significant degree than cuts in personal income taxes."

When I asked him in 1978, Laffer was unable to recall exactly when or where he first drew the curve, but Wanniski later told me that the event occurred in 1974 on a cocktail napkin in a Washington restaurant. "It hit me as a wonderful propaganda device" for persuading policy makers to lower tax rates, Wanniski said.

Martin Feldstein agrees with this appraisal. The Laffer curve, Feldstein says, is "something a Congressman can digest in about 30 seconds and then talk about for months." Like many academic economists, Feldstein was deeply skeptical of Laffer's economic ideas from the start. "There's absolutely no indication that Laffer's ideas will work in the way he suggests," Feldstein told me in 1978, well before the Reagan White House and an accommodating Congress gave Laffer a chance to test his ideas. With evident disdain, the Harvard economist added that he had "never seen Laffer in attendance at any meeting of professional economists where serious economic issues were under discussion."

Similar comments have come from other leading academicians. In the fall of 1988, soon after Bush had won the race for president, I interviewed several Nobel laureate economists about the challenges confronting the president-elect. To a man, they regarded the legacy of supply-side economics among the most difficult. Particularly outspoken was MIT's Paul Samuelson. He worried that "supply-side economics, which is kind of scatter-brained, was supposed to provide us with more incentives for investment and saving, but the private saving rate has actually declined, and on top of that, the government has dissaved as a result of the tax give-aways." Stressing that "our basic problem is that we're a very low-saving nation," Samuelson added rather glumly that, with the arrival of Reagan in the White House, "we used the rare opportunity for tax reform for not a very good tax reform."

FROM THEORY TO PRACTICE

Without the editorial page of *The Wall Street Journal* as a platform, it is doubtful that Laffer's economics would ever have gained such wide support in Washington or among so many of the nation's business leaders. And it was Jude Wanniski, his friend from Washington, who played a key role in gaining the supply-siders their invaluable *Journal* platform. Through his articles in the *Journal* and elsewhere, and through his salesmanship, Wanniski was so persuasive that finally the cautious Bartley himself became convinced that Laffer's free-lunch economics made eminent good sense.

Bartley's conversion, however, was not immediate. Initially, Wanniski's enthusiasm for the supply-side idea was greeted with considerable skepticism by his conservative editorial-page colleagues. Still, Wanniski persevered, managing to plug the tax cut idea in signed op-ed pieces as well as in articles for other influential publications with smaller circulations. His most notable freelance effort was a long article in *Public Interest*, which was edited by the conservative academician Irving Kristol, a frequent *Journal* contributor who, like Wanniski, was largely untrained in economics but all too ready to pontificate about the subject. The Wanniski article was brought to the attention of Ronald Reagan, then heading the American Conservative Union and challenging President Ford, unsuccessfully as it turned out, for the Republican party's 1976 presidential nomination. Intrigued by the Wanniski piece, Reagan sought out Laffer, who naturally was featured along with Mundell in the article.

At the *Journal*, meanwhile, Wanniski had begun correspond-ing with Jack Kemp, the conservative New York congressman. By and large sharing Laffer's and Wanniski's supply-side views, Kemp hired for his staff in 1975 an economist with a doctorate from the University of Virginia, Paul Craig Roberts, who, with Laffer, was to become a driving force in the supply-side move-ment. To his credit, however, Roberts never signed on to the notion that tax cutting would readily eliminate budget deficits. Roberts later joined the *Journal* as an editorial-page columnist, and in occasional conversations with me and other colleagues at the paper, the former Kemp aide seemed skeptical about much of what his fellow journalist Wanniski was preaching.

Kemp and Wanniski met in 1976 and soon became friends. Before long, Kemp was making political speeches endorsing Laffer's call for lower taxes. In early August, a *Journal* edi-torial strongly supported a Kemp proposal calling for some business-tax reductions. The editorial seconded the Laffer view—anathema to old-line conservatives such as Joe Evans—that budget deficits need not generate inflationary pressure. Moreover, the editorial maintained, "It is far from clear that a tax cut will always cause a deficit. It depends on whether it succeeds in stimulating the economy enough that the lower rates yield a larger net revenue."[3]

Since unsigned articles under the heading "Review and Out-look" represent the paper's official position on issues, the 1976 editorial indicated Bartley's conversion to the economics of Laf-fer, Mundell, and Wanniski. To this day, Bartley makes no secret about his conversion. In his 1992 book titled *The Seven Fat Years*, he recounts in great detail his early meetings with Laffer and Mundell, instigated by Wanniski. Often, these were held at what Bartley correctly describes as "a restaurant for Wall Street wannabees" who were not yet, and perhaps never would be, members of private business clubs in the area.

The restaurant, called Michael One, is situated near the American Stock Exchange. Michael One, Bartley recalls, served on many evenings in the mid-1970s as "the site of extraordinary seminars in economics" from which were "spawned, at least to my mind, what later became known as supply-side economics—if not indeed what later became the Reagan administration's economic policy." Bartley adds: "Beside the luminous plumage of the Mundell-Laffer-Wanniski trio, the rest of us were drab."[4]

Drab perhaps, but in the converted Bartley with his recently acquired control over the *Journal*'s editorial page—the op-ed contributions of freelancers such as Laffer as well as the unsigned editorials—the promoters of supply-side economics had a rare opportunity to spread their gospel. The paper's daily circulation was fast approaching 2,000,000, and as issues were passed from hand to hand, the daily readership was estimated to be several times the circulation. There was nothing quite like it in American journalism. Its readership, particularly within the higher corporate echelons, was the envy of most other major publications. Even on the political front, the paper's reach was remarkable. There were loyal subscribers in all of Washington's power centers and in important offices abroad as well. At one point, the Kremlin alone accounted for 73 subscriptions.

In the late 1970s, there was a foretaste of the supply-side revolution that would occur under Reagan. In October 1978, Congress passed a $19.7 billion tax-reduction package. The legislation, spearheaded by Wisconsin Congressman William Steiger, cut the maximum tax rate for large corporations from 48% to 46% and also reduced the tax rates on the first $100,000 in profits for smaller businesses. In addition, a 10% investment tax credit was extended to a number of new areas, ranging from greenhouses to pigpens. There were new tax breaks for individuals as well, including a higher personal exemption, a reduced rate for capital gains, and more generous tax rules on home sales by people over fifty-five.

Still, supply-side economics had not yet become fully established as policy in Washington, and for that to happen, strong political support was needed that neither Wanniski nor Laffer nor even Bartley could supply. But Jack Kemp, aided by Craig Roberts, could and did supply it. As early as 1977, the congressman had introduced a bill calling for a 30% across-the-board cut in marginal income-tax rates. To gain the support necessary in the Senate, where Senator William Roth of Delaware was urging a similar proposal, Kemp consented to a three-year phasing in of this reduction. As the 1980 presidential election drew close, the congressman weighed running for the White House himself as the candidate who would cut taxes sharply.

Kemp dropped out of the race, however, after Reagan, the leading Republican contender, promised that he, too, would press for lower tax rates. And, to ensure that Reagan stayed the supply-side course after his arrival at the White House, Kemp and his supply-side friends carried out what Wanniski has described as "guerrilla warfare." When a Reagan speech suggested, for example, that his administration was perhaps cooling to the supply-side push for lower taxes, Wanniski recalls, "We would call Kemp and scream, Deviation! Deviation! And he would call people and scream, Deviation! Deviation!"[5]

Rowland Evans and Robert Novak, the widely circulated and very influential syndicated Washington columnists, also helped in the promotional effort after the persuasive Wanniski managed to convince Novak, a former *Journal* reporter, of the virtues of supply-side economics. Some support was even supplied, if gingerly, by such luminaries of the monetarist movements as Milton Friedman. Friedman hardly regarded Laffer and the other supply-side promoters as seminal practitioners within the economics profession; there was even some concern that Laffer had once misled a promotion panel at Friedman's University of Chicago about his academic credentials, which Laffer has repeatedly denied.

In any case, Friedman and several other leading monetarists consented to lend a degree of support, and with it some respectability, to the supply-side cause—not because the monetarists shared Laffer's sanguine views about the blessings that would flow from tax cutting but in the belief that tax reductions would force a shrinkage in the federal government as its revenues dwindled. In this calculation, as in so many other of their estimates, the monetarists proved to be very wide of the mark. Their support, however, encouraged Reagan, a long-time fan of Friedman's, to press ahead with the tax-cut plan.

The early 1980s may have been a dismal time for the monetarists, with the Fed's unsuccessful shift in operating procedure, but it was the start of a fine time for the supply-siders. With their screams of "Deviation! Deviation!" they had managed to win the day in Washington. And the victory came precisely as the economy, under the Fed's new monetarist approach, was reeling.

"Supply-side economics came of age on July 31, 1981," recalls Michael Evans in his detailed 1983 account of the supply-side movement.[6] July also happened to be when the harsh recession of 1981–1982 was settling in. On July 31, Congress sent President Reagan a plan to cut taxes by $749 billion over five years. The legislation, which dwarfed the earlier Steiger tax reductions and focused mainly on personal income tax rates, called for a 5% cut in personal tax rates on October 1, 1981, and a further 10% cut in personal rates on July 1, 1982, by which time the economy was deep in the long recession. In all, the 1981 legislation, known officially as the Economic Recovery Tax Act, slashed marginal tax rates on given levels of income in three stages by 23% by 1984. Beginning in 1985, moreover, the personal income tax structure was indexed against upward "bracket creep" due to inflation, and the top rate on income from capital gains was lowered from 70% to 50%.

The supply-side proponents of this tax cutting, as Evans notes, promised that the economy, which actually was entering a slump, would shortly experience "the nirvana of more rapid growth and declining unemployment simultaneously with lower inflation and interest rates." The supply-siders also claimed that some two decades of budget deficits would soon end. In addition, President Reagan's 1982 Economic Report to Congress boasted that "the series of tax cuts enacted in 1981 provides the foundation for increased employment, spending, saving and business investment." The report stated that the "key elements" of the president's program were "reducing personal income tax rates and creating jobs by accelerating depreciation for business investment in plant and equipment."[7]

Laffer and his supply-side cohorts were riding high. But for all the promised supply-side benefits to materialize, the economy would have to perform, as Evans puts it, "not one but three unnatural acts." First, the GNP would have to grow far more rapidly, even while the Federal Reserve maintained a tight monetarist lid over the growth of the money supply. Second, economic growth would have to speed up sharply amid a steep deceleration in the rate of inflation. And third, the budget would have to swing into balance despite the Reagan administration's enormous increases in defense spending along with massive, multistaged reductions in tax rates.

Within a year, reality had already begun to set in. The Reagan White House remained optimistic about its supply-side policies, but less so than earlier. The tone of the President's 1983 Economic Report, for example, was a good deal more cautious. The report asserted that "the tax programs put in place in the last two years should play an important role in increasing capital formation in the United States." But it then hastened to add, "Yet, much more can be done to ensure a rapidly growing standard of living in coming years [and] it is crucial that we take action to reduce large federal deficits and to further stimulate private saving and investment."[8]

Far from fading away as the Reagan presidency unfolded, the budget deficits remained enormous. Topping $221 billion, the shortfall in 1986, five years after the enactment of the supply-side tax cuts, was far greater than the $74 billion of red ink in 1980, just before the arrival of Reaganomics. In the same five years, as a result of the swelling yearly deficits, the amount of federal debt outstanding more than doubled, increasing some $1.2 trillion.[9]

The nation's rate of savings, by no coincidence, dropped substantially as the Reagan presidency went along. In the course of the 1980s, savings as a percentage of after-tax income fell to the lowest levels since the 1930s. At 7.5% when Reagan assumed office, the rate declined progressively—to 6.8% in 1982 and on down to rates of less than 4% in 1987 and 1988. For perspective, the rate of savings in Japan in these years exceeded 20%, more than five times the comparable U.S. level.[10]

This shrinkage of savings, in turn, limited the amount of money being invested, which, of course, ultimately depends on what is being saved. As Benjamin M. Friedman noted near the finish of Reagan's second term, in the three decades leading up to the Reagan presidency the United States on average had "invested 3.3% of our total income in net additions to the stock of business plant and equipment [but] thus far during the 1980s the average has been just 2.3%; in no single year since 1981 have we achieved even 3%."

Between 1950 and 1980, the professor went on to estimate, the value of plant and equipment behind the average nonfarm worker in the United States rose from roughly $26,000 to $43,100, expressed in terms of the dollar's 1987 buying power to eliminate "growth" due merely to inflation. By 1987, however, this total had climbed only to $45,900, just slightly higher than at the decade's start. If business capital formation had merely continued in the 1980s at the pace of the prior 30 years, Friedman estimated that "by 1987 the average worker would have had not $45,900 in capital behind him but $49,100."[11]

In the 1970s, before the arrival of supply-side economics in Washington, roughly one-fifth of the nation's savings was absorbed by the financing needs of the federal budget deficit, and the rest was available for new capital investment. By the end of the 1980s, after two terms of Reagan, about two-thirds of the savings total was absorbed by the budget deficit, leaving only one-third for investment. In addition, savings amounted to only about 5% of the GDP, down from about 10% during the 1970s.

RIDING HIGH

It would be years before the full, unpleasant implications of supply-side economics became plainly visible. Meantime, the most widely followed statistics of economic activity suggested that whatever the policy makers in Washington were beginning to do was reasonably successful. The recession that had begun in July 1981 ended in November 1982, and what followed proved to be the longest peacetime upswing in the history of the U.S. business cycle. Over its course, the unemployment rate was cut in half, from about 11% of the labor force to slightly over 5%. By the time the expansion finally ended, Reagan was safely ensconced at his retirement home in California, and his successor George Bush was left to deal with a slumping, debt-burdened economy.

In retrospect, the way was paved for the long 1982–1990 expansion not by the economics of Laffer and Mundell but through the simple evolution of the business cycle. Deep, long recessions, economic history shows, tend to be followed by relatively long expansions. The reason is straightforward: recessions serve to cleanse the economy of the excesses—from severe inflation and shortages to excessive debt—that invariably build up during the preceding expansion phases of the cycle. As a rule, the worse the recession, the more thorough the cleansing process and, therefore, the more sustainable the subsequent economic revival. It is no coincidence, for example, that the supershort expansion of 1980–1981, which lasted only 12 months, followed the supershort recession of 1980, which, at only six months, was the briefest cyclical downswing in U.S. history. The 1981–1982 recession, by comparison, cleansed the economy of the double-digit rates of inflation and interest that were suffocating business activity as Carter left the White House.

The real basis for the long expansion of 1982–1990 notwithstanding, the supply-side economists and their allies in the press and in government were widely seen as the architects of the long upturn. The message that free lunches were indeed available if only taxes were reduced was sweet music to countless corporate chieftains and politicians. Whatever doubts they harbored about the economics of Laffer and his friends, they were all too ready to endorse tax cutting that promised to fatten bank accounts and delight constituents. As early as 1978, the politi-

cians invoking Laffer's name or seeking his counsel ranged from
California Governor Edmund G. Brown, Jr., and Louisiana Senator Russell B. Long, both Democrats, to California Senator
Samuel I. Hayakawa and, of course, New York Congressman
Jack Kemp, both Republicans.

Responding to his popularity, the indefatigable Laffer
bounced through an awesome travel schedule, carrying out
scores of speaking engagements. In a 24-hour period in the fall
of 1978, for example, he flew from Los Angeles to New York
to meet with clients of H. C. Wainwright, a Boston securities
firm for which he was producing economic analyses. Then he
was off to Puerto Rico for talks with officials there about the
island's tax plans. He was off again that evening for meetings
in Washington. Then, finally, there was the return flight to his
home in Los Angeles.

"I sleep like a log on planes," Laffer once told me, adding
that he avoided any alcohol on these flights because "it dehydrates you and is bad for the prostate gland. I also try to do
exercises—lots of deep knee-bends in the cabin bathroom." Altogether, Laffer, by his own count, was delivering some 200
speeches a year; for roughly a quarter of these, mainly to private groups, he was paid an average of $4,000 per appearance,
plus first-class travel costs; the other appearances, he reported,
were generally of a "public service nature" and were given free.
"He's taken five days of vacation in 16 years," his wife Patricia
reported when I visited their home in 1978. Laffer himself
added with great enthusiasm, "I'm getting my thoughts across
in Washington and that's good enough for me. I'm asked to
testify all the time, but I'd rather make converts in my area of
interest than worry about such things as the Panama Canal
treaty."

There was little doubt that Laffer's frenetic efforts to promote supply-side economics were successful. "Art's ideas have
been enormously influential in this office, as well as elsewhere,"
claimed Spencer Reibman, an aide to Jack Kemp, in 1978. A
former Laffer student, Reibman added that "Art was instrumental in getting me this job."[12] Other former Laffer students

were scattered through other congressional staffs or were taking on teaching assignments at universities around the country.

By the time the tax cutting was under way in the early 1980s, Laffer and the other supply-side leaders had become much sought-after gurus of economic wisdom. Laffer's performances at the lectern captivated his audiences, which often consisted of leading corporate executives only too happy to hear that by lowering their taxes Washington could somehow make the economy bloom and the deficit fade away. I twice served as the moderator in debates set up by the American Institute of Textile Manufacturers between Laffer and other economists whose academic credentials were at least the match of his own. The first of these debates was held at the Greenbrier resort in West Virginia, where Laffer's opponent was Otto Eckstein. The second debate was held at the Homestead resort in Virginia, where Laffer debated Lester Thurow of the economics faculty at MIT. Thurow later became the dean of MIT's prestigious Sloan School of Management. Both Eckstein and Thurow were skilled debaters as well as eminent economists, and both, in my view, won the day against Laffer and his supply-side arguments. Yet, there was no mistaking the audience's favorite in each debate: the textile executives, more than 1,000 of them, clearly were with the fast-talking Laffer all the way.

Around the same time, articles appeared in such magazines as *Newsweek* and *Esquire,* hailing Laffer as the high priest of a new economic religion based on the virtues of tax reduction. "Supply-side economics is a new economic religion whose time has pretty much come," enthused Barton Biggs, the chief investment strategist of Morgan Stanley, the investment banking concern, in a letter to clients. Biggs went on to describe Wanniski's book in praise of tax cutting, *The Way the World Works,* as the "most important" economic tome since the seminal writings of Karl Marx more than a century before.

A survey by *The Wall Street Journal,* taken early in Reagan's presidency, reported that Laffer's recently formed consulting firm, A. B. Laffer Associates, already boasted some 150 clients and had yearly revenues of about $2.5 million. Another supply-side consulting outfit, Polyconomics Inc., was dishing out advice to some 75 corporations and collecting some $500,000 in annual revenues; its head was Jude Wanniski, who had recently left the *Journal* for this far more remunerative pasture.[13]

Both Laffer and Wanniski, the report noted, managed to capitalize on their close ties to Kemp and other Washington policy makers. David Marvin, a manager of DuPont's pension fund and a fan of both supply-siders, praised them for serving as invaluable conduits "between the investment community and the political community." Wanniski's business particularly benefited from his links to Bartley at the *Journal*; in this period, articles carrying the views of two important Wanniski clients— the Independent Petroleum Association of America and Chrysler—appeared on the paper's editorial page. Wanniski and Laffer also issued topical newsletters for their clients that could be highly entertaining as well as, in the case of Wanniski's, remarkably offensive.

Early on, a favorite Wanniski target was the monetarists. One Wanniski missive called for a "public flogging" of Treasury Under Secretary Beryl Sprinkel, Milton Friedman's monetarist admirer. Another Wanniski report suggested most ungraciously that Anna Schwartz the respected monetarist who coauthored with Milton Friedman his most famous book, *A Monetary History of the United States, 1867–1960,* was too old to be taken seriously in her role as the head of a committee formed in Washington to study gold's possible monetary role; in the newsletter, Wanniski went so far as to list the age of Schwartz, who was in her sixties.

When challenged, Wanniski was an expert at glibly defending his positions in a manner that made further reasonable discussion difficult. Around the time that the tax-cut proposals were being debated, for example, I questioned him about his contention that the federal budget deficits that might ensue posed no problem. His response was typical of his ability to dismiss doubts with catchy rejoinders that would leave skeptics with little to say. His answer was: "How long does it take you to stoop down and grab a ten-dollar bill you see lying on the street?"

Such was the impact of the supply-siders in the early 1980s

that even the more established economic consulting firms began to incorporate supply-side assumptions about the benefits of tax cutting in their computer-based forecasting models. These firms included Data Resources, Chase Econometric Associates, Wharton Econometric Forecasting, and Evans Economics. It was quite an accolade for an economic movement that Karl Brunner, was later to characterize as "a largely nonsensical concept that has emerged through an interaction between the media and a small group of advocates."[14]

SUPPLY-SIDE SLIDE

The impact of Reagan's experiment with supply-side economics was less traumatic than the experiment of Volcker's Federal Reserve with monetarist operating procedures. Paul Krugman, a bright young economist at MIT, summarizes the supply-side adventure well. "When Ronald Reagan was elected," Krugman recalls, "the supply-siders got a chance to try out their ideas. Unfortunately, they failed."

Krugman, however, is quick to add, "it was not an abject failure [like the monetarist experiment] that left the economy in ruins—the American economy clearly did well enough in the 1980s to satisfy most voters." Rather, Krugman contends, the problem with supply-side economics was that the results proved to be "so far short of what it promised." That promise, of course, was "free lunches—a chance to invigorate the economy without pain."[15]

Krugman is perhaps too gentle in his criticism of supply-side economics. In the wake of the supply-side experiment, the damage to the economy was less acute and subtler, to be sure, than the shambles that followed the monetarist experiment. But in the long term, it may have been far more difficult to undo. By the time the full repercussions were becoming evident, many of the chief supply-side advocates had departed from the Washington scene.

Perhaps the most comprehensive assessment of the repercussions of the supply-side policy is contained in a retrospective critique conducted by two economists of the New York Federal

Reserve Bank. Published in the spring 1992 issue of the bank's *Quarterly Review,* the appraisal concludes that "on the whole, developments in U.S. fiscal policy during the 1980s were unfavorable for the long-run performance of the economy."

The study notes that "supply-side economics had an important influence" in the setting of this policy. It recalls that the supply-siders "argued that reducing marginal tax rates would encourage economic growth by creating incentives [and] believed that the tax cuts would pay for themselves—that is, the rise in the tax base resulting from lower rates would be sufficient to prevent tax revenue losses." But in fact, the analysis finds, the "large and persistent federal budget deficits" that accompanied the supply-side tax cutting "lowered the level of [the economy's] potential output by roughly 2-1/2% to 3-1/2% and, assuming no significant change in fiscal stance, the negative impact will continue to build over time."[16]

The reasons for the economy's reduced potential as a result of supply-side economics are so basic that it is remarkable the policy's failure was not more widely anticipated. The persistently large budget deficits that occurred worked inevitably to reduce savings and investment. The budget deficits during the 1980s averaged close to 4% of the GNP, roughly double the rate in the 1970s. In the process, the share of federal debt held by the public climbed to 45% of the GNP in 1990, up from 27% a decade earlier. Since, as the New York Fed's study observes, "each dollar of deficit represents a dollar of lost national saving," it is no surprise that the federal red ink was an increasing drag on savings during the Reagan years. The accompanying table, based on data compiled by the New York Fed, traces this trend.

National Savings
(as percentage of GNP)

	Total	Private	Federal	State-Local	International Inflow-Outflow
1961–1970	7.9	8.3	−0.4	0.0	−0.6
1971–1980	7.0	8.0	−1.8	0.8	−0.2
1981–1990	3.5	6.1	−3.6	1.0	1.9

Since savings make investment possible, the inevitable result of the decline in savings in the 1980s, traced in the table, was a corresponding falloff in investment, though the magnitude of the decline was less because of the rising influx of money from abroad, shown in the table's far righthand column. The bank's study estimates that "overall, the deficits cost the nation about 7% of its [potential] capital stock" in the 1980s, which in turn underlies the estimated drop in potential output. Even with the influx of savings from abroad, private investment as a percentage of GNP fell to 5.2% in the 1980s, down from 7.1% in the 1970s and 7.2% in the 1960s. The investment rate also declined as the 1980s progressed and the full impact of supply-side policy was felt. It fell from an average of 5.5% of GNP in the first half of the decade to 5% in 1986–1990.

In absolute terms, to be sure, investment did expand after the economy emerged from the 1981–1982 recession. But this growth was feebler than the normal pickup that occurs in the course of a new upswing in the business cycle after a full-scale recession. In the course of the 1975–1980 expansion, investment in business structures rose about 40%, and in the course of the 1961–1969 expansion it increased nearly 60%. The comparable gain in the 1982–1990 expansion was only about 15%.

The influx of savings from abroad, it should be added, transformed the United States in a single decade from the largest creditor nation to the largest debtor nation. And, while the influx helped to prevent a steeper fall in investments, it also represented a future debt-servicing obligation that continues to consume an appreciable share of the economy's resources, including new savings. "In the long run," the bank states, "the continued inflow of foreign capital places an additional burden on the economy." Part of this burden, of course, is the persistent outflow of interest and dividend payments to foreign investors. Unlike interest and dividend payments to U.S. investors, much of this money may be reinvested elsewhere and thus does not tend to benefit the U.S. economy.

When Milton Friedman and the other monetarists lent their support to the supply-side movement, they imagined unrealistically that cutting taxes would force a simultaneous reduction in federal spending. This was hardly the case; little did they appreciate Washington's determination to keep spending. (Paul Samuelson calls this monetarist notion "the tape worm theory— the idea that the way to get rid of a tape worm is stab your patient in the stomach.") Instead of the frugality that the monetarists had hoped for, there were only more Brobdingnagian budget deficits.

As a percentage of GNP, federal spending rose to 23.4% in 1981–1990, up from 21.1% in 1971–1980 and 19.2% in 1961–1970. Despite all the publicity about building up the military, defense outlays, at 6.1% of GNP, were actually below the 8.3% rate that prevailed in 1961–1970, years that of course encompassed the Vietnam War. Categories in which federal spending did rise to new highs in the 1980s included federal entitlement programs, such as Social Security and Medicare, and interest payments on the mounting federal debt. Entitlement spending came to 11% of GNP in the 1980s, up from 9.8% in the 1970s and 6% in the 1960s. Interest payments amounted to 2.9% in the 1980s, up from 1.5% in the 1970s and 1.2% in the 1960s.

Perhaps the best explanation of the continued rise in spending during the Reagan years can be found in the memoirs of his early director of the Office of Management and Budget, David Stockman. As Stockman relates, neither the leaders of Congress nor the officials in Reagan's administration, who should have led the way, were willing to accept the specific spending reductions that Stockman's office deemed necessary as a counterpart to the supply-side tax cuts. The Reagan White House's antispending rhetoric could not be taken seriously, Stockman notes, remarking that "the Reaganites were, in the final analysis, just plain welfare politicians like everybody else." Stockman concludes that the supply-side advocates, whom he initially admired, were really only "half-revolutionaries," ready to slash tax rates but lacking the stomach to institute spending reductions as well. "They stuck their heads in the sand and pretended that the deficit either didn't exist or it didn't matter," Stockman claims, and they "ended up creating an economic fantasy theory."[17]

"The normal boundaries of prudent financial behavior were

breached dramatically during the 1980s," concludes a study by a Montreal-based team of economists. "The resulting economic and financial stress and instability will not be corrected just by a temporary slowdown in growth and by a reduction in interest rates. The effects of the debt excesses are long-lasting and will be unwound only with time."[18]

The failure of supply-side economics is apparent in other ways. If supply-side theory were valid, the reductions in marginal tax rates should have induced people to work more and take less leisure time. However, the length of the average work week declined throughout the 1980s. From a high of 35.7 hours in the 1979, it fell to 34.9 hours in 1985 and to 34.6 hours in 1989. While the rate of participation in the labor force increased among females during the decade, the rate for males, the largest group with most of the breadwinners and the group most likely to benefit from reductions in the highest marginal tax rates, declined substantially.

For all this, diehard supply-side advocates have continued to regard their concept as an untarnished success. As late as the spring of 1991, Martin Anderson, a senior fellow at the Hoover Institution who served as Reagan's domestic policy adviser in the crucial period of 1981–1982, proclaimed that "the Reagan boom of the 1980s was the greatest economic expansion this country has ever had."[19] In fact, it was nothing of the sort. The expansion of the 1960s was appreciably longer, and in terms of economic growth and income growth, there were a number of brisker upswings.

The economy's average annual growth in 1982–1989, the supply-side years, was 3.7%. This was a decent rate of increase, to be sure, but it still trailed behind comparable expansionary gains of 4.2% a year in the 1970s and 4.1% in the 1960s. The average annual growth of personal income in the supply-side years was only 3.1%, after subtracting government transfer payments. This was far short of comparable yearly gains of 4.5% in the 1970s expansion and 4.4% in the 1960s.

Even so, in *The Seven Fat Years*, published in 1992, Bob Bartley maintains that "from 1983 to 1990, we enjoyed Seven Fat Years," during which, he contends, there was "unleashed

. . . a wave of sustained growth and a dynamic outburst of
entrepreneurial creativity."[20]

Many supply-side advocates who are less sanguine than Bartley or Anderson about the economy's performance in the Reagan years nonetheless maintain that the supply-side *concept*
remains valid because it has not received a true test. They note
that much of the tax cutting that took place in the early 1980s
was offset in the latter part of the decade by ill-considered tax
increases. They cite, for instance, a 1984 tax measure that made
depreciation rules less beneficial and legislation in 1986 that
abolished an investment tax credit and cut back still more on
depreciation allowances, although it also further reduced corporate and personal rates. Moreover, these advocates note,
state and local governments were steadily increasing their own
tax demands.

The upshot was that the average worker in the latter years
of Reagan's presidency was laboring a good deal longer to earn
enough to pay his total yearly tax bill than he did in the early
Reagan years. The National Tax Foundation, a Washington
research group, found that in the early Reagan years, after the
initial rounds of tax cutting, the average worker had to labor
through April 28 to cover a year's taxes, while at the end of
Reagan's presidency this "tax freedom day" was as late as
May 5.

Still, marginal tax rates were far lower at the end of the
decade than at the start, and to bring down the level of these
top-bracket rates was the crucial concern of the supply-siders.
It also should be noted that although the budget deficits remained enormous throughout the 1980s, they did begin to diminish moderately in the last few years of the Reagan presidency when taxes were again raised. In contrast, the red ink
kept rising relentlessly during the earlier Reagan years of unrestrained supply-side tax cutting.

While the supply-siders have been slow to concede the failure
of their theory, most economists long ago abandoned whatever
faith they may once have placed in the promises of Laffer,

Mundell, Wanniski, Bartley, and the other leaders of the supply-side movement. Indeed, rare is the economist today who will admit that the supply-side idea ever seemed to make much sense. Even so, it is a fact that a remarkably large number of economists engaged in business forecasting once endorsed and professed to believe the supply-side promises—no doubt to the delight of their high-tax-bracketed corporate bosses.

For example, as the Reagan administration settled into power in March 1981 and as the supply-side tax cuts were being mapped, a survey of several dozen leading corporate economists by Blue Chip Economic Indicators found that more than two-thirds believed that the federal budget, then deeply in deficit, would be safely back in balance by 1984 with supply-side tax cutting.

As it turned out, the deficit in 1984 was slightly over $185 billion, more than double the 1981 total of about $79 billion. The diehard advocates of supply-side economics were by no means the only members of the profession to have peddled the bogus notion that there was indeed such a thing as a free lunch.

7

Looking Ahead, Seeking a Role

Those of us compelled occasionally by our livelihoods to travel about pontificating in public on the economic outlook—a dreadful assignment, to be sure, after which it is sound practice to leave town quickly—must depend for openers on an assortment of old jokes about the economics profession. These tales, which are plentiful, are designed to warm up audiences, usually of the captive variety, to a subject not renowned for intrinsic allure.

Perhaps the most successful tale from this stable, at least in my experience, involves a noted noneconomist: the late Albert Einstein. The nonpareil physicist, according to the story, arrives in heaven and soon is introduced to three angels. Attempting to strike up a conversation, he politely asks them to recite their IQs. The first angel responds that his is 180, which leads Einstein to smile broadly and remark, "Oh good, we can have some interesting discussions about my theory of relativity." The second angel duly reports that his IQ is 130, to which Einstein replies, after a brief hesitation: "Well, that's fine, perhaps we can have a good chat about world politics." Finally, the third angel steps forward to report somewhat haltingly that his IQ is only 80. There is a very long pause before Einstein, ever the gentleman, quietly inquires: "Tell me, my friend, what do you think about the economic outlook?"

The story is worth employing on the rubber-chicken circuit

not only for its ability to produce some laughs but also to adorn the teller, about to pontificate on the economic outlook, with a protective mantle of self-effacement. The Einstein story also seems worth recalling for what it says about the sorts of problems that confront the economics profession as the twentieth century nears a close. The third angel notwithstanding, economists are as a rule intelligent individuals, with IQs well above the benighted 80 level. Still, too many of these bright people have become mired in a pretty dumb endeavor: trying to forecast with reasonable accuracy the economy's twists and turns not only over a month or a quarter, but over a full year or two or three or even, as I have occasionally witnessed in material arriving from such outfits as Data Resources, over an entire decade.

Hubris may be too kind a word to characterize such exercises. Robert Solow may put it best. The present state of forecasting the economy's course, is such, Solow says, that perhaps economists should not attempt to prognosticate at all. "The world wants to judge our profession by our ability to forecast six months or a year ahead and that's not something we're very good at," he remarks, since "the economy simply isn't very predictable."

Nearly 30 years ago, by way of illustration, *The Wall Street Journal* foolishly launched a series of articles under the title of "Here Comes Tomorrow." While the series occupied page one and accordingly attracted a great amount of reader attention, as well as perhaps a bit of additional advertising, its estimates of what the future held, particularly within the economic arena, proved pitifully wide of the mark; environmental considerations, for instance, received not a mention.

As author of the lead article in the series, I was obliged to interview at length the chief economist of the National Planning Association, an organization based in Washington. Its primary mission was to peer far down the economic road and tell its business and governmental clients precisely what it saw there. The chief economist's predictions, precise and long range, are not worth recounting now except to report that they turned out to be woefully inaccurate. So great was their inaccuracy, in fact, that the same economist 10 years later confided to me that the research outfit was no longer in the long-term forecasting business. "There's not much interest in long-range forecasts around here any more," he said, explaining that "we've been wrong too often."[1] This was a remarkably candid confession, I reflected, for an individual paid by an organization whose very name indicated a high degree of concern—and perspicacity— about the economic future.

A PROFESSION IN DIFFICULTY

As a new century nears, the U.S. economy, after yet another recession in the long post–World War II string of slumps, finally seems after the Bush presidency to have come, however briefly, on better times. This is not true, however, for those attempting to make a living as experts on the economy—the economists themselves. For them, the bad times persist. Their wide-ranging troubles are perhaps most visible in the forecasting arena. So many of them have miscalculated the economy's moves so badly for so long that planners in and out of government increasingly disregard their counsel. The profession's difficulties even extend to the academic arena, where the subject's once-high popularity is eroding and confusion mounts over how the economy works and how best to manage it.

"The profession is humbled and at odds with itself," comments Mary S. Rosenblum, vice president and senior economist at the Atlanta Federal Reserve Bank. Peter Lynch, the legendary former manager of Fidelity Investment's Magellan Fund, has remarked on several occasions, most recently at the start of the Clinton presidency, "If you spend over 14 minutes a year on economics, you've wasted 12 minutes." In 1991, a short while before his retirement, Ken Olsen, the founder of Digital Equipment, stated emphatically, "We have no reason whatsoever to believe economists. First of all, as pseudo-scientists, they really don't follow the tradition of stating the truth or being analytic [but instead] just want to influence the outcome, particularly the government ones."[2]

The economists' woes come amid increasing concern over such troubling long-term trends as mounting debt, relentless foreign trade deficits, and perhaps an end to the long postwar rise in the nation's standard of living. By their training, economists appear well suited to lead the charge against these problems. But this hasn't happened. At corporations, economists are an endangered species. Their clout also is waning in Washington. Eschewing economists, Clinton's first four choices for his "economics team" were a Texas senator to head the Treasury Department, a California congressman to run the Office of Management and Budget, and two New York investment bankers, one to serve as the president's assistant for economic policy and one as deputy Treasury secretary.

This snubbing followed a dismal performance by many forecasters. In early October 1992, for instance, 50 leading economists, polled by Blue Chip Economic Indicators, estimated on average that the economy had grown only 1.8% annually in the third quarter. Soon after, the Commerce Department reported growth of 2.7%. Still, many forecasters remained unconvinced. On November 16, for example, Gary Ciminero, the chief economist of Fleet Financial Group in Providence, Rhode Island, cautioned that the 2.7% growth reported for the third quarter seemed way too high. "Don't believe this optimistic data—it could be hazardous to your health," he wrote to clients, proclaiming in boldface type that "actual growth about half the 2.7% reported pace" was likely after revisions.

"Some economic tooth fairy took pity on President Bush just prior to the election," Ciminero added, "at least until postelection" revisions of the early data. On November 25, the third-quarter rate was indeed revised—but the change was sharply *upward* to 3.9%; yet another revision on December 22 placed the final third-quarter number at 3.4%, still far higher than the consensus had forecast.

Faulty forecasting is by no means limited to the private sector. At the start of 1992, economists in the Bush administration estimated that the budget deficit in the fiscal year to September 30, 1992, would reach about $400 billion. When the results were in, the actual shortfall was $290 billion, due in part to lower-than-expected federal spending to close down failed savings-and-loan associations.

The inability of economists to anticipate the economy's ups and downs more accurately may have cost George Bush the presidency. As Lester C. Thurow of MIT says, "Economists kept saying there's going to be a clear turnaround" before the election, "but I'm sure if they had told Mr. Bush instead that there would be fewer people on private payrolls the first Tuesday of November 1992 than there were on the first Tuesday of November 1988, he would have tried to do something about it, rather than letting events take their slow course."

The failure to gauge the economy's performance more accurately has led to a great deal of flip-flopping in the advice that many economists offer. Consider Alan S. Blinder, a Keynesian economics professor at Princeton University, the coauthor of a best-selling economics textbook, a noted *Business Week* columnist, and a member of President Clinton's CEA. Early in 1992 Blinder refused to join in the calls by many other prominent Keynesian economists for sharply increased fiscal stimulus to spur the economy. He cited the recession's mildness and the Federal Reserve's ability to induce growth. But in late August he reversed his stand, claiming the economy was far sicker than he initially believed. In a *Business Week* column titled "O.K., I Was Wrong," he urged "fast action," including large temporary tax breaks for businesses and "emergency fiscal relief for beleaguered cities and states."[3] Months later, after the Commerce Department's third and final estimate of third-quarter economic growth, the professor's original advice appeared in retrospect a lot sounder than his subsequent counsel after his flip-flop.

The use of ever more powerful computers presumably should improve forecasting. However, the output of computers very much depends on the quality of data that go into them, and it's widely agreed that this has deteriorated in recent years. Some federal statistical series—several, for instance, on labor force turnover—have been eliminated to hold down spending. Another problem, as the saga of the 1992 third-quarter report indicates, is the extensive revising of data that goes on, often long after the initial reporting. Forecasters, as a result, frequently discover that their painstakingly constructed estimates are founded on faulty numbers that will be changed and changed again.

A further hazard is the manner in which data are adjusted for seasonal factors. For instance, retail sales tend to be higher in December, because of pre-Christmas shoppers, than, say, in the early months of a new year, when the Christmas bills arrive and tax time is drawing near. Accordingly, federal statisticians deliberately reduce the raw volume of December sales by a factor that they believe will make the month comparable to the months without shoppers. In a perfect statistical world, this adjustment would make good sense. But the sad reality is that to seasonally adjust most data in a realistic function is well-nigh impossible.

Take the employment numbers that Washington issues each month. Near the end of 1992, for example, the Bureau of Labor Statistics (BLS) reported that "perhaps the most important [recent labor force] development was an increase of 35,000 manufacturing jobs" in November. However, these were in fact mostly phantom jobs, created by adjusting for seasonal factors in what may have been a faulty manner. In an actual, unadjusted count of individuals, "the manufacturing sector probably lost more than 30,000 jobs in November," notes Gene Epstein, a writer for *Barron's*.[4] Epstein explains that the BLS uses the record of the three previous Novembers as a guide to seasonally adjust the manufacturing-employment numbers. But these were months, he notes, "when the economy was stagnating" or undergoing an outright recession; in fact, companies were shedding manufacturing workers in both November 1990 and 1991. Had the BLS instead used as a reference point a more typical span of Novembers, incorporating as well the 1987–1989 period when the economy was clearly on the rise, the seasonal adjustment for manufacturing jobs in November 1992 would have been a *minus*—perhaps by as much as 40,000—instead of the reported increase of 35,000.

Another difficulty for forecasters is that service industries play a far larger role in today's economy, and it is exceedingly hard to maintain an accurate statistical tab on the service sector. If many economic forecasters were unduly gloomy about the prospects for recovery from the 1990–1991 recession, they were so because they believed that productivity within the service sector was stagnating. "The greatest single challenge facing managers . . . is to raise the productivity . . . of service workers," warned Peter F. Drucker, a renowned management authority at The Claremont Graduate School, in the lead of a long article lamenting the service-sector situation in the *Harvard Business Review*.[5] However, the statistics prompting such concern appear deeply flawed, painting an overly depressing portrait of service-sector productivity and, therefore, of the U.S. economy as a whole.

"At our current state of knowledge, we don't really know what's happening to service-sector productivity," says Michael Darby, an economics professor at the University of California in Los Angeles and a former chief economist for the Commerce Department, one of Washington's most prolific number mills. Service-sector productivity, Darby thinks, "could well be growing faster than manufacturing productivity, instead of much slower as is generally supposed." Ronald H. Schmidt, a senior economist at the San Francisco Federal Reserve Bank, goes further, saying that "while the evidence is not conclusive, productivity is growing faster in services than in manufacturing." Schmidt adds: "The fuzziness of the service sector, whose role keeps expanding, makes it harder to get accurate readings on the performance of the economy as a whole."[6]

Economists who pull together the data in Washington do not dispute such criticisms. "Government statistical programs have failed to keep pace with the growth and change in the service sector," concedes Susan M. Keehan, a business analyst at the Census Bureau, which collects much of the raw data used for gauging service productivity. "In many cases," she adds, "these programs have actually declined." Michael Harper, chief of productivity research at the Bureau of Labor Statistics, offers the insurance industry as an illustration of why productivity is "simply impossible to measure" in some services. "Do higher premiums, which tend to boost an insurance company's revenues, also serve to boost its productivity?" he asks. "Or are higher premiums merely a signal of higher policy risks? Perhaps, in reality, lower premiums signify greater efficiency and productivity, but we simply don't know."[7]

For these reasons, the BLS deliberately provides no productivity statistics for the insurance industry. Other service businesses in which the BLS finds it impossible to measure productivity include such major fields as health care, real estate, and securities brokerage. In all, services for which no productivity measures are available employ some 70% of the people who hold jobs within the service sector—far higher than the comparable rate in manufacturing industries.

Various clues suggest that service-sector productivity may be far healthier than available numbers and articles such as the one by Peter Drucker indicate. In some services, such as banking, pay has risen sharply over the years, and yet productivity, at least as reported by Washington, has stagnated. This disparity makes no sense, since growth in pay must be tied in the long run to growth in productivity. If productivity is so poor in a service industry like banking—where, it should be noted, unionization is relatively low—then why are employers willing to grant consistently large pay boosts? Still another sign that service-sector productivity may be healthier than generally supposed appears in foreign trade data. For years, the United States has boasted large service-sector trade surpluses; such success in global markets would seem to indicate a high level of competitiveness and, therefore, relatively robust productivity. The trade balance for goods, in sorry contrast, has been in deep deficit, erasing the service-sector surpluses and causing an overall shortfall for the United States in its foreign trade account.

Difficulty in gauging service productivity leads to bewildering situations. In a recent 15-year period, railroad productivity rose at a brisk annual rate of 4.7%, according to the BLS. But another government agency, the Commerce Department's Bureau of Economic Analysis (BEA), which also tries to measure productivity in some service businesses, found that railroad productivity for the same period rose only 2.3% a year. For airlines, the two agencies are even further apart; the BLS reports a gain of 3.6% annually during the 15 years and the BEA reports a *decline* of .2% a year.

Economists face daunting difficulties in trying to gauge productivity in rapidly expanding service industries. Daycare centers are handling more and more children per worker, which suggests a gain in productivity. But some observers dispute any such conclusion, arguing that the trend also signifies an offsetting decline in the quality of care provided for each child. Conversely, surgery now often requires much larger operating-room teams than years ago, suggesting a productivity decline. But these difficult operations, which are performed more and more frequently and save lives that once would have been lost, obviously represent vast strides in health care quality.

With the growth of international trade and finance, moreover, the economy is affected increasingly by developments abroad, which tend to be especially difficult for economists to anticipate and assess. "We've got a world economy now and it's just not possible for forecasters to understand and take into account all the resulting complexities and uncertainties," says Lester Thurow.

Making matters even riskier for forecasters is any shifting of the economy's gears, which has happened repeatedly in recent years. Typically, economists project recent economic trends forward. This may yield fairly accurate forecasts when the economy is on a steady course, but not when it is shifting, for instance, from a downturn in the business cycle to an upturn. At such times—which, of course, are when the need for accurate forecasting is greatest—users of forecasts should "think carefully about plausible outcomes far from the consensus view," cautions Stephen K. McNees, a Boston Federal Reserve Bank vice president who keeps close track of forecasters' accuracy.

With about 3,700 members, the NABE has some 300 fewer members now than two decades ago. Moreover, a NABE spokesman reports, "A smaller portion of our membership is engaged in actual forecasting and more are working in profit-making units" of corporations.

A case in point is New York's Citibank, which now employs only four economists for the broad-scale forecasting that a decade ago occupied about 50 economists. Moreover, this quartet's output is largely for in-house use, for example, to provide guidance on the course of interest rates for the bank's securities traders. "I don't know a single outside client who's interested in our forecasts anymore," says Rham Bhagavatula, the leader of the quartet. While many on the bank's original economic team were laid off, 22 have relocated within the bank in jobs directly tied to making a profit; one survivor, for instance, is now an executive in the bank's credit-card unit.

Some economists laid off by corporations have managed to find jobs at service firms that supply forecasts for a fee. One such firm is Data Resources. Roger Brinner, the executive research director there, reports that "as corporations have cut back their economic staffs—some of whom we have hired—they have more need for outside vendors of broad economic data, such as us." As a result, he says, 1992 turned out to be "our best year ever in terms of revenues and profits."

Though the demand may have risen for the services provided by these firms, many businesses are simply relying less on forecasts in their operations. "One way that companies are reducing their dependence on forecasts is by responding more promptly and flexibly to unforeseen changes" in the business climate, says Victor Zarnowitz of the University of Chicago. In tracking the accuracy of forecasters, he notes the increased use of just-in-time inventory procedures that help companies cope better with unexpected changes in customer demand.

Geoffrey H. Moore, the Columbia economist who directs its Center for International Business Cycle Research, believes that "the trend to leaner inventories lends a new degree of stability to the U.S. business cycle." The cycle, Moore says, has been subject in the past to some pretty wide swings "as companies have overstocked and then had to scramble to pare down excessive inventories often built up as a result of listening to unduly optimistic forecasts."

A few statistics make clear how remarkably trim most businesses were keeping their inventories in the early 1990s.

Around the start of the Clinton presidency, retail, wholesale, and factory inventories—taken together and adjusted for inflation—stood at only 1.4 times monthly sales, the lowest such reading in more than 40 years. This was also well below the inventory-to-sales ratios recorded in the early stages of earlier post–World War II upswings in the business cycle.

Meanwhile, a study of nearly 400 manufacturing plants in the United States by Paul Swamidass, a professor of operations management at Auburn University, shows 16% of the plants to be "extremely skilled" in just-in-time procedures, turning over their inventories, on the average, once a month, nearly twice the turnover rate for the group as a whole. The study, sponsored by the National Association of Manufacturers, also shows that an additional 44% of the factories have programs under way to enable them to "excel" soon in just-in-time operations. As such trends progress, businesses will find they require far less in the warehouse to cover a given jump in demand. This in turn will enable them to depend less on what the economic forecasters may be predicting.[8]

Even economists with superior forecasting records have felt the lay-off ax. "Accurate forecasting does not generate job security," says Richard B. Hoey, the chief economist of Dreyfus. Hoey lost his job at the New York subsidiary of a London-based securities firm in April 1991, though he had predicted the 1990–1991 recession. Hoey maintains, in fact, that before his firing he had "the best forecasting record of any Wall Street economist." After several months of unemployment, he was hired by Dreyfus, where he still works but divides his time between forecasting and managing the $120 million portfolio of a Dreyfus mutual fund.

Hoey is among the lucky ones. Another forecaster who was generally on the mark during his years as a business prophet is Robert H. Chandross of South Orange, New Jersey. Chandross was let go in 1991 by London-based Lloyds Bank and was still job hunting more than a year later. With a doctorate in economics from Princeton and experience at the New York Federal Reserve Bank and at the securities firm of Kidder Peabody, Chandross was the chief economist at Lloyd's headquarters for North America in New York. He was hired by Lloyds in 1984 with instructions to hire other economists and set up an economics department to help advise the bank's expanding North American operations. But Chandross soon found that economics wasn't viewed as a necessity at Lloyds. When business slowed in the 1990–1991 recession, the economist recalls that "there was a need to cut back my area, which wasn't regarded as a profit center and was thought of as a sort of nonessential adjunct to the sales force."

Asked if he would study economics again if he were back at Princeton, Chandross says that he still enjoys the subject greatly. However, on whether or not he would again pursue economics as a lifetime endeavor, he says, "I don't know—but I do know that the economics profession has sold people a bill of goods on which it can't possibly deliver—the notion that economists have the ability to make good long-range forecasts with any degree of consistency."

TROUBLE ON THE CAMPUS

On campuses, meanwhile, student interest in economics has ebbed. In 1991, for example, 1,042 doctorates were awarded in economics. While up slightly from the previous year, the 1991 figure was below the peak of 1,062 in 1989 as well as the totals for several earlier years. The number of master's degrees awarded in economics has also been edging down, and the number of bachelor's degrees with economics as the major field of study has leveled off after a long, sharp climb in the 1970s and 1980s. At Harvard University, the subject recently fell behind government as the most popular undergraduate major. In the mid-1980s, economics was easily number one, with government a distant third. In the mid-1980s, by no coincidence, investment firms recruited aggressively with lucrative pay offers aimed particularly at students majoring in economics. This practice abated, however, with the belt-tightening that occurred at financial services firms after the 1987 stock-market crash.

Economics, it should be added, is becoming a more rigorous major at some universities, which may deter students. In the mid-1980s, the subject, considered relatively easy, was a favorite major of Harvard athletes, especially football and hockey players; 18 of the 28 members of Harvard's varsity hockey team in the winter of 1984–1985, for example, were economics majors. At that time, Harvard students majoring in economics were not required to take any calculus; now they must do so. "Now, when you look at a football or hockey program telling about the team members, you no longer can draw any close connection between economics and the players," says Benjamin Friedman, chairman of Harvard's economics department.

Another deterrent to studying economics may be the subject's evident failure, as we have seen, to provide clear answers to the array of long-term problems facing the economy. After World War II, when the ideas of John Maynard Keynes prevailed in classrooms, it was widely accepted, as we have seen, that the economy could be made to prosper through the well-timed application of fiscal measures. The economy's difficulties in the 1970s gave rise to the monetarist school, led by Milton Friedman, which claimed that carefully controlled growth of the money supply was the key to prosperity. In the 1980s, the supply-side economists, under Arthur Laffer, gained clout with their notion that tax-cutting would induce prosperity.

The economy's continuing problems have cast doubt over all these prescriptions. Yet, new answers are not emerging. "As far as I know, there's nothing very new on the theoretical front going on," says Thurow. "It's lamentable," he adds, "that nobody seems to be doing much research on what happens in a modern economy like ours when you have falling real estate prices. I've called three our four universities and the answer I get is that nobody seems to be working on this very pertinent question." Mary Rosenbaum of the Atlanta Fed finds it disheartening that "there has been so little effort by economists to construct good models that could provide some guidance for the newly independent countries of Eastern Europe" as they adjust, often painfully, to market-oriented economic systems.

As doubts about the validity of prescriptions have grown, internecine quarreling at universities has sharply increased within the different schools of economic thought. Some monetarists claim that the Federal Reserve has tended to be too restrictive, keeping too tight a lid on the money supply. However, other monetarists hold a very different view. In August 1992, Milton Friedman told an interviewer that the money supply was growing "much too slowly," and he warned as a consequence of the "danger that we are going to have another recession." The situation, he proclaimed, "looks very scary."[9] But around the same time, other monetarists, monitoring other versions of the money supply, maintained that Fed policy was, if anything, too loose. They deemed M2 a misleading indicator because, they believed, its sluggishness largely reflected a shifting of funds from high-yielding certificate of deposits, as they came due, to other monetary categories not embraced by M2.

Jerry Jordan, now president of the Cleveland Federal Reserve Bank, is a leader of this contingent of monetarists. In December 1992, with the economy clearly on an expansionary course, he argued in a speech to the Cleveland Chapter of the NABE that the Fed policy, contrary to Milton Friedman's claim, was loose enough "to promote economic growth." Jordan questioned Friedman's worry about a new recession and his perennial focus on the broad M2 version of the money supply. Jordan contended in his speech that "it is not clear that M2 is still a reliable indicator of the thrust of monetary policy."[10] Predictably, Friedman was unimpressed by such arguments. In March 1993, though his predicted recession still had not materialized, he complained, "The Fed has only been paying lip service to meeting its monetary targets." And, he went on, "Alan Greenspan would have no trouble meeting the targets if that were truly his first priority."[11]

At the root of this squabbling among the monetarists, as Robert Giordano of Goldman Sachs observes, is that the "money supply becomes increasingly difficult to define as the financial system develops . . . substitutes for bank deposits as a means of payment." This is "especially true," Giordano adds, recalling Charles Goodhart's dictum, "if the central bank diligently follows a money-supply targeting policy."[12]

The Fed, in fact, appeared exceedingly confused about how to manage monetary policy as the Bush presidency neared an end. In October 1992, at a news conference in Tokyo, Greenspan told reporters, "No models can explain the types of patterns we are having." The American economy was remaining sluggish despite repeated reductions, induced by the Fed, in short-term interest rates. The Fed's customary techniques for analyzing the economy, Greenspan added, were "simply failing" to guide the monetary agency as well as they once had done—a comment reminiscent of Arthur Burns' claim years earlier that the "old rules" were no longer working as they once had.[13] (The Fed, as it happened, subsequently reduced, by a modest amount, its target for M2 growth in 1993, suggesting a victory of sorts for the Jordan monetarist camp.)

Disputes among monetarists over which version of the money supply is best and should serve as a policy guide has even inspired some Federal Reserve poetry. In the June 1992 issue of the Cleveland Federal Reserve Bank's monthly review, an anonymous staff member (whose boss, of course, is Jerry Jordan) offers a poem about the quarrel, presented in the style of Edgar Allen Poe's classic *The Raven*. Called *The Maven*, the poem tells of a weary, worried "Fed economist." He wonders in the first person if M2, which grew so slowly through much of 1992 that it was a cause of the squabbling between monetarists, is still a valid measure. The economist is visited late one night by a stately "money Maven." The last few verses of the poem are not designed to please all monetarists, but they do fairly capture the confusion and discord within the group:

> Was this stern, gaunt man a theorist or a much more
>   practiced realist
> In the ways of tracking money and the relationships it
>   bore?
> How many forecasters had he seen wander, countless
>   numbers in need of launder,
> Through deposit shifts escaping ponder of the man
>   planted on my floor?
> "Tell me why you've come to visit," I pleaded, shaking to
>   the core:
>   Quoth the Maven, "M2 no more."

"Prophet!" said I, "Curse of Fed! Speak not of funds rate
and money unwed!
Whether supply-sider sent, or whether fine-tuner's cloth
you wore,
Allay my fears! Deny M's broken; don't leave me with my
compass croakin'—
Of M2's growth rate there's no jokin'—tell me truly, I
implore:
Is there solace in some measure, pleasure found, my faith
restored?"
Quoth the Maven, "M2 no more."

And the Maven, still he hovers, present as I reach for
covers
Of dusty tomes on M1A and control schemes I must
explore.
Bears no witness, reserves nor base; Milton's bust and
unknowns I face.
And the lamp-light o'er him streaming throws his shadow
on the floor:
And my soul from out that shadow that lies floating on
the floor
Shall be lifted—I've found M4![14]

Not to be outdone, economists generally favoring Keynesian
concepts have a quarrel of their own over how harmful the
perennial federal budgets deficit may be—though the dispute
has not yet been poeticized. Many share the view of President
Clinton's advisers that the deficit is too large, tends to suppress
savings and investment, and should be reduced. But some, such
as Robert Eisner of Northwestern University, take a very different position. Eisner calls the government's measuring of the
deficit "outrageously misleading" and argues that the shortfall
"is probably too small" for the good of the economy, rather than
too large. Eisner claims that much of the deficit reflects outlays
for physical assets—roads, bridges, buildings, schools, and military hardware. These expenditures, he contends, should be
taken out of the budget's expense column and treated instead
as capital investments, as would happen on a corporation's bal-

ance sheet. The budget deficit, he declares, "is completely misunderstood; most people literally don't know what they're talking about."

However, many other academics of Keynesian persuasion disagree strongly, with this view. Harvard's Benjamin Friedman, for example, sharply differs with the Eisner argument that the deficit is largely a bogeyman created by improper accounting. "Eisner says all this building of roads and highways should be a capital expense, but in the Reagan and Bush years there wasn't much of that sort of spending by the government going on, except perhaps in the military," Friedman says. "Moreover, what really matters is the trajectory of the budget deficit, and however you measure it, the deficit is a lot bigger than it used to be before Reagan; the direction in peacetime always used to be down, but now it's up, with the result that the national saving rate is a lot smaller." A Goldman Sachs study supports the idea that little of what the government spends is for the purposes that Eisner mentions. The study finds that in 1991 and 1992, for instance, nondefense capital investments, after depreciation, averaged only about $11 billion a year, a relatively tiny amount when the annual budget deficits were ranging far above $200 billion.[15]

The supply-side economists have tended to argue with one another since Wanniski first met Craig Roberts. But the decibel level has increased since the economy's troubles in the wake of Washington's experiment with supply-side theory in the 1980s and the supply-siders' loss of influence at the White House. Such is the supply-siders' disarray and confusion, in fact, that it is difficult to ascertain exactly where many of them stand. Laffer, for instance, announced in 1992 that he planned to vote for Bill Clinton rather than George Bush. Yet, Bartley's editorials in *The Wall Street Journal* indicated a clear preference, albeit with serious reservations, for Bush. Meanwhile, attempting to rewrite history, Roberts claimed in *Commentary* magazine that "no supply-side economist inside or outside the Reagan administration ever said that tax cuts would pay for themselves."[16]

Disagreement and confusion have occurred even among the

small group of academic economists who make up the Business Cycle Dating Committee of the National Bureau of Economic Research. These seven economists, headed by Robert Hall of Stanford University, are charged by the government with deciding when the business cycle has changed direction. Drawn from Yale, Harvard, Columbia, the University of Chicago, and Northwestern as well as Stanford, these professors meet periodically to assess the business scene and determine—presumably without political bias—whether the economy is expanding or in a recession. To decide, the group carefully studies dozens of economic indicators, and usually there is fairly prompt agreement about the economy's condition.

However, the economy's prolonged sluggishness in the early 1990s left the professors uncertain over whether the recession that clearly began in July 1990 was still under way or whether a feeble new recovery was in progress. Finally, after much indecision and debate, the committee ruled in December 1992 that the economy in fact had been in an upswing of the business cycle since March 1991. Thus, a full 21 months elapsed between the start of the recovery from the 1990–1991 recession and the committee's recognition of the event. "We waited much too long and were too indecisive," remarks Geoffrey Moore, the committee member from Columbia University.

Amid all the academic squabbling, economists such as Stephen Marglin feel—perhaps for good reason—left out in the cold. Marglin, a tenured economics professor at Harvard, has long believed that economic policy should be conducted along Socialist, if not Marxist, lines, a conviction he came to after working years ago in India. However, the demise of leftist regimes in Eastern Europe and the Soviet Union has left him "suffocated" at Harvard, he says. He notes, for example, that he no longer is invited to serve as a guest lecturer in the university's famous EC10 economics course, a part of Harvard's core curriculum that undergraduates must take. Marglin has complained about this snubbing to Martin Feldstein, the professor in charge of EC10, but to no avail. "Feldstein wants little to do with opinions about the economy that are far different from the standard, conventional ones," Marglin says. As a result, he claims, "our students aren't being exposed to a broad enough spectrum of economic alternatives."

NEW DIRECTIONS

Over 60 years ago, John Maynard Keynes was taunted by a colleague for having altered his views on how the economy worked. In the 1920s, Keynes had emphasized the importance of monetary policy, but in the 1930s, as the Great Depression deepened, he changed his position, stressing instead the paramount role of fiscal policy and downplaying the importance of monetary policy. When his colleague chided him, Keynes paused briefly and then responded: "When the facts change, I change my mind. What do you do, sir?"

The Great Depression was, of course, the overwhelming new fact that prompted a change in Keynes' analysis. He concluded that monetary policy would not be of much help in reviving business activity but that a sharp increase in government spending would indeed serve to spur demand. To a large extent, this strategy was employed in the United States and elsewhere, and as a result, Keynesian economics dominated policy making through the early post–World War II years.

However, the facts keep changing. Major developments in the 1970s were the big oil price increases initiated by OPEC and the severe inflation that accompanied them. Keynesianism could not cope with the new facts and this failure, says N. Gregory Mankiw, a Harvard economist, "caused a period of confusion, division and excitement that is still going on." The confusion is likely to continue into the indefinite future, adding to the uncertainty about what the economy will be like a decade or two from now. Economists simply cannot agree on how the economy works, and no new consensus seems likely any time soon. "We're all waiting for a new Maynard Keynes to lead us," says Robert Dederick, chief economist of Chicago's Northern Trust Co.

Another major change has been the increasing internationalization of the American economy. David Hale, chief economist of Kemper Financial Services in Chicago, says: "In the 1990s, there will be only two kinds of business economists—those who follow the world economy and those who are unemployed." And Bob Dederick of Northern Trust notes that "the breakdown in fixed exchange rates in the early 1970s has made life more complicated for economists." At the same time, of course, floating exchange rates have created jobs for many economists who predict future currency exchange rates.

In the United States, there are roughly 100,000 men and women who either are or at least call themselves economists, and the increased confusion about the future is embarrassing for them. In the days of the Keynesian consensus, businesses had come to trust economic forecasts, and many had built up large staffs of economists. Federal, state, and local governments hired more economists to help set their agendas. But with the growing skepticism about what economists can do, such staffs have been cut or eliminated. At one anguished moment in his presidency, Ronald Reagan asked: "Do we really need a Council of Economic Advisers?"[17]

Looking to the future, businesses and governments still must plan, of course, so someone will have to make forecasts. The federal government, despite Reagan's question, still has a CEA for the president to turn to. Business planners increasingly subscribe to advisory services, which are less costly than maintaining economists in-house, and just-in-time inventory procedures, which make companies less vulnerable to bad forecasts, seem bound to come into ever wider use.

Economic consultants, meanwhile, are striving to keep their models abreast of changing economic conditions. Vincent J. Malanga, the president of LaSalle Economics in New York, reports, for example, that "I have reduced the weight I assign to residential home construction, whose importance in the overall economic picture has diminished as a result of tax-law changes that discourage real-estate speculation." At the same time, recognizing the greater role of foreign trade in the American economy, Malanga says he has increased the weight he assigns to exports and imports.

The upheaval in the economics profession also has deeply affected academic economists. "Arguments have become in-

Keynesian	James Tobin Paul A. Samuelson Robert Solow	The market occasionally fails, producing high unemployment and requiring fiscal stimulus. Monetary policy isn't much help.
Monetarist	Milton Friedman Karl Brunner	Monetary policy is more powerful than fiscal policy, but it works with long and unpredictable lags.
Supply-Side	Jude Wanniski Paul Craig Roberts Arthur Laffer	Cutting marginal tax rates gives individuals incentive to work, save, and invest.
Real Business Cycle	Charles Plosser	External shocks mainly determine economy's course.
New Classical or Rational Expectations	Robert E. Lucas, Jr.	The market works well and government intervention may do more harm than good.
Austrian	Friedrich A. Hayek	Stresses dangers of any intervention.

Figure 7-1   A Glance at Some Economic Schools

creasingly sophisticated," says Allan H. Meltzer, who teaches at Carnegie-Mellon University and remains a monetarist, though far less strict a one than in the 1970s. "Keynesians used to assume that wages were rigid," Meltzer recalls. "But now economists ask, why is that so? Bad ideas get killed—the idea that monetarism can be used to make reliable forecasts, for instance."

Academic economists, it should be stressed, recognize full well that their work ultimately must be of value in the world beyond their campuses. Noting the continual emergence of new ideas, Harvard's Gregory Mankiw is hopeful that "at least some of these recent developments will permanently change the way in which economists of all sorts think about and discuss economic behavior and policy." (See Figure 7-1 for a digest of economics schools.)

One view that has gained adherents in recent years is that governmental intervention in the economy—whether through shifts in fiscal or in monetary policy—cannot greatly alter the general situation. The logic underlying this theory of "rational expectations" is that the public inevitably will see through the government's efforts to change the economic course. The so-called New Classical economists subscribing to this view, led by Robert E. Lucas, Jr., of the University of Chicago, hold that individuals, taken as a whole, will respond immediately to policy changes and in so doing will render any new policy ineffective. If, for example, the government plans to raise taxes six months down the road in order to trim the budget deficit, people will curtail their spending in anticipation of having to pay for the tax boost. The reduced spending level, in turn, will serve to increase the budget deficit since, as the economy slows, tax revenues will ebb and federal outlays to help the newly jobless will rise.

Another emerging concept, not unrelated to the idea of rational expectations, is the "real business-cycle" theory. This doctrine holds that periods of exceptional growth and periods of economic contraction basically stem from external developments that jolt the economy from time to time, rather than from shifts in fiscal or monetary policy. These jolts from the outside may range from earthquakes to technological breakthroughs to the impact of cartels on the availability of key materials, as happened in the case of the oil-price surge in the early 1970s. In fact, Charles Plosser of the University of Rochester, an early advocate of the real business-cycle idea, cites external factors, rather than federal policies, as the main reason for recent recessions: oil-supply squeezes for the recessions of 1973–1975 and 1981–1982 and the savings-and-loan debacle and the Persian Gulf crisis for the milder 1990–1991 recession.

The message of real business-cycle theory, much like that of rational expectations, is that there is little policy makers can do to change the economic picture and, as a result, the best policy for the government is to leave things pretty much alone. The Federal Reserve's reluctance to spur monetary growth when the economy was so lackluster in the early 1990s, some economists believe, may have reflected this reasoning more than any fear at the Fed of resurgent inflation.

Still another concept attracting interest is the idea—called "new growth" theory—that more attention should be focused on how economic growth is best achieved. Less doctrinaire than other emerging concepts, new growth theory asks many more questions than it answers: What, for instance, will be the precise impact on economic growth of such diverse factors as federal regulations, technological advances, and pricing practices in, for example, the auto industry? The goals of new growth theorists are ambitious indeed: to determine more clearly what makes economies grow and to see whether or not economies that start out, say, poorer than other economies may eventually achieve equal status. Through the use of increasingly sophisticated computers, new-growth theorists are optimistic that they can eventually supply such answers.

A CONTINUING INFLUENCE

For all their miscalculations and the distrust that now surrounds their profession, economists will continue to exert a powerful influence over how we live. Practitioners of the dismal science are not about to retreat behind Trappist walls or trade in their hard-earned advanced degrees for licenses as haruspices. They will continue to play a crucial, if diminished, role because, as Keynes' response to his colleague's taunt suggests, they are willing and able to change as facts change.

A recent illustration of this flexibility is supplied by Robert Reich, a Rhodes Scholar at Oxford with President Clinton and now secretary of labor, as well as a former lecturer at Harvard's Kennedy School of Government. His advanced degree happens to be in law rather than economics, but his distinguished academic career at the Kennedy School was devoted largely to teaching economics. His influence within the economic arena during Bill Clinton's drive for the presidency was substantial: before signing on as President Clinton's labor secretary, Reich was in charge of the Clinton economic transition team.

During much of his early academic career, Reich preached that the United States sorely needed an industrial policy. He argued that Washington, in its wisdom, should channel resources to the industries deemed most likely to secure a competitive, prosperous American economy. But Reich prudently altered this position. Perhaps he was influenced by Hayek, who cautioned long ago that such a policy in an economy as vast and diverse as America's was not possible; no single mind or planning authority, the Austrian economist held, could possibly "survey the millions of connections between the ever more numerous interlocking separate activities which have become indispensable for the efficient use of modern technology."[18]

The Reich who emerged as Clinton's close adviser urged a policy for the Clinton administration that bore little resemblance to what he had advocated a decade earlier. Taking account of the increased globalization of corporations, Reich now urged measures designed to make the United States a more attractive place for footloose companies, free to move about the globe and set up shop where circumstances seemed most appealing. There was little place in this new Reich prescription for channeling funds to those American businesses seen as the most promising by all-knowing central planners. Rather, the new focus was to put resources into education, in the belief that a well-trained work force will attract global companies, and into the infrastructure, in the belief that good roads, bridges, airports, and so on will also serve as an international magnet.

"This change of mind on Bob Reich's part is a good thing," says Robert Solow of MIT. "It's proof that people in our business can learn and change our minds."

Plowing funds into roads and educational facilities is a more practical matter for economists than esoteric arguing over what version of the money supply may prove most meaningful or just how freely currency exchange rates should be allowed to fluctuate in relationship to one another. Practicality, in fact, is crucial to the profession's assuming a more beneficial role in helping to manage the nation's affairs. A shift in this direction is evident, I should add, in a recent survey to determine the most cited economist in the United States. The winner, with 676 citations in scholarly journals during a 12-month period, is hardly a household name: Richard A. Posner. Posner is a senior lecturer at the University of Chicago—but at the university's law school rather than in its economics department. He also is a judge on the Seventh U.S. Circuit Court; his popularity as an economist lies in his ability to apply an economic perspective to legal issues. Milton Friedman, with 467 citations, was a distant sixth and Keynes, with only 358 citations, was seventeenth on the list of 25.[19]

Greater practicality is evident as well in classrooms. Guest lecturers in Harvard's EC10 economics course are now more apt to deal in highly practical concerns than to ponder, for example, whether monetarism makes more sense in treating today's economy than a fiscal approach. Typical of this new fashion was a lecture delivered on November 18, 1992, by David Ellwood, a Kennedy School expert on labor and poverty issues who has joined the Clinton administration. "How can we help the working poor today?" he asked the several hundred Harvard students assembled in the large, multitiered auditorium of the university's Memorial Hall. Ellwood went on to propose very specific remedies, including precisely targeted tax credits, educational incentives, and a higher minimum wage. He also put forward, in considerable detail, a program to train welfare recipients and get more of them working. Along the way, he found time to joke about "old-fashioned macroeconomists" who continue to focus on the "big picture" and, he said, "must take a secret blood oath by which they vow" to focus only on such things as endorsing free trade.

I recall, by way of comparison, attending an EC10 lecture on foreign trade given by Martin Feldstein during the mid-1980s. The professor talked in very general terms about how shifts in trade balances develop, and the effects of such developments on the overall level of economic activity. In contrast to the rapt attention accorded Ellwood in 1992—including a burst of applause at the end of the lecture—the student reaction to Feldstein's trade lecture was somnolent.

The profession's shift away from macroeconomics and its greater emphasis on a microeconomic approach to specific problems signifies a return of sorts to previous practice rather than an entirely new trend. Microeconomics typically focuses on the economy's many individual facets, how they interact to determine particular price, production, and income levels, and how various resources are allocated. Macroeconomics, in contrast, focuses on the overall level of economic activity, as seen through such aggregated data as the GDP.

"Macroeconomics is a relatively young field," notes Mary Rosenbaum. Like many economic historians, she credits Keynes with the emergence of macroeconomics in the 1930s as a new approach to dealing with the severe economic problems of the time. But now, she believes, "We're witnessing a return to a better balance between the macro and the micro approach to economic challenges, and I have to believe that's a welcome change, given the failures of the various macro schools in recent years."

A bold effort to bring classroom economics closer to specific issues and problems was launched recently at Middlebury College in Vermont. The college introduced EC475, Monetary Policy and Financial Institutions, for seniors majoring in economics. Taught by Dewey Daane, a retired Federal Reserve Board governor, assisted by a former executive of Marine Midland Bank, the course features guest lectures with extensive practical experience in both Washington and the corporate world. Among the visitors in 1991–1992, the first year of the course, were Paul Volcker, the former Fed chairman; Dennis Weatherstone, the chairman of J.P. Morgan; Stephen H. Axilrod, the New York-based vice chairman of Nikko Securities International; Albert Wojnilower, a managing director of First Boston; and Scott Pardee, the chairman of Yamaichi International in New York.

"These are people talking about how the real economic world works—how actual technical aspects of the implementation of economic policy work," says David Colander, the chairman of Middlebury's economics department. The students, Colander claims, will end up knowing more about the operations behind monetary policy than many of the professors in the field. "Most colleges teach generalities," he says, "without acknowledging that presidencies are made or broken on the specifics" of economic management. Keith Reardon, a graduate of the course, agrees, saying it was "the most fascinating economics course I've ever taken; you really learn how policy is set, on a practical, nontheoretical level."

Even in the theoretical realm, economists not engaged in internecine squabbling are trying harder to address real-world problems, and the approaches beginning to emerge seem a good deal more practical than in the recent past. Consider new growth theory. Among its leading advocates is Paul M. Romer. Still in his thirties, he teaches at the University of California at Berkeley. However, Romer is not content to devote his energies only to academia. He has drafted specific policy recommendations and urged them on real-world planners—including his own father, Roy Romer, who happens to be the governor of Colorado and the chairman of the influential National Governors' Association. The proposals include one that would compel taxpayers to place part of their incomes in savings accounts. Another proposal spells out a payroll savings plan for relatively young employees that the government would match and pay for through new sales taxes.

A powerful influence on Wall Street, meanwhile, has been Fischer Black, an MIT economist who left the ivory towers of Cambridge, Massachusetts, for a partnership at Goldman Sachs in New York. Working with Myron Scholes, another former academic, Black's mathematical work has provided a foundation for pricing a range of sophisticated financial products, such as various sorts of options now widely used at Wall Street's busy trading desks.

Departing his ivory tower at the University of Chicago's economics department, Jacob A. Frenkel, a native of Israel, first moved to Washington, where he served as research director of the IMF, and then, in 1991, to Israel, where he serves as governor of that nation's central bank. Utilizing his expertise in monetary economics, Frenkel has since waged a difficult but remarkably successful campaign to bring down Israel's high inflation rate. The challenge of the central-bank job, he says, more than makes up for a huge cut in pay—to about $30,000 a year in Israel from a tax-free salary of over $150,000 at the IMF.

Traveling abroad as well has been Jeffrey Sachs, who became a tenured professor in Harvard's economics department at the remarkably young age of twenty-nine. Immensely popular with students, Sachs, now in his late thirties, spends much of his time providing practical advice to foreign governments struggling with troubled economies. These assignments have ranged from advising Mongolia how best to privatize a herd of 24 million yaks to helping Bolivia design a debt buy-back plan to rein in that nation's runaway inflation.

"My life's work is to try to help desperately hurt countries get out of serious economic crises," Sachs says, adding, "I am a technically trained mathematical economist, and what I do is based on economic history; I'm not just a preacher."[20] He does not attempt to estimate, however, what is the most helpful to him—preaching, economic history, or mathematics—when it comes to dealing with Mongolian yaks.

A greater emphasis on practicality can be detected also in President Clinton's choice for the chairmanship of the CEA. Bypassing such leading macroeconomists as Princeton's Alan Blinder, Clinton tapped Laura d'Andrea Tyson, a professor at the University of California at Berkeley who, as one pundit puts it, "chooses to work in English rather than algebra and to study the real economy rather than build sand castles."[21] Tyson's expertise is in the interaction of governmental policies and trade flows, with an emphasis on what constitutes fair play. Much of her work has been to examine how to level the international playing field in trade. This is a very far cry from taking a secret blood oath endorsing the principle of free trade.

Economists and baseball players have little in common. Baseball players usually are paid far more than economists, retire much sooner, and, by and large, are brawnier if not brainier. But there is a common thread linking the two professions: trading cards. Yes, today economists too are celebrated in trading cards. Indeed, those whose visages and histories appear on cards range across the ideological spectrum—from John Kenneth Galbraith to Milton Friedman, whose work and academic background are neatly synopsized alongside the Friedman dictum, "Inflation is always and everywhere a monetary phenomenon."

As such attention indicates, economists may have a somewhat brighter future than it would seem from all the problems engulfing their profession. Any profession that warrants trading-card celebrity assuredly must have a decent future—though the cards admittedly are selling for a good deal less than, for example, a Mickey Mantle card will command; a set of 29 economist cards can be purchased for only $5 from the economics department of the University of Michigan at Flint.

The profession's resilience is evident, moreover, in the determination of many economists to make their voices heard during the 1992 presidential campaign. As many as 110 economists endorsed a widely circulated advertisement supporting Bush's economics and warning that Clinton's would "hurt the American economy." A short while later, 556 other economists countered with an answering statement in support of Clintonomics.

As a new century approaches, the general level of prosperity will depend in no small measure on the extent to which policy makers continue to heed economists' advice and on the soundness of that advice. There is no sure way, unfortunately, to test beforehand the wisdom of what may be proposed.

Only this much is certain: economists, for all their mistakes, will continue to exert a major influence. However wrong Keynes may have been about how best to treat the economy's ills, he was correct about the power of economists themselves. "Practical men who believe themselves to be quite exempt from any intellectual influences," he wrote in 1936, "are usually the slaves of some defunct economist."[22] Keynes is now defunct himself, but his statement stands. At home and abroad, for better or worse, the ideas of present-day practitioners of the dismal science may some day enslave practical men.

Conclusion

The adventures of the modern economists, from such early luminaries as Paul Samuelson and Milton Friedman to today's young comers, inspire varied reactions. The off-target forecasting prompts skepticism, even cynicism, about the profession's very worth. There is bewilderment at such disparate assessments of an economic landscape that seems in essence not really all that difficult to survey. And there is concern about the economy's prospects in the longer term when no expert's counsel—Keynesian, monetarist, supply-side, or whatever else—presents a valid formula for sound economic management.

In sum, the profession's record in the half century since Keynes and White sat down at Bretton Woods provokes dismay. My sagacious colleague Lindley Clark has even urged that the Nobel Prize for economics be discontinued—and he is absolutely right. (In fact, the Nobel Prize for economics is not a prize endowed in Alfred Nobel's will but a Johnny-come-lately award, instituted in 1969 and endowed by the central bank of Sweden.) Robert Dunn, an economics professor at George Washington University, is not among the more than 30 economists to have won or shared the prize, but he surely deserves some sort of award for his observation that some three-quarters of the recipients are from either the United States or Britain, nations with relatively poor economic records. Meanwhile, there have been no winners from Germany, Japan, or any of the fast-growing smaller Asian nations, all of whose economies have performed in superior fashion.

As ineffective and misguided as the modern economists by and large have been, useful lessons can still be drawn from the economy's record in the difficult postwar decades, and the most valuable of these is simply, I submit, that the business cycle endures. It has survived fixed and then floating exchange rates, fiscal fine-tuning and then rigid monetary rules, and even tax slashing in the name of a balanced budget. It no doubt will continue to endure, surviving prescriptions yet to be devised.

Textbooks devote countless pages to examining the business cycle: this tendency of the economy to expand, go into a recession, and then expand once again—a sort of two-steps-forward and then one-step-back progression. But my favorite analysis of why the business cycle endures comes from a noneconomist, a *Wall Street Journal* reader named Russell Fowler, who recently retired from a county-government job in upstate New York. Fowler says: "Maybe the reason the business cycle endures is the economy is solidly based on human nature. When things are going good, some human reactions occur: overconfidence, complacency, poor workmanship, greed, overexpansion, mistakes; all bad and leading to a downturn. Then, when things are going bad, there's a tendency to shape up and turn things around. Maybe that's all there is to it."

Amen. That is as sound an explanation of the why of the cycle as I have encountered. The message is clear: so long as human nature is with us, so will be the business cycle. And Fowler could have said more. To focus on the business cycle affords economy watchers—be they ink-stained journalists or powerful planners setting policy—a degree of perspective not readily achieved if one becomes too closely wedded to a particular economic doctrine.

I am reminded, in this regard, of two very different assessments of the economic outlook made during 1992. One was by the oft-quoted monetarist, Milton Friedman, and the other was by Geoffrey Moore, who labors in relative obscurity at Columbia University. Concentrating on the sluggish behavior of M2,

Friedman publicly and repeatedly expressed concern over the staying power of the young recovery. He characterized the outlook as scary, warning that the economy could sink back into a recession.

As director of Columbia's Center for International Business Cycle Research, Moore tended to take a broader view of factors shaping the economy's course as 1992 went along. M2 was but one of the many economic indicators that he monitored closely and sought to place within a business-cycle framework. He reminded worried callers—and I was one—that unemployment, for instance, is usually slow to recede after a recession and may even increase for a while after the rest of the economy has begun to recover. When Friedman and other noted economists were worrying loudly that the recession might soon resume, Moore was quietly reassuring people that the economic up-swing, albeit a relatively weak one, would probably persist, at the least, through 1992 and on into 1993. And, of course, he was correct.

My own appreciation of the business cycle's importance in economy watching dates back more than three decades, to my days as a young reporter in the *Journal*'s Chicago bureau. Among other ignominious chores, my duties included covering the annual conventions of dealers in household appliances, which was held each year in the city's cavernous Merchandise Mart. My practice was to try to buttonhole as many dealers as possible during the several days of the convention, in search of exceed-ingly specific information about how business at the various dealerships was faring. After perhaps 50 or 60 such interviews, I would attempt to pull my notes together into a trend-catching feature article, summarizing the overall condition, at least at the retail level, of the nation's appliance industry. The dealers, as I recall, were remarkably candid with me, to a point where they would often disclose precise data on recent sales, prices, and even profits, all compared with levels several months, as well as a year, earlier.

Reviewing my notes, I soon detected a striking pattern. After several years when the appliance business had been relatively good, the dealers would tell me that business was good, no

matter the current situation. Usually, I would press on, asking
for instance whether sales in the last several weeks were actually running as much ahead of year-earlier rates as, say, they
had six months ago. More often than not, the happy-sounding
dealer who had just told me how good business was would
hesitatingly report that as a matter of fact sales in the last few
weeks were, well, actually down a fraction from the year-earlier
level. If I pressed on a bit more, I would also find that the
dealer's inventories had taken an unexpected jump in the past
few weeks. "No doubt a fluke" was the usual comment.

A similar pattern emerged, but in reverse, when I interviewed the dealers after a long spell of poor business. Invariably, the initial response was that things were terrible. However,
further questioning often turned up reports that sales, while
perhaps still weak, were no longer lagging quite as badly as
three months ago and that inventories, while still excessive,
were getting a little leaner. In the end, it was a tricky endeavor
to make sense out of what the dealers had to say. Usually, their
initial pronouncements about the business situation proved, on
closer questioning, to be almost wholly backward looking, and
of course, my concern as a reporter was with the present and
the future. Complicating the job was the fact that the dealers
tended to tailor their planning—buying appliances, expanding
stores, hiring help, and so on—to their experiences over the
past year or so rather than to recent sales and inventory developments.

I recall a particularly difficult series of interviews in early
1960. Invariably, the dealers first would tell me—and I believe
they meant it—how great things were. But then it developed
that, yes, inventories were climbing sharply and, no, sales in
the last few weeks really were no longer running ahead of a
year earlier. Eventually, I produced a quite gloomy article that
bore little resemblance to the expressions of optimism that I
had heard initially. The headline on the *Journal*'s front page
was: "Appliance Anxiety—Worried Dealers Cut Prices as Sales
Lag, Inventories Pile Up." The story, which ran in January
1960, proved, as things turned out, well worth the effort. It
was among the first articles anywhere to suggest that the econ-

omy, which had been expanding, might soon enter a new recession. In fact, a full-blown recession started in April 1960. Was it any wonder, I later thought, reflecting on the misplaced ebullience of those appliance dealers, that the economy periodically gets ahead of itself and winds up in a recession?

There is a footnote to the story that seems worth adding. To supplement what I had learned at the Merchandise Mart from the dealers and to round out my reporting, I decided to phone several key appliance manufacturers. To my surprise, I found that the manufacturers, far from cutting back their production schedules in response to rising inventories and slackening sales at the dealerships, were sharply expanding their output. I recall, for instance, that the refrigerator division of Hupp was setting its first-quarter production schedule for a huge 57% increase over the comparable rate a year earlier.

After my article appeared, the chairman of Owens-Corning Fiberglas, a major supplier of insulation to the appliance industry, was so upset with its gloomy tenor that he complained to the publisher of Dow Jones, which owns *The Wall Street Journal* and on whose board the Owens-Corning chairman then sat. He claimed that his own executives were very bullish about the appliance industry's near-term prospects and, in fact, had just told him that demand from appliance makers was strong and rising. My publisher backed me up, to my great relief, and wisely suggested that perhaps we should simply let events take their course—which soon led to the 1960–1961 recession. The Owens-Corning chairman never apologized, but why should he have? He had supplied me with a valuable illustration of how myopic business planners, in this case at a supposedly well-run, blue-chip corporation, can be. I concluded that as long as there is an appliance industry—never mind automobiles—the business cycle will surely endure.

The greatest benefit that an appreciation of the business cycle brings to those of us condemned to scrutinize the economy's behavior is, I am convinced, its value as a compass. Its accuracy, while hardly of pinpoint precision, is nonetheless sufficient to prevent too great a degree of confusion over what may be evolving on the economic scene. By appreciating the importance of the business cycle, we know to be humble. Armed with humility, economic planners will suffer no dashed hopes if their prescriptions fail to produce a recession-free era. We also know to be patient. Expansions and recessions will run the course in their own good time, with remarkably little regard for policy shifts. The economy will tend to expand, for instance, until it runs up against too many constraints to further growth. These may take many forms: high interest rates, painful inflation, limited plant capacity, labor shortages, burdensome debt, excessive inventories, insufficient savings—the list goes on. Inevitably, the economic pace will slow. Perhaps business activity will even begin to retrench, precipitating a recession. Policy initiatives may delay the downturn by weeks or even months, but not indefinitely: the business cycle endures.

Doubtless, most economists will continue to disregard the business cycle as they go about mapping new pathways to utopia. A wonderful family doctor, who actually made house calls every day, used to give some sound advice to his patients. "Enjoy life," he would say. "Have some fun and do everything— but do it in moderation." That may be good advice, in a different context, for economists.

Have some fun. Continue to issue your forecasts, seeking to make them more accurate. Keep dreaming up ways to make the economy sounder and increase prosperity. But be moderate in what you claim and in what you expect, and remember that the business cycle, like human nature, is here to stay.

Notes

Chapter One

1. Charles A. Coombs, *The Arena of International Finance* (New York: John A. Wiley & Sons, 1976).

2. For a chronology of these events, see Peter M. Garber, "The Collapse of the Bretton Woods Fixed Exchange Rate System." Paper presented at the National Bureau of Economic Research conference, Retrospectives on the Bretton Woods System: Lessons for International Monetary Reform, Bretton Woods, N.H., October 5, 1991.

3. Darryl R. Francis, "Monthly Review," St. Louis Federal Reserve Bank, November 1971.

4. For a detailed report on these arrangements, see Kathryn M. Dominguez, "The Role of International Organizations in the Bretton Woods System." Paper presented at the National Bureau of Economic Research conference, Retrospectives on the Bretton Woods System: Lessons for International Monetary Reform, Bretton Woods, N.H., October 5, 1991.

5. See Michael Bordo, "The Bretton Woods International Monetary System: An Historical Overview." Paper presented at the National Bureau of Economic Research Conference, Retrospectives on the Bretton Woods System: Lessons for International Monetary Reform, Bretton Woods, N.H., October 5, 1991.

6. Ragnar Nurkse, *International Currency Experience—Lessons of the Inter-War Period* (Geneva, Switzerland: League of Nations, 1944).

7. Bordo, "The Bretton Woods International Monetary System."

8. *Post-War Currency Policy: The Collected Papers of John Maynard Keynes, vol. 25* (Cambridge, England: Cambridge University Press, 1980).

9. Harry Dexter White, March 1942 Draft, Box 8, White Papers, Mudd Library, Princeton University, Princeton, N.J.

10. G. John Ikenberry, "The Political Origins of Bretton Woods." Paper presented at the National Bureau of Economic Research conference, Retrospectives on the Bretton Woods System: Lessons for International Monetary Reform, Bretton Woods, N.H., October 5, 1991.

11. John Kenneth Galbraith, *Money: Whence It Came, Where It Went* (Boston: Houghton Mifflin, 1975).

12. Ibid.

13. Ikenberry, "The Political Origins of Bretton Woods."

14. Coombs, *The Arena of International Finance.*

15. Henry Kaufman, *Interest Rates, the Markets, and the New Financial World* (New York: Times Books, 1986).

16. Ibid.

17. Coombs, *The Arena of International Finance.*

18. Alfred L. Malabre, Jr., "Friedmanism: One Big Catch," *The Wall Street Journal*, January 2, 1970.

19. Alfred L. Malabre, Jr., "The Outlook," *The Wall Street Journal*, March 24, 1969.

Chapter Two

1. John Kenneth Galbraith, *Economics in Perspective* (Boston: Houghton Mifflin, 1987).

2. Ibid.

3. Michael Harrington, *Socialism* (New York: Saturday Review Press, 1970).

4. John Maynard Keynes, *The General Theory of Employment, Interest and Money* (New York: Harcourt Brace Jovanovich, 1965).

5. Robert Heilbroner, "After Keynes," *The New School Commentator* (February 1992).

6. Galbraith, *Economics in Perspective.*

7. Robert Sobel, *The Worldly Economists* (New York: The Free Press, 1980).

8. Walter W. Heller, *New Dimensions of Political Economy* (Cambridge, Mass.: Harvard University Press, 1966).

9. Raymond J. Saulnier, *Constructive Years: The U.S. Economy Under Eisenhower* (Lanham, Md.: University Press of America, 1991).

10. Arthur F. Burns, "Wesley Mitchell and the National Bureau," National Bureau of Economic Research, May 1949.

11. Saulnier, *Constructive Years.*

12. Sobel, *The Worldly Economists.*

13. Ibid.

14. William Greider, *The Secrets of the Temple: How the Federal Reserve Runs the Country* (New York: Simon & Schuster, 1987).

15. Milton Friedman, *Free to Choose* (New York: Harcourt Brace Jovanovich, 1980).

Chapter Three

1. Robert Sobel, *The Worldly Economists* (New York: The Free Press, 1980).

2. Arthur M. Schlesinger, Jr., *A Thousand Days: John F. Kennedy in the White House* (Boston: Houghton Mifflin, 1965).

3. Sobel, *The Worldly Economists.*

4. Walter W. Heller, *New Dimensions of Political Economy* (Cambridge, Mass.: Harvard University Press, 1966).

5. Sobel, *The Worldly Economists.*

6. W. Carl Biven, *Who Killed John Maynard Keynes?* (Homewood, Ill.: Dow-Jones Irwin, 1989).

7. Robert L. Bartley, *The Seven Fat Years* (New York: The Free Press, 1992).

8. William J. Barber, "The Spread of Economic Ideas," in *The Spread of Economic Ideas,* ed. David Colander and A. W. Coats (New York: Cambridge University Press, 1989).

9. Sobel, *The Worldly Economists.*

10. Doris Kearns, *Lyndon Johnson and the American Dream* (New York: Harper & Row, 1976).

11. William Greider, *Secrets of the Temple: How the Federal Reserve Runs the Country* (New York: Simon & Schuster, 1987).

12. Kearns, *Lyndon Johnson and the American Dream.*

Chapter Four

1. Alfred L. Malabre, Jr., "The New Uncertainty," *The Wall Street Journal,* November 17, 1967.

2. Michael K. Evans, *The Truth About Supply-Side Economics* (New York: Basic Books, 1983).

3. Alfred L. Malabre, Jr., "End of the Boom?" *The Wall Street Journal,* July 23, 1968.

4. Alfred L. Malabre, Jr., "Here Comes 1970," *The Wall Street Journal,* September 30, 1969.

5. Alfred L. Malabre, Jr., "The Outlook," *The Wall Street Journal,* August 11, 1969.

6. "Are Labor Costs Soaring?" An editorial in *The Advance,* December 26, 1970.

7. Alfred L. Malabre, Jr., "Heard in the Suite," *The Wall Street Journal,* December 5, 1985.

Chapter Five

1. Milton Friedman, "The Case for Monetary Rule," *Newsweek*, February 7, 1972.

2. Arthur F. Burns, interview with author, November 24, 1971.

3. Sam I. Nakagama, "Argus Weekly Staff Report," November 18, 1969.

4. Ibid.

5. Alfred L. Malabre, Jr., "The Outlook," *The Wall Street Journal*, December 22, 1969.

6. W. Gordon Lyle, interview with author, December 18, 1969.

7. Lindley H. Clark, Jr., "The Monetarist," *The Wall Street Journal*, October 7, 1981.

8. Karl Brunner and Allan Meltzer, *Monetary Economics* (London: Basil Blackwell, 1989).

9. Alfred L. Malabre, Jr., *Understanding the Economy: For People Who Can't Stand Economics* (New York: Dodd Mead, 1976).

10. Lindley H. Clark, Jr., "Federal Reserve U." *The Wall Street Journal*, July 20, 1972.

11. A. James Meigs, *Money Matters* (New York: Harper & Row, 1972).

12. Robert Giordano, "Economic Research: Financial Market Perspectives," Goldman, Sachs & Co., September 26, 1991.

13. William Greider, *Secrets of the Temple: How the Federal Reserve Runs the Country* (New York: Simon & Schuster, 1987).

14. William C. Melton, *Inside the Fed* (Homewood, Ill.: Dow-Jones Irwin, 1985).

15. Greider, *Secrets of the Temple.*

16. Paul Volcker and Toyoo Gyohten, *Changing Fortunes* (New York: Times Books, 1992).

17. Greider, *Secrets of the Temple.*

Chapter Six

1. Paul Blustein, "New Economics," *The Wall Street Journal*, October 8, 1981.

2. Alfred L. Malabre, Jr., "Tax-Cut Theorist," *The Wall Street Journal*, December 1, 1978.

3. "Review and Outlook." An editorial in *The Wall Street Journal*, August 4, 1976.

4. Robert L. Bartley, *The Seven Fat Years* (New York: The Free Press, 1992).

5. Blustein, "New Economics."

6. Michael K. Evans, *The Truth About Supply-Side Economics* (New York: Basic Books, 1983).

7. *Economic Report of the President*, February 1982.

8. *Economic Report of the President*, February 1983.

9. *Economic Report of the President*, February 1988.

10. Alfred L. Malabre, Jr., *Within Our Means* (New York: Random House, 1991).

11. Benjamin M. Friedman, *Day of Reckoning* (New York: Random House, 1988).

12. Alfred L. Malabre, Jr., "Tax-Cut Theorist," *The Wall Street Journal*, December 1, 1978.

13. Paul Blustein, "What's in Demand," *The Wall Street Journal*, October 12, 1981.

14. Alfred L. Malabre, Jr., *Beyond Our Means* (New York: Random House, 1987).

15. Paul Krugman, *The Age of Diminished Expectations* (Cambridge, Mass.: MIT Press, 1990).

16. M. A. Akhtar and Ethan S. Harris, "The Supply-Side Consequences of U.S. Fiscal Policy in the 1980s," Federal Reserve Bank of New York, *Quarterly Review*, Spring 1992.

17. David A. Stockman, *The Triumph of Politics: Why the Reagan Revolution Failed* (New York: Harper & Row, 1986).

18. "Escaping the Debt Trap," *The BCA Interest Rate Forecast*, September 1992.

19. Martin Anderson, "The Great American Tax Debate," *Policy Review* (Spring 1991).

20. Bartley, *The Seven Fat Years*.

Chapter Seven

1. Donald Moffitt, ed., *America Tomorrow* (Princeton, N.J.: Dow Jones Books, 1977).

2. "Olsen Speaks from Experience," *Informationweek*, October 21, 1991.

3. Alan S. Blinder, "O.K., I Was Wrong," *Business Week*, August 24, 1992.

4. Gene Epstein, "Labored Statistics," *Barron's*, December 21, 1992.

5. Peter F. Drucker, "The New Productivity Challenge," *Harvard Business Review*, November–December 1991.

6. Alfred L. Malabre, Jr., and Lindley H. Clark, Jr., "Dubious Figures," *The Wall Street Journal*, August 12, 1992.

7. Ibid.

8. Alfred L. Malabre, Jr., "Firms' Inventories Are Remarkably Lean," *The Wall Street Journal*, November 3, 1992.

9. Peter Brimelow, "An Interview With Milton Friedman," *Forbes*, August 17, 1992.

10. Jerry Jordan, speech delivered at the Cleveland Chapter of the National Association of Business Economists, December 24, 1992.

11. Gene Epstein, "Economic Beat," *Barron's*, March 8, 1993.

12. Robert Giordano, "Economic Research," Goldman, Sachs & Co., December 1992.

13. James Sterngold, "Fed Chief Says Economy Is Resisting Remedies," *New York Times*, October 15, 1992.

14. "The Maven," Cleveland Federal Reserve Bank, *Review*, June 1992.

15. William Dudley, "Economic Research," Goldman, Sachs & Co., March 1992.

16. Paul Craig Roberts, "What Everyone 'Knows' About Reaganomics," *Commentary*, February 1991.

17. Alfred L. Malabre, Jr., and Lindley H. Clark, Jr., "Dismal Record," *The Wall Street Journal*, March 27, 1989.

18. Alfred L. Malabre, Jr., *Beyond Our Means* (New York: Random House, 1987).

19. Cindy Kelly, "The Most Cited Economists," *The Margin*, Fall 1992.

20. "Poland's Mr. Fixit," interview with Jeffrey Sachs, *Best of Business Quarterly*, Fall 1991.

21. Robert Kuttner, "Real-World Economists," *Washington Post*, January 7, 1993.

22. John Maynard Keynes, *The General Theory of Employment, Interest and Money* (New York: Harcourt Brace Jovanovich, 1965).

Suggested Reading

Anderson, Martin. *Revolution: The Reagan Legacy.* Stanford, Calif.: Hoover Institution Press, 1988.

Bartley, Robert L. *The Seven Fat Years.* New York: The Free Press, 1992.

Biven, W. Carl. *Who Killed John Maynard Keynes?* Homewood, Ill.: Dow-Jones Irwin, 1989.

Blinder, Alan S. *Hard Heads Soft Hearts.* Reading, Mass.: Addison-Wesley, 1987.

Buccholz, Todd G. *New Ideas from Dead Economists.* New York: Plume, 1989.

Collander, David, and A. W. Coats, eds. *The Spread of Economic Ideas.* New York: Cambridge University Press, 1989.

Coombs, Charles A. *The Arena of International Finance.* New York: Wiley-Interscience, 1976.

DeRosa, Paul, and Gary H. Stern. *In the Name of Money.* New York: McGraw-Hill, 1981.

Eisner, Robert. *How Real is the Federal Deficit?* New York: The Free Press, 1986.

Evans, Michael K. *The Truth About Supply-Side Economics.* New York: Basic Books, 1983.

Friedman, Benjamin. *Day of Reckoning.* New York: Random House, 1988.

Friedman, Milton, and Rose Friedman. *Free to Choose*. New York: Harcourt Brace Jovanovich, 1980.

Friedman, Milton, and Walter W. Heller. *Monetary vs Fiscal Policy: A Dialogue*. New York: W.W. Norton, 1969.

Friedman, Milton, and Anna J. Schwartz. *A Monetary History of the United States 1867–1960*. Princeton, N.J.: Princeton University Press, 1963.

Galbraith, John Kenneth. *The New Industrial State*. Boston: Houghton Mifflin, 1967, 1971.

———. *Money: Whence It Came, Where It Went*. Boston: Houghton Mifflin, 1975.

———. *The Age of Uncertainty*. Boston: Houghton Mifflin, 1977.

———. *The Galbraith Reader*. Boston: Gambit, 1977.

———. *Annals of an Abiding Liberal*. Boston: Houghton Mifflin, 1979.

———. *Economics in Perspective*. Boston: Houghton Mifflin, 1987.

Gilbert, Milton. *Quest for Monetary Order*. New York: Wiley-Interscience, 1980.

Greider, William. *Secrets of the Temple: How the Federal Reserve Runs the Country*. New York: Simon & Schuster, 1987.

Harrington, Michael. *Socialism*. New York: Saturday Review Press, 1970.

Harris, Marvin. *America Now: The Anthropology of a Changing Culture*. New York: Simon & Schuster, 1981.

Heilbroner, Robert. *The Worldly Philosophers*, 6th ed. New York: Touchstone, 1986.

Heilbroner, Robert, and Lester Thurow. *Economics Explained*. Englewood Cliffs, N.J.: Prentice-Hall, 1982.

Heller, Walter W. *New Dimensions of Political Economy*. Cambridge, Mass.: Harvard University Press, 1966.

Kearns, Doris. *Lyndon Johnson and the American Dream*. New York: Harper & Row, 1976.

Klamer, Arjo. *Conversations with Economists*. Totowa, N.J.: Rowman & Allanheld, 1983.

Klein, Philip A., ed. *Analyzing Modern Business Cycles*. Armonk, N.Y.: M.E. Sharpe, 1990.

Krock, Arthur. *Memoirs: Sixty Years on the Firing Line.* New York: Eagle Books, 1968.

Krugman, Paul. *The Age of Diminished Expectations.* Cambridge, Mass.: MIT Press, 1990.

Malabre, Alfred L., Jr. *Beyond Our Means.* New York: Random House, 1987.

————. *Within Our Means.* New York: Random House, 1991.

Meigs, A. James. *Money Matters.* New York: Harper & Row, 1972.

Melton, William C. *Inside the Fed.* Homewood, Ill.: Dow Jones-Irwin, 1985.

Moffitt, Donald, ed. *America Tomorrow.* Princeton, N.J.: Dow Jones Books, 1977.

Niskanen, William A. *Reagonomics: An Insider's Account of the Policies and the People.* New York: Oxford University Press, 1988.

Regan, Donald T. *For the Record.* New York: Harcourt Brace Jovanovich, 1988.

Saulnier, Raymond. *Constructive Years: The U.S. Economy Under Eisenhower.* Lanham, Md.: University Press of America, 1991.

Schlesinger, Arthur M., Jr. *A Thousand Days: John F. Kennedy in the White House.* Boston: Houghton Mifflin, 1965.

Silk, Leonard. *The Economists.* New York: Basic Books, 1974.

Sobel, Robert. *The Worldly Economists.* New York: The Free Press, 1980.

Solomon, Robert. *The International Monetary System 1945–76.* New York: Harper & Row, 1977.

Stockman, David A. *The Triumph of Politics: Why the Reagan Revolution Failed.* New York: Harper & Row, 1986.

Thomson, Dorothy Lampen. *Adam Smith's Daughters.* New York: Exposition Press, 1973.

Thurow, Lester. *The Zero-Sum Society.* New York: Basic Books, 1980.

Volcker, Paul, and Toyoo Gyohten. *Changing Fortunes.* New York: Times Books, 1992.

Wanniski, Jude. *The Way the World Works.* New York: Basic Books, 1978.

Index